PROFESSIONAL STUDIES FOR SECONDARY TEACHING

Sara Miller McCune founded SAGE Publishing in 1965 to support the dissemination of usable knowledge and educate a global community. SAGE publishes more than 1000 journals and over 800 new books each year, spanning a wide range of subject areas. Our growing selection of library products includes archives, data, case studies and video. SAGE remains majority owned by our founder and after her lifetime will become owned by a charitable trust that secures the company's continued independence.

Los Angeles | London | New Delhi | Singapore | Washington DC | Melbourne

PROFESSIONAL STUDIES FOR SECONDARY TEACHING

EDITED BY
ED PODESTA & LEIGH HOATH

Learning Matters
A SAGE Publishing Company
1 Oliver's Yard
55 City Road
London EC1Y 1SP

SAGE Publications Inc.
2455 Teller Road
Thousand Oaks, California 91320

SAGE Publications India Pvt Ltd
B 1/I 1 Mohan Cooperative Industrial Area
Mathura Road
New Delhi 110 044

SAGE Publications Asia-Pacific Pte Ltd
3 Church Street
#10-04 Samsung Hub
Singapore 049483

Editor: Amy Thornton
Senior project editor: Chris Marke
Marketing manager: Dilhara Attygalle
Cover design: Wendy Scott
Typeset by: C&M Digitals (P) Ltd, Chennai, India
Printed in the UK

Editorial arrangement © Ed Podesta and Leigh Hoath, 2023. Chapter 1 Ed Podesta and Leigh Hoath; Chapter 2 Charlotte Wright and Natasha Raheem; Chapter 3 Elizabeth Nassem and Natasha Reynolds; Chapter 4 Kathryn Cameron and Ian Needham; Chapter 5 Naziya O'Reilly and Siobhan Simms; Chapter 6 Christina Turner and Alison Mansfield; Chapter 7 Heena Dave and Sophie Wilson; Chapter 8 Amy Thompson and Leigh Hoath; Chapter 9 Jane Essex; Chapter 10 Andrew Chandler-Grevatt and Charlotte Sawyer; Chapter 11 Amanda Nuttall and Tom Shaw; Chapter 12 Julian Burkinshaw and Rachel Rudman; Chapter 13 Amanda Meier, Mark Deacon and Leigh Hoath.

Apart from any fair dealing for the purposes of research or private study, or criticism or review, as permitted under the Copyright, Designs and Patents Act 1988, this publication may be reproduced, stored or transmitted in any form, or by any means, only with the prior permission in writing of the publishers, or in the case of reprographic reproduction, in accordance with the terms of licences issued by the Copyright Licensing Agency. Enquiries concerning reproduction outside those terms should be sent to the publishers.

Library of Congress Control Number: 2023930607

British Library Cataloguing in Publication Data

A catalogue record for this book is available from the British Library

ISBN 978-1-5296-1068-0
ISBN 978-1-5296-1067-3 (pbk)

At SAGE we take sustainability seriously. Most of our products are printed in the UK using responsibly sourced papers and boards. When we print overseas, we ensure sustainable papers are used as measured by the PREPS grading system. We undertake an annual audit to monitor our sustainability.

CONTENTS

Acknowledgements vii
About the editors and contributors ix
About this book xiii

1 What does it mean to be a professional? 1
   Ed Podesta and Leigh Hoath

2 Developing knowledge, identity and relationships as a teacher-learner 15
   Charlotte Wright and Natasha Raheem

3 Pupils' safeguarding and wellbeing 35
   Elizabeth Nassem and Natasha Reynolds

4 Teacher wellbeing 51
   Kathryn Cameron and Ian Needham

5 Behaviour in schools 69
   Naziya O'Reilly and Siobhan Simms

6 Planning your teaching 89
   Christina Turner and Alison Mansfield

7 The curriculum and the teacher 111
   Heena Dave and Sophie Wilson

8 Adaptive teaching 139
   Amy Thompson and Leigh Hoath

9 Teaching for inclusion 159
   Jane Essex

10 Developing effective assessment 179
    Andrew Chandler-Grevatt and Charlotte Sawyer

11 'What if …?' Schools and society 205
    Amanda Nuttall and Tom Shaw

Contents

12 Accountability and governance   225
    Julian Burkinshaw and Rachel Rudman

13 Your professional future: getting a job and developing your expertise 241
    Amanda Meier, Mark Deacon and Leigh Hoath

Index   261

ACKNOWLEDGEMENTS

We would like to thank the team of authors who have contributed to this book. We are grateful that they have shared their expertise and given their time and energy to this publication.

ABOUT THE EDITORS AND CONTRIBUTORS

ABOUT THE EDITORS

Leigh Hoath is a Professor of Science Education at Leeds Trinity University where she leads on science-focused initial teacher education across primary and secondary post- and undergraduate programmes. Her other work includes developing outreach and engagement in the chemical industry and being a consultant to BBC Teach.

Ed Podesta is an Associate Professor at Leeds Trinity University, where he has led the Secondary Initial Teacher Training (ITT) team, taught on the MA Education and supervised MA dissertations. His research interests are focused on teachers' professional agency and autonomy, particularly in relation to curriculum. He is studying for a PhD at Leeds University.

ABOUT THE CONTRIBUTORS

Julian Burkinshaw is Curriculum Leader for Personal Development at Temple Learning Academy, Leeds. His postdoctoral research investigated the role of flexible working practices on commuting to work. His current role seeks to develop the curriculum to support pupils in untangling complex and sensitive topics to provide clear learning experiences to support pupils in their everyday life and prepare them for future success in modern Britain.

Kathryn Cameron is a Senior Lecturer at Leeds Trinity University where she is the Programme Leader for Postgraduate Certificate in Education (PGCE) Business and for School Direct. Her published articles have focused on Business Education generally and supporting best practice of Business teachers.

Andy Chandler-Grevatt is a Senior Lecturer in the School of Education at the University of Brighton and an Assessment Editor for Oxford University Press. He is an author of over 60 publications that support classroom assessment in the UK and internationally.

Heena Dave is a Senior Curriculum Designer at the Teacher Development Trust and oversees the design and development of the charity's leadership programmes. As a former Head of Science, Heena is an experienced Middle Leader and co-author of *Cracking Key Concepts in Secondary Science*. She is currently completing a Doctorate in Education at the University of Stirling.

About the editors and contributors

Mark Deacon had a 30-year school teaching career finishing as Vice Principal in a secondary academy. He is now Senior Lecturer in Science Education at Brighton University and Lead Biology Tutor at the University of Buckingham.

Amanda Meier is currently a Head Teacher of Alternative Provision (pupil referral unit) in Brighton and Hove. Amanda has worked in secondary education for 26 years, starting off as a teaching assistant and qualifying as a teacher and Special Educational Needs Co-ordinator (SENCO) in 2008. She was a SENCO/Executive SENCO for 14 years and has been in school leadership within mainstream and specialist settings for the last six years. With responsibility for managing teams of up to 40 people, Amanda has extensive experience of looking for and appointing teaching and support staff. Prior to working in education, Amanda held numerous roles in the hospitality industry.

Elizabeth Nassem is a Lecturer in Special Needs, Disability and Mental Health, and Programme Leader for Education Studies at Leeds Trinity University. Her research over the last ten years has focused on bullying in schools and pupil voice.

Ian Needham is a Senior Lecturer in Education and also Senior Tutor for the PGCE in Computer Science with Information and Communication Technology (ICT) at Leeds Trinity University. He has worked with Science, Technology, Engineering and Maths (STEM) learning to deliver extensive subject and pedagogy Continuing Professional Development (CPD) for teachers of Computer Science, including a role as the Secondary Lead for the North Yorkshire, Leeds and Wakefield Computing Hub.

Amanda Nuttall is Associate Professor in the School of Teacher Education at Leeds Trinity University and a DPhil student at the Department of Education, University of Oxford. Her research interests include examining the impact of poverty and disadvantage in education, teachers' knowledge creation work, and theorising professional development for educators through a lens of identity.

Naziya O'Reilly is a Lecturer in Education and PGCE module co-ordinator of Primary Professional Studies at Leeds Trinity University. She is currently researching the marginalisation of student voice for Black and minority ethnic students in teacher education. Naziya's doctoral research focused on the ethics of restorative practice in UK primary schools, specifically writing on the ideas of voice, risk and self-transformation in pupil behaviour. Her previous publications include the *Journal of Ethics and Education* and the *International Journal of Educational Research*.

Natasha Raheem has worked in inner-city schools in London and Bradford for the past 15 years. She is an English teacher at Dixons City Academy in Bradford and Assistant Vice Principal at Dixons Centre for Growth. She leads on the Dixons Academies Trust School Direct Programme and delivers professional development programmes to staff across the Trust.

Natalie Reynolds is a Senior Lecturer in the Faculty of Education at Edge Hill University. Her specialisms are English education and student wellbeing. Prior to this, Natalie had an extensive school teaching career as an English teacher and Head of Faculty.

About the editors and contributors

Rachel Rudman was a secondary English teacher before becoming a Senior Lecturer at Leeds Trinity University, where she now teaches on the English secondary PGCE course. Her work aims to make connections between the nature of English as a discipline and pedagogy in practice to support students' development in the classroom.

Charlotte Sawyer is Head of History and a Professional Tutor at an 11–18 Comprehensive School. She has previously worked in the Independent Schools sector as well as teaching in further and higher education institutes.

Tom Shaw is Director of Research and Development at Carr Manor Community School in Leeds. Over the last 25 years, he has worked to develop relational and restorative cultures as an Religious Studies teacher, Senior Leader in education, community work and churches. On behalf of the Leeds Learning Alliance (LLA), Tom leads on the promotion of 'inclusion, collaboration and ambition' to a wide range of education-facing organisations across the country.

Siobhan Simms has over 20 years' teaching experience in a range of different secondary and through schools across the country. Over the years she has been a classroom teacher, Head of Year, Head of Department and works closely with trainee teachers and early careers teachers. She relishes the opportunity to work with young people.

Amy Thompson is Deputy Principal at Temple Learning Academy, a through school in Leeds. Her career to date has been spent in inner-city Leeds. She's passionate about the role education plays in social justice and the life-changing opportunity school provides for our nation's most vulnerable children.

Christina Turner is a Senior Lecturer (PGCE Maths Tutor) at Leeds Trinity University. She is also a Lead Maths Specialist for White Rose Maths. Christina continues to enjoy mastering the craft of teaching, with every lesson being an opportunity to 'do things better'. She particularly loves maths and maths pedagogy!

Sophie Wilson is a Senior Lecturer and Course Lead in Secondary Geography at St Mary's University, Twickenham. As a former Head of Geography and Head of House, she is currently the Gi Pedagogy Project Lead and Chair of the Geographical Association's ICT Special Interest Group (GAICT SIG). Her research interests are in curriculum, Geographic Information Systems (GIS) and Sustainability.

Charlotte Wright is a Senior Lecturer in Education and Programme Co-ordinator for the MA in Education at Leeds Trinity University. She has taught English for 25 years in a range of schools, and trains new teachers and researchers. She is currently engaged in a Doctorate in Education looking at the theorising practice of English teachers.

ABOUT THIS BOOK

The beginning of a teaching career is challenging, exciting and on a very steep learning curve. As well as learning how to teach your subject you are also tasked with developing a professional identity, meeting the demands of your training and then the demands of the Early Career Framework. In addition, you will be observing experienced teachers and being observed, teaching, creating lesson plans and marking work, to name just a few of the tasks ahead. You will find yourself spinning lots of plates and as you master one skill another will be introduced, or you may find that you need to revisit a part of your teaching you thought was secure.

As experienced teachers and teacher educators, we know what these early years are like – they are dynamic, pressured and rewarding. Perhaps one of the most difficult elements of our roles in developing and supporting trainees and Early Career Teachers (ECTs) is that there is not one, neat, fixed answer that means you will do things 'right'. There are however things that are to be avoided and some ways that are established as good practice. Throughout this book we will outline what we believe is helpful to you, identify some of the common pitfalls of the early stages and share experiences that trainees and ECTs have brought to us in our time of working in education. We are not for one moment telling you the one way to approach your professional life, but hopefully enabling you to think about the decisions you make as you develop in those early career years.

WHY NOW?

The demands of the Core Content and Early Career Frameworks will be of great concern to you. They shape the training you receive in the first three years of your career, and therefore the ways in which you will work with your mentors and training providers. The purpose of this book is to support you in those discussions and progression with your development as a secondary teacher. As part of your Initial Teacher Training (ITT) it is likely that you will have to complete assignments and work that relate to Professional or Education Studies – the name varies depending on your place of study. This book will pull together many of the key elements relating to your professional and academic development throughout your training and help you address those assignments. Most importantly the authors' diverse experiences and approaches mean that the book can help prepare you to teach in a wide variety of settings, and provide you with the professional perspective that your new career demands.

About this book

USING THE BOOK

Within most chapters there are a number of key features that will support different elements of your training and ECT years. You will read theory and academic work that relates to the theme of the chapter but also be presented with practical tips which will enable you to translate this theory into practice within your teaching. All of the case studies presented are with kind permission from the trainees who shared them with us.

THE TEAM

The authors of the chapters have been carefully selected – all work in Initial Teacher Education (ITE) and/or schools. We have established teams of authors with different experiences in order that your reading is not just one perspective but is synthesised from different stances. Our collective hope is that this book supports your academic work, your professional development and your classroom practice.

1

WHAT DOES IT MEAN TO BE A PROFESSIONAL?

ED PODESTA AND LEIGH HOATH

▪▪▪— KEY WORDS

- Profession
- Conduct
- Ethics

CHAPTER OBJECTIVES

In this chapter we want to explore the meaning of 'profession' and how becoming a professional is at the centre of your experiences in your training year. We draw out some lessons from the way that the meaning of the word 'profession' has changed over time, and then think about how being a 'professional' involves consideration of the values and purposes of education – and the relationship between *what* you teach and *who* you are teaching. With that in mind, we look at the regulation of the teachers' profession through the Teachers' Standards (2021) and the expectations of professional conduct that they require of us. Finally, we complete a quick tour of the book, through the lens of the Core Content Framework (2019), and set out how we hope you will use our work.

▪▪▪— LINKS TO THE CORE CONTENT FRAMEWORK

All of the Core Content Framework themes are referred to and applied in this chapter, but the following are the most relevant:

Standard 1 – Set high expectations

1. Teachers have the ability to affect and improve the wellbeing, motivation and behaviour of their pupils.

(Continued)

2. Teachers are key role models, who can influence the attitudes, values and behaviours of their pupils.

Standard 8 – Fulfil wider professional responsibilities

1. Effective professional development is likely to be sustained over time, involve expert support or coaching and opportunities for collaboration.
2. Reflective practice, supported by feedback from and observation of experienced colleagues, professional debate, and learning from educational research, is also likely to support improvement.

THE IDEA OF A PROFESSION – A VERY BRIEF HISTORY

The word 'profession' has an interesting history. It started with a religious meaning, referring to the vows or explanations of faith that people made when becoming nuns, priests or monks. Only later, especially since the 1700s, has it been connected with the idea of knowledgeable or skilled work. We still talk about 'entering a profession', which suggests that becoming a professional brings with it a different kind of work, and even different kinds of duties and responsibilities than you might get with other 'jobs'. Of course, just because a word used to mean something in the past doesn't necessarily suggest that it still has that meaning. However, if we consider some of the ways in which we have thought about what a profession has meant, we can perhaps understand some of the different meanings it has now.

The historian of professionalism, Harold Perkin, suggested that during the Industrial Revolution there was a shift in the way that we thought about some kinds of work, which amounted to a kind of new professional ideal, *based on trained expertise and selection by merit* (2002). This meant that some kinds of professional work required specialised knowledge and specific practical abilities, and that entry to the profession should be controlled so that only people who possessed this knowledge and these skills should be allowed to join. Alongside this status of 'professional' came better conditions of work and pay and, in some senses, a higher social status.

At first this kind of professional status was not attached to the job of being a teacher. From the late nineteenth century, as mass education developed (before 1870 school attendance was not compulsory), teaching was seen as being a simple job of telling pupils the correct information, often in large groups. Indeed, many children were taught by 'pupil teachers' – older children who had been previously taught the material by a teacher or head teacher (Robinson, 2017). These 'pre-professional' ideal teachers have been described as *enthusiastic people, who know their subject matter, know how to 'get it across' and can keep order in their classes* (Hargreaves, 1994: 157). There is a sense in which these aspects of the work of teaching still apply. However, our concept of the work of the teacher has grown more complex since then.

Starting in the early twentieth century and picking up pace in the period after the Second World War was a process of 'professionalisation'. During this period there was a growing perception of the need for teachers to have specialised knowledge. This developed partly out of a shift towards training teachers at university and partly in the demand from the public for all pupils to receive more than a basic education (Mandler, 2020). This desire led to an expansion of schooling and raising of the school leaving age, so that by 1972 pupils had to stay until they were 16. This increased the need to recruit and train teachers, in colleges and universities, which in turn led to higher wages and higher status and helped further develop teachers' sense of professional autonomy and specialised knowledge. Furthermore, teachers faced difficulties in working with more and more pupils, often from backgrounds where their parents might not have attended school much beyond the age of 11 or 12 (Burgess and Hardcastle, 2000). These difficulties spurred many of them on to think about new ways of teaching such pupils and new ways of discussing and explaining their practice as professionals.

By the 1960s the professional freedom which developed from this new status and developing language of practice started to clash with the need of government to show value for money in their public spending on education. At the same time there was a growing tendency for politicians to see education as being a way to improve the country's economic efficiency and growth and an answer to social problems. There was a series of scandals and battles between teachers and politicians (especially English teachers for some reason!) in which control over the curriculum and methods of education was at stake (McCallum, 2021). Over a period of more than 20 years, governments of different political parties experimented with different kinds of regulation of teachers' work. By the 1980s policy makers were more determined to take more control, and the Conservative government led by Margaret Thatcher introduced a 'National Curriculum' in 1988 which specified what each subject needed to teach.

Since the introduction of the National Curriculum, the concept of professional autonomy has therefore shifted away from freedom over curriculum and towards autonomy in choices made about methods of teaching. In more recent years this has also changed. Starting with the introduction of the National Strategies by the New Labour government led by Tony Blair in the early 2000s, policy makers have become more interested in the way teachers teach their subjects (Helsby and McCulloch, 2002). Most recently this professional autonomy has shifted into a professional duty to keep up to date with 'what works', and the most effective 'research-led' or 'evidence-informed' teaching methods (Mockler, 2005). This has been enthusiastically boosted by grass-roots teacher movements such as ResearchEd and more informal networks using social media, such as 'teachmeetIcons'.

Teachers' Standards, introduced in 2006 and significantly simplified in 2012, have codified this shift in the meaning of 'professional' in relation to the 'what' and 'how' of curriculum, but they also show that during this period the state has taken an increasingly important role in defining and overseeing other aspects of teachers' professionalism (Knight, 2017). The Standards currently in force are in two parts. Part One relates to the kinds of competencies that are expected of teachers. Part Two, entitled 'Personal and Professional Conduct', or PPC for short, sets out the kinds of restriction on behaviour that are required by entering the teaching profession. Teachers have been sanctioned and even 'struck off' – banned temporarily or permanently – for behaviour which fell short of these rules. This has included conduct which occurred out of school and the classroom, including recreational drug taking, financial misconduct and claiming false expenses (Gibbons, 2019).

REFLECTION POINT

- What does this brief history of the idea of professionalism in education tell us about the different aspects of professionalism which might apply today?

Persistent themes in thinking about professionalism

From our brief history of the idea, we hope that you can see that 'professionalism':

- refers to the development of an ethic of teaching that marks it out from other forms of work
- includes a sense of responsibility for choices about curriculum, pedagogy and being able to explain and justify these choices
- retains some sense of agency autonomy but is also increasingly about a commitment to continually improve your practice
- is highly regulated by the state
- brings duties and responsibilities within and beyond those of your immediate workplace.

YOUR OWN PROFESSIONAL IDENTITY AND THE CHALLENGES OF LEARNING

Your own understanding of the professional expectations and duties of teaching will also change over time (Day, 2021). It will be affected not only by your personal history, and the developing character traits which you bring to your initial training, but also the experiences and tuition that you receive on the course. In this section we want to talk a little about the challenges of the early stages of this journey, but you can also read more about this in Chapter 2, in which you'll be introduced to the idea of a 'teacher-learner' identity, which we think is especially important for trainee teachers.

WORKING WITH EXPERIENCED TEACHERS

During your training you will work with a mentor, and with other teachers. They will be expected to observe your lessons, provide you with feedback and guide your development. The role and status of these teachers have some important implications. In most of your lessons, a more experienced teacher will already have an established relationship with the pupils in the class. Establishing yourself as the 'teacher' in this space can therefore be challenging. Equally, you will have met the majority of your classes in a non-teaching capacity to begin with, either via observing, supporting or small group work. Making the transition to the person who leads that class may be a challenge. And, as we've already mentioned, an additional layer of complexity in establishing yourself is your position as a *learner* in the classroom as well as that of the teacher.

DEVELOPING YOUR AGENCY

Working closely with experienced teachers can also make it difficult for trainees to have the confidence to make decisions about planning and teaching. Often trainees will try to be like their mentors in class and be reluctant to try something different. We are not for one moment suggesting that you ignore advice about how to teach from more experienced teachers. While there is no one right way to teach your subject or specific aspects of it, there will be some ways which are better than others. However, it is important that you recognise the need to develop the agency to make decisions about teaching your subject. This sense of agency, of empowerment to move ideas forward, will be boosted if you're able to develop a sense of your own professional identity (Beauchamp and Thomas, 2009: 183).

BEING CAREFUL WITH 'REFLECTION'

Reflection forms an integral part of teacher training, before and after qualifying: a process described by Selmo and Orsenigo (2014) as enabling *a better understanding of the skills, knowledge and self-awareness conditional for being a teacher*. Similarly, Protassova (2020) argues that *reflection is a key to learning and also to formation of one's identity*. Becoming a 'reflective teacher' is therefore often something that training providers emphasise. However, reflection brings its own challenges.

While it might seem straightforward to reflect on a lesson, beginning teachers often lack the knowledge they need to be able to go beyond superficial evaluation of how they 'feel' when thinking about how well a lesson was taught. Especially at the start of the training year, you might focus on whether you felt:

- like a teacher;
- as if the pupils saw you as a teacher;
- that lots of work was done;
- that the pupils behaved well.

These things are all important, especially as ingredients in your developing confidence. However, they are not central to a reflection on how well the pupils are learning, or how well your understanding and practice of teaching is developing. Unless reflection is systematic, it can be a fuzzy term, which could lead you to overemphasise your feelings about how well a lesson went and fail to understand how a mentor or experienced teacher would like you to develop your practice. Instead, we recommend that trainee teachers rely on several different sources for and ways of evaluating their teaching (Beauchamp, 2015; Brookfield, 2017). For instance, you might use the following lenses to reflect on and evaluate a lesson in different ways.

DIFFERENT LENSES FOR EVALUATING OR REFLECTING ON YOUR TEACHING

Equity perspective: what might the limitations of this approach be, in terms of things that the pupil might miss or not experience or be given the opportunity to achieve?

Practical perspective: what are the workload or organisational implications of these strategies?

Autobiographical perspective: how do your experiences shape your view of the planned teaching/interventions? Have you tried things successfully in the past and therefore believe they might work here? Have you seen others try similar things which affect your beliefs about whether they would be effective? Do you have other personal experiences which help you reflect on what might happen if you did teach your pupil?

Students' perspective: try to put yourself in your students' shoes – what might they have experienced if you had carried out this plan? How might they have reacted based on your knowledge of them as people and learners?

Colleagues' perspectives: would you tweak or change anything based on your colleagues' views or experiences? You could seek views of a variety of colleagues, including peers, mentors, host teachers, subject and/or Special Educational Needs (SEN) specialists.

AN 'ETHIC' OF PROFESSIONAL TEACHING

Part of the process of identity formation and professionalism that teachers have been through (collectively and individually) is the development of a language that allows them to control and crucially to explain and examine their practice (Hopmann, 2015). You can already see, from the last section, that this is also an important theme of this book.

A recurring image that many of our chapter authors have explicitly used, or implicitly called upon, is one that shows an evolving relationship between teachers, the subject they teach, and the pupils they are teaching. This relationship is often described in the European didactic tradition as a 'didactic triangle' [see Figure 1.1] (Zierer, 2015).

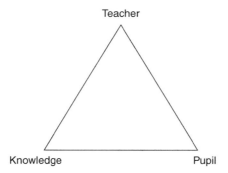

Figure 1.1 The didactic triangle

The triangle suggests that the teacher is acting as a bridge between the word (represented by the content and subject you teach) and the pupil. This model sees the student not as something to be given powerful knowledge to learn, or even only as something to which knowledge must be made more approachable or learnable. The student in this tradition is seen as a human, with all the un-developed potential that humans have. The role of the teacher is to create educational experiences which enable the *cultivation of human powers by means of knowledge* (Deng, 2021: 1658).

This view emphasises that the teachers' role is more involved, and more satisfying, than merely explaining or presenting pre-selected items of knowledge. In acting as a bridge through which pupils encounter new ideas, experiences and information, teachers help bring about new perspectives, abilities, ways of thinking and looking at the world in their pupils. The triangle also implies that teachers should be actively thinking about *what* they are teaching and *how* they are teaching it in lots of different ways (Ametller et al., 2007; Deng, 2016):

- How will this knowledge be received by pupils?
- How can I connect this knowledge with their previous understanding and experience?
- What, in these new ideas, might conflict with their previous understanding and experience?
- What new ways of thinking, acting, creating and/or understanding does this new knowledge represent?
- How can I help pupils express and use this new knowledge?
- How can I help my pupils connect this knowledge with the ways in which my subject discipline understands the world?

In some ways this resembles the concept of Pedagogical Content Knowledge (PCK, see Shulman, 1986: 9), which is described as *the most useful forms of representation of the most*

1 What does it mean to be a professional?

powerful analogies, illustrations, examples, explanations and demonstrations – in a word, the ways of representing and formulating the subject ... that make it comprehensible to others, but what we are suggesting is that there is more than just the subject content to be considered and making choices around the best approaches to use to teach it. Central to the ways that pupils in your class develop in encountering the content you are teaching is you as a teacher. You are not just a conduit of the content but also an interpreter and broker of it, and in order to make this as accessible as possible to your pupils, you must have a good understanding of both the pupils and what you are teaching, and just to be clear – secure subject knowledge is non-negotiable.

Goodchild and Sriraman (2012) suggest that thinking about your role as teacher in this way *serves as a starting point to theorise the dynamics of teaching-learning, as well as situating and contextualising each element in relation to the others* (2012: 581). In relation to you as a teacher and your professional journey, it is worth unpicking what this means. We can start by thinking about the kind of reflection, discussed above, that new trainees often engage with when they first start planning and teaching. Perhaps you have already planned a lesson, or even a starter. It is likely that you spent some time thinking about how well the lesson went, quite possibly by thinking about whether the pupils worked hard or behaved well. These are all valid concerns of new teachers – and totally understandable things to reflect on when you first start your training year, and perhaps when you move to a second placement school or teach a new group.

What we encourage trainees to do is go beyond this level of reflection, so that we are thinking about *what* we are teaching and *who* we are teaching it to – by keeping in mind the developmental potential of the content we are teaching – and the purposes of education that underpin potential (see Chapters 7 and 11).

This leads us onto the other recurring theme that this book develops – the need for trainees and teachers to address and re-evaluate how their actions (their preparations, marking, feedback, teaching, etc.) contribute towards broader purposes of education. As you read through the book, especially Chapters 2 and 7, you will see many references to Biesta's exploration of the purposes of education, and the role of teachers in relation to those purposes (Biesta, 2009, 2020a, 2020b). These ideas have been a very important influence on our thinking, and on the thinking of many of our authors.

Biesta suggests that knowledge is an important part of one of the key purposes of education – that of qualification. He has a wider definition of that word than is in general use, however, seeing it as not only teaching pupils to get qualifications, but also equipping them with knowledge that allows them to do things in the world. Knowledge also has a role in the other two purposes of Subjectification and Socialisation. Subjectification refers to the development by pupils of an idea of themselves – who they are, and how they can become more independent individuals with autonomy and a sense of self. Socialisation, on the other hand, means the way that education helps us learn how to live together with others – a sense of our communities, and how we live in what Biesta calls *social, cultural and political 'orders'* (Biesta, 2009: 40). The argument is that education involves all these purposes, that they often overlap, but can also be in tension with each other. The teachers' role is partly to make decisions that address these tensions in specific circumstances and decision making.

As we will see in the next section, becoming a teacher is partly about meeting the requirements of your course, and the regulatory requirements that society and governments place on new teachers to show competence. However, as we hope we have started to show you here, becoming a teacher is also about learning to see the relationship between big issues, such as the purposes of education, and the specifics of your practice and choices in the classroom. We hope that by setting out the challenges of thinking in this way, as well as some ways of helping you face those challenges, our authors will help you navigate your training year in a way that gives you confidence and autonomy as new professionals.

TEACHERS' STANDARDS AND QUALIFIED TEACHER STATUS

Some of you will have already achieved professional status. Perhaps you have changed careers from one of the more traditional professions such as medicine or law. You might have been working in public service professions such as social work or similar professions. Teaching, just like these sectors, has professional expectations and rules. Some of these are set out in the Teachers' Standards, some are written in contracts of employment or in your programme handbook, and some are unwritten expectations that society or schools might have. Because it's an easier way to think about the flow of this book, we will think first about 'Part Two' of the Teachers' Standards, which ask trainees and qualified teachers to maintain professional behaviours and standards, in school and out of it. After that we will look in more detail at the requirements of Part One of the Teachers' Standards, which are focused on the knowledge and skills that trainees are required to achieve during their training year. We will outline how our chapters address each standard (which is also a theme of the Core Content Framework).

PART TWO – WIDER PROFESSIONAL EXPECTATIONS

Learning to recognise, navigate and sometimes comply with the professional expectations of teachers is one of the tasks of your course. You might sometimes get these wrong – much of the time professional errors are something that you can receive feedback about, so that you can learn from that experience. A good example might be professional dress, or standards of spoken English. Some professional rules and expectations are more fundamentally important, however. Breaking rules that affect children's safety or wellbeing, or acting dishonestly or fraudulently, will in most cases see a trainee being suspended from a course, with a requirement to do further study or training on specific issues. Particularly serious cases can result in trainees being removed from a course, sometimes permanently.

1 What does it mean to be a professional?

> ▰▰▰ **EXTRACT FROM PART TWO OF THE TEACHERS' STANDARDS (2021)**
>
> Teachers uphold public trust in the profession and maintain high standards of ethics and behaviour, within and outside school.

You can see from this extract that the professional obligation to 'uphold public trust' does not stop at the door of your school, or even at the university or training provider's entrance. Teachers are public figures in their communities, and individual teachers represent the profession as a whole. It follows that you take some professional responsibilities with you as you carry on the rest of your life. You will get advice (and probably also be asked to comply with some rules) from your provider and from school about things like the use of social media, for instance. These should be straightforward things to think about and put into practice. You should also know that teachers have been 'struck off' or banned from teaching in England for things that happened outside of their school, such as dishonesty, drugs, drink driving and other offences, as well as for more obvious 'educational' misdemeanours, such as exam cheating.

MEETING THE TEACHERS' STANDARDS (2021) AND THE CORE CONTENT FRAMEWORK

At the end of the training year, you have to show that your knowledge and practice meet the Teachers' Standards. Your provider will have procedures and expectations about how you do this so that they can then recommend you to the Department of Education for the award of Qualified Teacher Status and enable you to start your two-year ECT period. You can find out more about this in Chapter 13. Part One of this document sets out eight linked standards which relate to your practice and knowledge, and to your professional conduct. The Core Content Framework, which underpins the curriculum that you will be taught in your training year, is also made up of eight interrelated curricular themes, each of which has the same focus as the Teachers' Standards.

We have set out each of these eight themes below and suggested at least one chapter of this book for each of them. However, this book is not intended to be the only thing you read (!), and in your course you will be taught far more than professional studies. You will also be taught about the subject you are teaching – its approaches, traditions and specific ways of thinking. This book tries to give some flavour of these, but can only do so briefly, with the understanding that you will also need to engage with your subject studies, tutors and mentors.

THE CORE CONTENT FRAMEWORK (CCF, 2019) AND THIS BOOK

1 – set high expectations

Chapter 6 on planning and 7 on curriculum outlines how important teachers' expectations are, especially the way that they impact on pupils' learning, and how well they achieve in school. However, this theme is also picked up in Chapter 11 on social justice, which argues that we need to think more widely about what our pupils get from their education.

2 – promote good progress

An important theme of 'promoting good progress' is accountability. This chapter, and Chapter 2 on developing a 'teacher-learner' identity, asks you to consider different ways of reflecting on what good teaching might mean, and how to approach your own development. Chapter 5 on behaviour and Chapter 12 on accountability further contextualises how schools think about how the promotion of progress takes place, in the classroom and at a whole school level.

3 – demonstrate good subject and curriculum knowledge

This theme goes right to the heart of the didactic relationship that teachers foster between subject content and pupils' development. Chapters 6 and 7 about planning lessons and curriculum thinking are the most obvious places in which we develop your thinking about what your subject knowledge is, and how you engage with it in your practice as a teacher. It is also picked up in Chapter 10 on assessment.

4 – plan and teach well-structured lessons

Chapters 6 and 7 on planning and curriculum also focus on this issue – but you can also probably see links between a well-structured lesson and a lesson in which there is a good environment for learning, and behaviour, which are covered in Chapter 5.

5. adapt teaching

This theme, of the CCF and the Teachers' Standards, is probably the one which best illustrates the interrelations between all the others. Adaptive teaching, covered in Chapter 8, benefits all pupils, but especially those who have not found school, or learning, to be easy. Teachers who can adapt lessons, resources and their teaching are drawing on aspects of good subject knowledge (so they can understand and re-explain topics that are misconceived by their pupils), but they also carefully sequence and structure their lessons and curricula so that pupils can build knowledge, skills and confidence. At the same time teachers are using assessments of pupils' understanding to help them make these adaptions, plan next steps and work out what barriers still prevent the progress they are looking for.

6 – make accurate and productive use of assessment

This is another theme in the book which you will see over and again: the interconnected nature of teachers' expertise. Chapter 10, for instance, on assessment, looks at the formal, summative assessments that teachers, and the education system, uses to consider children's achievements, and also provides challenging thinking and excellent advice

1 What does it mean to be a professional?

about how teachers use more formative, and informal, methods of assessment *as they teach* to help them understand pupils' growing knowledge, and what help they might need to understand the things they are learning. But you will also see these issues discussed in the chapters on planning (Chapter 6) and adaptive teaching (Chapter 7).

7 – manage behaviour effectively

You will learn a great deal about how each of your placement schools manages and conceives of issues relating to pupil conduct and behaviour. Chapter 5 considers this issue, and you will also see that pupils' behaviour and relations with school and teaching runs as a theme through many other chapters – specifically Chapter 6 on planning, but also Chapter 11 on school and society and Chapter 3 on safeguarding.

8 – fulfil wider professional responsibilities

In many ways this is the clear theme that underpins the whole of our book. We are asking you to think about your developing expertise as practitioners, but also the role and obligations that society sets out for the education system more broadly, so while this current chapter has obviously focused on some of these aspects, you will also see clear links in Chapter 3 on safeguarding, Chapter 9 on inclusion and Chapter 11 on school and society.

HOW TO USE THIS BOOK

Each chapter of the book has the same design, even if the authors sometimes take different approaches to the themes that we have outlined. This is to help you use the book in different aspects of your ITT course. Where appropriate for each topic the authors will provide you with:

- Case studies – that explain or illustrate the key issues, dilemmas, practices or experiences related to the theme of the chapter

- Reflection points – to give you some interesting perspectives from which to consider your views, or the views of others, in relation to the issues in the chapter

- Key things to look for when observing lessons – so that you can spot key moments in teaching that we hope will help you better understand the issues that teachers are facing or working with

- Ideas for guided practice and feedback – that we hope will help you practise and develop skills that you can use in your own teaching

- Assignment links – to show you how this chapter might support you with specific assignments in your training year

- Further reading – so that you can take further and develop your study of the issues in any chapter

- Discussion points for tutorials and seminars – so that you, your peers and your tutors can use each chapter as the basis of session discussions or activities.

Each chapter also sets out the most important links with the Core Content Framework, and by extension the Teachers' Standards. It is important to know what the main focus of each chapter is in relation to these standards. However, it will be clear to you already – just from this first chapter – that one of our key themes is how interrelated each of these aspects of teaching really are.

Of course we hope that you enjoy reading our work, but we are not expecting you to sit and read from cover to cover in one sitting. You might be asked to cover a chapter for a specific session or seminar, or because you have focused on a topic for one of your assignments, for instance. However you use our book, we want the chapters to be an introduction to the issues that they cover – and hopefully one that encourages and enables you to take your studies further.

REFERENCES

Ametller, J., Leach, J. and Scott, P. (2007) Using perspectives on subject learning to inform the design of subject teaching: an example from science education. *The Curriculum Journal*, *18*(4): 479–492. DOI: 10.1080/09585170701687928

Beauchamp, C. (2015) Reflection in teacher education: issues emerging from a review of current literature. *Reflective Practice*, *16*(1): 123–141. DOI: 10.1080/14623943.2014.982525

Beauchamp, C. and Thomas, L. (2009) Understanding teacher identity: an overview of issues in the literature and implications for teacher education. *Cambridge Journal of Education*, *39*: 175–189. DOI: 10.1080/03057640902902252

Biesta, G. (2009) Good education in an age of measurement: on the need to reconnect with the question of purpose in education. *Educational Assessment, Evaluation and Accountability (Formerly: Journal of Personnel Evaluation in Education)*, *21*(1): 33–46.

Biesta, G. (2020a) *Educational Research: An Unorthodox Introduction*. Bloomsbury Academic.

Biesta, G. (2020b) Risking ourselves in education: qualification, socialization, and subjectification revisited. *Educational Theory*, *70*(1): 89–104. DOI: 10.1111/edth.12411

Brookfield, S. D. (2017) *Becoming a Critically Reflective Teacher*. John Wiley & Sons.

Burgess, T. and Hardcastle, J. (2000) Englishes and English: schooling and the making of the school. *School Subject Teaching: The History and Future of the Curriculum*, 1.

Day, C. (2021) The new professionalism? How good teachers continue to teach to their best and well in challenging reform contexts, in *Good Teachers for Tomorrow's Schools*, pages 37–56. Brill.

Deng, Z. (2016) Bringing curriculum theory and didactics together: a Deweyan perspective. *Pedagogy, Culture & Society*, *24*(1): 75–99.

Deng, Z. (2021) Powerful knowledge, transformations and Didaktik/curriculum thinking. *British Educational Research Journal*, *47*(6): 1652–1674. DOI: 10.1002/berj.3748

Gibbons, A. (2019) Revealed: the top 10 reasons for banning teachers, *Tes Magazine*. Available at: www.tes.com/magazine/archive/revealed-top-10-reasons-banning-teachers

Goodchild, S and Sriraman, B. (2012) Revisiting the didactic triangle: from the particular to the general. *Mathematics Education* (44): 581–585.

Hargreaves, D.H. (1994) The new professionalism: the synthesis of professional and institutional development. *Teaching and Teacher Education*, *10*(4): 423–438. DOI: 10.1016/0742-051X(94)90023-X

Helsby, G. and McCulloch, G. (2002) Teacher professionalism and curriculum control, in *Teachers' Professional Lives*, pages 64–82. Routledge.

Hopmann, S. (2015) 'Didaktik meets Curriculum' revisited: historical encounters, systematic experience, empirical limits. *Nordic Journal of Studies in Educational Policy*, *2015*(1), 27007.

Knight, B. (2017) The evolving codification of teachers' work: policy, politics and the consequences of pursuing quality control in Initial Teacher Education. *Teacher Education Advancement Network Journal*, *9*(1), Article 1.

Mandler, P. (2020) *The Crisis of the Meritocracy: Britain's Transition to Mass Education Since the Second World War*. Oxford University Press.

McCallum, A. (2021) Who gets to be creative in class? Creativity as a matter of social justice in secondary English lessons, in A. Ross (ed.) *Educational Research for Social Justice: Evidence and Practice from the UK*, pages 79–95. Springer International Publishing. DOI: 10.1007/978-3-030-62572-6_4

Mockler, N. (2005) Trans/forming teachers: new professional learning and transformative teacher professionalism. *Journal of In-Service Education*, *31*(4): 733–746. DOI: 10.1080/13674580500200293

Perkin, H. (2002) *The Rise of Professional Society: England since 1880*. London: Routledge.

Protassova, E. (2021) Teacher's identity development through reflection. Conference: International Scientific and Practical Conference Education in a Changing World: Global Challenges and National Priorities, pages 67–77. DOI: 10.15405/epsbs.2021.07.02.9

Robinson, W. (2017) Teacher education: a historical overview, in *The SAGE Handbook of Research on Teacher Education*, pages 1, 49–67. London: Sage.

Selmo, L. and Orsenigo, J. (2014) Learning and sharing through reflective practice in teacher education in Italy. *Procedia – Social and Behavioral Sciences*, *116*. DOI: 10.1016/j.sbspro.2014.01.496

Shulman, L. (1986) Those who understand: knowledge growth in teaching. *Educational Researcher*, *15*(2): 4–14.

Zierer, K. (2015) Educational expertise: the concept of 'mind frames' as an integrative model for professionalisation in teaching. *Oxford Review of Education*, *41*(6): 782–798. DOI: 10.1080/03054985.2015.1121140

2

DEVELOPING KNOWLEDGE, IDENTITY AND RELATIONSHIPS AS A TEACHER-LEARNER

CHARLOTTE WRIGHT AND NATASHA RAHEEM

▪▪▪ KEY WORDS

- Learning disposition
- Dialogue
- Learning continuum

CHAPTER OBJECTIVES

As you read this chapter, you will learn about the importance of seeing yourself as a learner as well as a teacher, at the start and throughout your career. This may sound challenging, but we will share the sources of knowledge that will be available to you within and beyond your school, in training and in employment as an ECT. We will also suggest ways in which you might nurture your 'teacher-learner disposition' and, in doing so, increase your confidence, expertise and feelings of belonging in the workplace. Throughout this chapter (and the book as a whole) you will determine the fact that schools are networks of social relationships, and we will outline how you can strengthen those relationships by making conscious contributions which add to a rich conversation about learning.

▪▪▪ LINKS TO THE CORE CONTENT FRAMEWORK

All of the Core Content Framework themes are referred to and applied in this chapter, but the following are the most relevant:

Standard 8 – Fulfil wider professional responsibilities, with particular relevance to:

1. Effective professional development is likely to be sustained over time, involve expert support or coaching and opportunities for collaboration.

(Continued)

> 2. Reflective practice, supported by feedback from and observation of experienced colleagues, professional debate, and learning from educational research, is also likely to support improvement.
> 3. Teachers can make valuable contributions to the wider life of the school in a broad range of ways, including by supporting and developing effective professional relationships with colleagues.

WHY LEARNING ABOUT YOUR TEACHING IS AS IMPORTANT AS LEARNING HOW TO TEACH

In the Core Content Framework and Early Career Framework, 'seeking', 'engaging', 'reflecting', 'participating' and 'contributing' are emphasised as a key part of 'Professional Behaviours'. These dynamic verbs act as a reminder that 'professionalism' is not just about outward-facing image and behaviours; it also means cultivating an active learning disposition. You will benefit from supportive structures around you as you begin your career, moving from the initial training phase into your first years of teaching with a network of peers and mentors around you. In tandem with the structured learning opportunities for Early Career Teachers, this network can help you maintain the core job satisfaction that comes from renewing and building your pedagogical knowledge and understanding of the social world of the school and wider educational community.

As your career progresses, you are likely to move between different school contexts – you may well already be experiencing contrasting contexts as part of your training year. Therefore, it is important to develop a 'vari-focal lens', that is, to learn about the close-up detail of best practice in your current school setting while also keeping wider horizons and possibilities in view. This might mean taking time to learn how different schools are responding to national policy changes or investigating how the teaching of your subject might look or feel different in other contexts. The cultivation of this kind of multiple perspective will help you avoid the kind of culture shock that teachers sometimes describe when moving schools (see Hancock, 2016, for example). It can take time to strengthen this lens.

Another use of the 'vari-focal' lens is to view the learning process from the perspective of the teacher *and* of the learner. Teaching requires a commitment to learning as well as to teaching: you will be required to update your subject and pedagogical knowledge with each new class and each curriculum change and will have to reinhabit your own 'learner identity' as you do so. This personal and professional renewal is an exciting and stimulating part of the job, which will give you a sense of self-efficacy (Glackin, 2019). It will help you to continue to understand your pupils' experiences when faced with learning challenges, as well as contributing to job satisfaction (Cochran-Smith and Lytle, 2009).

Successful cultivation of this learner disposition takes planning, and also a continuing alertness to learning opportunities. You will experience much learning at a tacit level as you immerse yourself in the fast-flowing river of school life – that is, you will continually pick up many incremental insights through your daily practice. But you will also need to take time to seek out formal or focused opportunities to participate in professional learning. That you do so is beneficial for your school: if you can see yourself as a potential contributor to, as well as recipient of, teacher learning, then you will help to represent the viewpoints and experiences of Early Career teachers, which are an important aspect of any school community. You may feel a little daunted at the thought of volunteering to say or present something in a staff training event, for example, but this kind of participation will build your professional confidence and voice and enrich the knowledge base of your colleagues and managers.

Brookfield (1995: 239) points out that *becoming a skillful teacher will always be an unformed, unfinished project – a true example of lifelong learning.* Teaching could be defined as professional problem solving, and if we accept that the job will always contain elements of uncertainty (Ball, 2021), we can use our commitment to exploring ideas to guard against potential frustrations.

The willingness and ability to recognise uncertainty can be considered a beneficial response in teachers and may also contribute to better instruction, especially when it allows teachers to reconsider their beliefs and practices that are at odds with the realities of their classrooms (Helsing, 2007).

CASE STUDY

Reflecting on the 'teacher-learner' identity

When asked to reflect on the challenges and benefits of maintaining an active teacher-learner identity, Leeds primary school teacher Helen offered the following pointers:

1. It remains really important to keep putting yourself in the position of the learner, and repeatedly asking yourself the question 'What would allow *me* to learn effectively?' After a few years in teaching, you could start to plateau in your development as routines and habits become embedded and lose sight of the complex ways in which different children might learn. Keep asking questions and keep aware of the capacity all of us have to forget we might have blind spots.

2. Seek stimuli that will take you outside of your familiar environment: explore online CPD, visit other classrooms or schools, listen to education podcasts, read, volunteer to be a governor. Where you find contrasts with your own practice, you will also find you reflect productively on what might be worth trying.

3. Look for opportunities to speak or write about what you do and think. I have just finished an MA in Education which I completed while teaching, and getting to talk

(Continued)

and to write about both my own practice and the research literature has helped so much with my professional confidence. Although the MA was hard work, it's been worth it: I've been able to share my dissertation findings with our staff and am now considering applying for promotion as I feel I have found a new kind of authority in how I think about education.

Re-read Helen's thoughts about the benefits of a 'teacher-learner' identity. Reflect on the following issues. What do you think the learning opportunities will be?

- In your 'centre-based training' (where you might have lectures, seminars, etc.)
- In your school placement
- That relate to your subject specialism – for instance, which aspects of the school curriculum will you need to learn most about?

You will start to shape your teacher identity during the training year, partly through the habits you develop. A healthy teacher habit to form is the willingness to seek out knowledge both within and beyond your school. This allows you to consider your personal values, preferences and the purposes of approaches that you use.

HOW TO ACCESS TEACHERS' KNOWLEDGE

Teacher knowledge is what a teacher uses to enable learning in the classroom. This knowledge base, and its use, is deeply complex and seemingly invisible. This is one reason why having a learning disposition as a teacher is essential; you have to lead on your own learning as well as draw on the expertise of teachers in and outside of your school. By actively seeking out and creating opportunities to engage in hard thinking, you will continually build and strengthen your knowledge base to meet the varying needs of pupils and changing curricula.

During your training year, you will learn from a range of former and current teachers during provider and school-based training. You will see teacher knowledge enacted by observing lessons, co-planning and by accessing central resources such as schemes of learning and planned lessons. Micro-moments (the asking of quick questions about an aspect of teaching) in shared workspaces will enable you to hear strategies to maximise pupil progress. You can also access teacher knowledge beyond the walls of your placement through EduTwitter, professional associations, conferences, online professional development (e.g. Seneca) and resources aimed at pupils, e.g. videos of teachers delivering remote lessons to pupils on Oak National Academy.

Accessing teacher knowledge may turn into a superficial exercise if the complexity of this concept is not considered. Understanding mental models is a useful starting point when thinking about knowledge and they refer to *what people know and how this knowledge is organised to guide decision and action* (Schempp et al., 2002, cited in Mccrea, 2018). These mental models are powerful because they generate action or inaction in the classroom. Once a mental model is strengthened, some actions become automatic and, consequently, this means teachers can be more responsive to the needs of learners in class. It is never beneficial to compare your teaching to that of an experienced teacher: you have not been privy to their teaching journey or their endeavours to constantly build their teaching knowledge. Great teachers are made, not born, and through reflection, analysis and hard thinking about how you can adapt your future practice, you are building a strong knowledge base, brick by brick.

As a trainee teacher, you may focus your time on primarily developing subject knowledge and, while this is important, you must also dedicate time to accessing other forms of knowledge. Mccrea breaks this knowledge down into four main domains:

- Knowledge of the curriculum – what pupils need to know at different stages to master it.
- Knowledge of pupils – what they know and don't know as well as their learning dispositions.
- Knowledge of pedagogy – how learning works, including cognitive, emotional, social and cultural aspects.
- Self-regulation – knowing how to adapt what you do, through analysis and evaluation, for maximum impact on pupils (Mccrea, 2018).

LEARNING OPPORTUNITIES DURING YOUR TRAINING

The knowledge base of a teacher is a 'complex tapestry' (Adoniou, 2015) and, as a trainee, you will be supported by expert teachers to unpick the tapestry so you can examine each individual thread and then weave them back together in ever-shifting patterns. This support will come in a number of ways. In this section we will describe just some of these, and how you can make the most of them.

OBSERVING EXPERIENCED TEACHERS

When you begin observing lessons, you will see expert teachers in action and their teaching will appear effortless and completely natural. What you will not see is the thinking that guides their action or inaction before, after and during the lesson, and it is this thinking you need to dig deeply for so you can develop and strengthen your mental model of teaching.

Observations do not need to be for a full lesson if agreed in advance with the teacher. When beginning placements, it is important that you understand how to observe a lesson. Training may be provided by your training provider and, if not, it is important that you seek the support of your mentor or ITT Lead so you know what to look for. If possible, ask to observe with a more experienced colleague or ask if you can film a lesson and then analyse parts of the lesson with your mentor. Whatever you observe, you always need to consider the impact of what a teacher says/does or does not say/do on pupils.

After lesson observations, ask questions to encourage the teacher you are working with to articulate their mental model and make the implicit, explicit. When asking questions, think carefully about how they are framed to encourage a teacher to talk honestly and really unpick what they did. You are not there to make judgements but, rather, to understand how to make quick decisions in the complex and fast-paced environment of a classroom. You also need to listen very carefully to what is said, notice precise details and make notes.

Useful sentence frames are:

- I noticed that you did/said .... Can you talk me through your thinking as I saw that it had real impact on ...?
- Could you tell me more about ...?

Make the time to observe other teachers, within and outside your subject specialism, even as your teaching load increases. One of the ways in which you can highlight your 'teacher-learner' identity is by being proactive – ask the teachers you are working with to recommend someone to observe based on your weekly target, for instance.

REVIEWING LESSON PLANS AND SCHEMES OF WORK

As you will see from Chapter 6, you will be learning about planning lessons, even if you're working in a school with pre-prepared lesson plans and resources. These resources are an excellent opportunity to develop your teacher-learner identity because you are, at the same time, trying to understand how to teach the lesson, and why it was put together in this particular way.

The model of questioning outlined above is also very useful when learning, and teaching from, schemes of learning and centrally planned lessons. You need to understand the hard thinking behind curricula content and sequencing, and for that, rich dialogue with your mentor is needed.

LEARNING FROM MEETINGS

During your training year, you will attend meetings and professional development sessions in school and with your training provider. Maximise the time you spend in these spaces by being present, considering how you can apply the learning to your practice, making notes and asking questions. Discuss any sessions you attend with your mentor so you can be supported in consolidating your understanding. If possible, incorporate

2 Developing knowledge, identity and relationships as a teacher-learner

your new learning into planning for the following week and write a reminder in your teacher planner to return to the new strategy at a later point. Always have a notebook and pen with you as you never know when a teacher might share a rich strategy or approach with you. It is worth reflecting on any notes you have made at the end of each day and considering which aspects of the Core Content Framework (CCF) they relate to. By doing this, you can start to prioritise the knowledge you still have to access and consider how you can continue to build your emerging knowledge in other areas.

LEARNING FROM MODELLING

In the classroom, modelling is when a teacher demonstrates a new concept or approach to learning and pupils learn by observing it. Learning from having good practice and technique explicitly modelled for you is another good way of developing your teacher-learner identity. While watching an expert teacher using a technique, you are finding out about effective approaches, while also learning about the use of modelling to help someone learn.

CASE STUDY

Modelling effective practice

Faatimah, a trainee in Bradford, received feedback following a lesson observation where she modelled annotating a text using a visualiser (a camera that can capture, record and save images and videos). Before Faatimah's next lesson, she asked the teacher she was working with to model using the visualiser effectively for her so she could check her understanding. Faatimah was then able to see what she had to do and the impact these actions would have on pupils. Next, the teacher asked Faatimah to write a script detailing how she would approach modelling and then rehearse it with her. Throughout the process, Faatimah received feedback so, when she did this in the classroom, she felt confident. By taking ownership of her learning by asking for an approach to be modelled and then having the opportunity to rehearse, she had accessed the teacher's knowledge and, consequently, strengthened her mental model.

- Think about how you have used approaches to teaching you have seen modelled.
- Which worked best for you and why?
- How can you better identify what you would like to see modelled for you to develop in your own teaching?

LEARNING FROM FEEDBACK

As a trainee, you will get a lot of feedback; you will get feedback from teachers, senior leaders, parents and instant feedback from pupils in the classroom. This feedback may affect your confidence and self-concept, especially if it is not as positive as you would have hoped and when you have spent a long time planning a lesson. It is important to see such feedback as a treasured gift and not let it affect your perception of colleagues. While feedback may be packaged in different ways, its aim is to improve you as a teacher and, in the long term, pupils' learning. It can be challenging and demoralising to not always receive positive feedback, but that is the reality of teaching. Perfection is an impossible dream because we are teaching children who respond in ways we cannot always anticipate. This is the challenge of teaching, but it is also the joy. Colleagues will appreciate your response to feedback, especially if you seek it out when you do not need to and you strive to implement your weekly targets. There may be times when you do not understand or agree with the feedback, and it is important to be honest to check your understanding is secure. While it is not always easy to voice concerns or a lack of understanding, this is essential to maintain a strong rapport with the teacher you are working with. These sentence frames can help you to remain respectful when receiving feedback.

Thank you for your feedback. I'm not sure I completely understand X, could you please explain it to me again?

Thanks so much for the feedback. You mentioned X. I thought I'd done this here (give a specific example linked to pupils). Could you talk me through how I could improve it so I can check my understanding?

MAKING THE MOST OF LEARNING OPPORTUNITIES

Below are some scenarios for you to think about. They are all quite common through the training period. Consider them and how you would respond.

1. You observe a lesson and notice the teacher using directed questioning (questions aimed at a named individual). All pupils answer the questions, and the pace of the lesson does not slow down. You want to talk to the teacher about this and find out more about any planning for questioning that the teacher might do. Script how you would approach this conversation.

2. You have taught a lesson and you're feeling disappointed because there was low-level disruption. In the classroom, you were not sure how to address it. You really want to learn more about different strategies you can use to create a supportive learning environment. What steps would you take before the next lesson to develop your knowledge base on creating a supportive learning environment?

3. You receive feedback from your mentor asking you to work on the pace of your lesson. Your mentor has suggested adding in times for each activity. You start to plan your next lesson, but you're not sure how long the main learning activity should take. You also find it hard to remember to stick to timings in class. What steps would you take before submitting your lesson plan to your mentor for feedback?

HOW TO USE THEORY TO SUPPORT YOUR PRACTICE

You will hear 'theory' talked about in many different ways: it can range in meaning from the individual and personal (ideas, opinions and beliefs, proposals, attitudes) to the institutional (a structured explanation of an educational philosophy or standpoint, a coherent model, a shared lens, developed ideas which are transferable to differing contexts within the field of education). It may be useful to take a moment to think about who you believe is authorised to 'count' as a theorist, and whose theories might matter most to you as a teacher. If we perceive theory as something abstracted and generated a long way from the classroom, perhaps 'owned' by academics and policy writers, it is easy to think of it as irrelevant – even a kind of intrusion or obstruction as we rush to get the complex immediate work of teaching done. Sometimes theory is even positioned as the opposite of practice, but beware of this false binary: we are *always already theorists* (McCormick, 1992) as well as practitioners, making hundreds of conscious and unconscious choices every day in school that are rooted in our own theories, and/or those promoted at school, local or national level.

To see 'theory' as a noun, a bank of abstracted material 'out there' to be mastered, is to forget our own agency. Rather, we would encourage you to think about theoris*ing* as a verb in motion as you teach, an important ongoing process of triangulation in which you bring your ways of seeing from the classroom into contact with ways of seeing offered by professionals from a range of contexts, in order to develop your ability to make 'good situational judgements' (see Orchard and Winch, 2015). In this way, the expertise you are acquiring by doing, practising and experiencing will be continually enhanced with expertise acquired by reading, listening, discussing, comparing, articulating and evaluating ideas and positions.

You are always engaged in a kind of research work as you teach as you watch and listen and adjust what you do in each unique class setting, which sets you on the same intellectual spectrum as those undertaking more formal, applied research towards specific practical aims and theory development (OECD, 2015).

Theory can also be a useful tool for 'productive estrangement' – that is, standing outside of your instinct or 'common sense' knowledge to consider alternative possibilities – and this is particularly useful if you are stuck on an aspect of educational problem solving. It's another example of a kind of 'vari-focal' lens, another way of looking at practice. Engagement with theory and active theorising is also an important facet of your work as a teacher because your practice will be more robust if it is underpinned by a strong rationale – *it is not just about knowing what you do and how you do it. It is also about why you do it* (Williams, 2004: 5).

REFLECTION POINT

An important set of theories that you carry around, perhaps without realising it, are about your subject. There will be many occasions when a pupil might ask you, *Why are we studying this?* What is your immediate response to this, if the question pertains to your subject as a whole? We will develop this thinking as we go through this section.

CASE STUDY

Why do we teach English?

In an article in a subject association magazine aimed at English teachers, John Perry discusses teacher theorising about why we should teach literature in schools. After conducting empirical research with a group of Heads of English, he presents their theorising in two strands: how they see 'the point of literature – for schools', and how they see 'the point of literature – for pupils', recognising that subjects as entities may have particular status both within and beyond the actual classroom. In the first strand, the Heads of English talk about the significance of the national 'Progress 8' measure and GCSE results for their work and decision making. In the second strand, the Heads of English offer three key ideas:

a. that the study of literature works as *a kind of passport to greater opportunities than the school's immediate community can offer*, with one describing English lessons as a chance to get them out of the area, to give them the opportunity to be somewhere else

b. that the study of literature is important for developing pupils' 'cultural awareness'

c. that the study of literature *helps pupils develop their understanding of local, national and global social concerns*, with race, gender and the effects of poverty offered as examples (Perry, 2022: 20).

- How far do you agree with what Perry reports? Now think back to your own schooling and encounters with literature there. How far did your own experience of learning about literature fulfil the ideals articulated by the participants in Perry's research?

- Now imagine a pupil is asking you "Why are we studying this?" in relation to your own subject or one subject that you teach. Make a list of your justifications.

- What might be the personal, local, national, practical and intellectual benefits of studying this subject? If this subject was removed from the curriculum, what would be lost to society, and how might different stakeholders be affected?

You will continue to engage in subject theorising as you move on through your career. You might go on to ask further questions about how your subject or a key subject that you teach is constructed and justified in local and national curricula and exam syllabi or tests. You might listen to hear how your subject is described in CPD such as conferences and webinars, or in the staffroom or department office. You might read research or other literature relating to your subject. As you engage in all of these activities, you will be triangulating theory with your own practice to refine or expand your subject theory and your answer to the 'why' question.

HOW TO GET THE MOST FROM WORKING WITH MENTORS, TEACHERS AND OTHER KEY STAFF IN SCHOOLS

During your placement, you'll work with a range of different members of staff. Your mentor, in most cases, will be the teacher who makes the biggest difference to your personal and professional development. You will, however, work closely with other teachers, Heads of Departments/Phase Leaders, Heads of Year (if relevant) and staff in the Special Needs department. You'll also work with non-teaching staff (catering staff, site staff, technicians and the administration team). Developing effective professional relationships is part of Teaching Standard 8 and the separate Personal and Professional Conduct (PPC) Teaching Standard. By being highly professional, you will develop qualities that will allow you to get the most from those you work with and contribute to a positive culture.

UNDERSTANDING YOUR PROFESSIONAL RESPONSIBILITIES

One of the main ways to get the most out of working with colleagues is to be respectful of their time and workload by acting in accordance with school policy and expectations. Teachers are expected to be highly professional, especially as we are role models for the pupils in our care. Sometimes, trainees can struggle with PPC, especially if they have not worked full-time in a professional environment before, and this can affect the quality of the relationships with the teachers you work with. You need to be aware of what is expected from you from your school and your ITT provider.

Taking up this responsibility begins with reading key documents such as the course handbook and key school policies such as: absence, equality and diversity, safeguarding, punctuality and the professional conduct policy. There may also be some PPC expectations which are not specified in policies, such as when and how you communicate with staff after the working day and at weekends. Trainees can struggle with managing competing deadlines, prioritising, organisation and knowing when and how to ask for help. A useful activity is to reflect on your personal skills and consider what you might need support with. For example, if you know you struggle with organisation, you can share this with your mentor and get advice with practical strategies to improve your organisation in school. If high standards of PPC are not maintained consistently, relationships are affected as your action and inaction has an impact on not only you but your mentor, other teachers you are working with, your ITT provider and ultimately pupils and their learning.

Part of being a learner is making mistakes; some of your mistakes will be known (e.g. missing a deadline) while other mistakes might be unknown (e.g. mishandling questioning in class so pupils start shouting out). Consider which mistakes require an apology. For example, if you don't organise your evidence folder despite being given a reasonable deadline by your mentor, you should apologise to your mentor, explain what happened and what you will do differently next time. An apology is needed because by not meeting a deadline, you have created additional work for other people. Based on this example, your mentor would have set aside time to review your folder and will have to then set aside more time to do this at a later date. Teachers you are working with will understand and respect you for taking responsibility and apologising. We are all human, mistakes happen, and people will move on if you show you are willing to learn and act on feedback.

CASE STUDY

Megan and Mandy

Megan, a trainee in Bradford, made sure she was organised and prepared for every mentor meeting. This meant she had to complete in advance the relevant documentation and send it to the mentor before the meeting. To ensure the meeting ran efficiently and was purposeful, Megan wrote a list of questions to be answered by her mentor in the meeting.

Another trainee at the same school, Mandy, spoke to her mentor about feeling worried about assignment deadlines and assessment visits. Mandy's mentor suggested that she added her deadlines to her planner, and to work backwards from there so that the work she needed to undertake on placement was done in good time. She was also able to suggest members of the teaching team who could model some relevant practice.

Megan's preparations meant that she was active in mentor meetings and showed her mentor she was organised and keen to learn. They also showed that Megan was respectful of her mentor's time. No question is ever a silly question; as a trainee teacher, you are still learning and you are not expected to know the answers without receiving help, but getting help will be easier if you're on top of the things that you can control, such as your preparatory tasks. Sometimes, though, you will struggle or be nervous about things. By being honest with her mentor about her feelings, Mandy demonstrated vulnerability. If you show vulnerability, you are not weak or a failure, you are engaging in help-seeking behaviour, a key protective factor of teacher resilience (Beltman et al., 2011). Mandy's mentor was then able to support her with managing her time effectively.

Asking for help is not about being excused from work or asking for expectations to be lowered; it is support being put in place to help you maintain a sense of balance and high performance. There can be many barriers to asking for help, such as not wanting to be a burden or not knowing how to talk about a challenging situation, but it is important to be comfortable being uncomfortable. You may need to demonstrate vulnerability when discussing interactions with pupils. For example, a young female trainee will need to be confident talking to her male mentor about gendered behaviour from male pupils which has left her feeling upset, angry and helpless. You may also need to demonstrate vulnerability by telling your mentor about something challenging in your personal life which has deeply upset you and is starting to affect you physically. If you don't ask for help, you isolate yourself and then situations can escalate, and behaviours may develop that do not represent you. As a trainee, you often don't just have a mentor's support; you have a whole team behind you. Be aware of your right to support and use it. Some schools also offer free access to Employee Assistance Programmes where you can get external advice. By asking for help and communicating concerns, you are showing you trust your mentor to help you and that you value your relationship.

- What is the impact of a trainee being late to school or lessons and not informing their mentor or the teacher they are working with?

  Impact on the trainee:

  Impact on the mentor:

  Impact on other teachers in the school:

  Impact on the ITT provider:

  Impact on pupils:
- How do you want to be described by teachers you work with?
- What steps are you going to take to ensure this description is what your mentor writes in your job reference?

THE IMPORTANCE OF DEVELOPING RELATIONSHIPS ACROSS YOUR SCHOOL PLACEMENT

On busy teaching days, you may interact with over a hundred pupils, but you might not have an in-depth conversation with another adult. If you choose to work and/or have breaks in a classroom, you then miss out on rich micro-moments and also more carefree moments with colleagues. Without the kindness, humour and support of fellow teachers, feelings of isolation can increase and teachers are less likely to feel like they belong to the school community. As teachers, we value the importance of developing strong relationships with our pupils, but we also need to place as much emphasis on developing strong relationships with our peers. Pupils pass through schools, but team relationships endure and are therefore worth the investment for the individual and the school community.

Self-determination theory (SDT) is one of the most robust and empirically supported theories of motivation (Udalowska, 2020) and it emphasises the importance of connection. It suggests that people are motivated to grow and change by three innate psychological needs: autonomy (the experience of volition and willingness), competence (the experience of effectiveness and mastery) and relatedness (connecting to and feeling significant to others) (Vansteenkiste, 2020). When each need is satisfied, there is *enhanced self-motivation and mental health* (Deci and Ryan, 2000: 68), contributing to feelings of fulfilment throughout your teaching career. Some examples of indicators of strong social connectivity in a school are:

- You are welcomed to the school community in a staff meeting.
- You feel like you belong to the team straight away through the kindness of colleagues and their frequent check-ins with you.
- You look upset and a teacher stops doing what they are doing to help you.
- You feel able to ask for help and show vulnerability.

These behaviours enhance relatedness because they contribute to your feelings of belonging and, consequently, your psychological safety. Strong social support enables you to be honest, ask for help and take risks so you have access to more opportunities for personal and professional growth, thereby strengthening your teacher-learner identity.

You can foster strong relationships with others from day one of your placement with these recommendations:

1. Treat all staff members with respect and courtesy no matter what their role is and never underestimate the power of saying hello and smiling. This behaviour may seem obvious, but it requires confidence, which is not always an easy trait to demonstrate as a trainee teacher. By doing this, you will, however, start to build your support network and also raise your profile within your placement school.

2. You can show you value the importance of relationships by being intentional in when and how you develop them. This means carving out space for them in your day and valuing how important they are to maintain balance and fulfilment at work. Work in the shared workspace (if available) and have lunch in the staffroom so you can interact with different colleagues. By doing this, you will not only be privy to rich conversations and micro-moments about teaching and learning, but the informal interactions will sustain you, relax you and make you smile. This will also provide you with the opportunity to ask colleagues to share their Early Career Teacher stories. It can be easy to fall into the trap of comparing yourself to others; you'll soon find that even the most amazing teacher struggled with aspects of teaching during their training year.

3. Be a team player. This might mean photocopying for a colleague who you can see is under pressure or even buying biscuits for your team on a dark, rainy day in November! It might also mean taking the time to find someone to say thank you or write a few words of thanks. You may not prioritise this behaviour or see it as your responsibility, but it is important that being a team player becomes part of your teacher identity. Staff working in schools are part of the same community and we help each other to succeed, contributing to the success of our pupils. By acting like a team player from day one, your willingness to support others will be noticed and greatly appreciated and staff are more likely to help you in return.

SOCIAL CAPITAL

Social capital is another concept that is useful to consider when thinking about fostering effective relationships. It refers to *connections among individuals – social networks and the norms of reciprocity and trustworthiness that arise from them* (Putnam, 2000, cited in Kiechel, 2000). While there are overlaps with relatedness, social capital places a strong value on social networks; the more people you know, the more people you have who can provide guidance and support, share opportunities (including job offers and promotions) with you and champion you within and outside of the school context. As a trainee teacher, you can increase your own social capital by making the most of the networking opportunities available in your placement school. Here are some examples of indicators of positive social capital in schools:

- There are regular opportunities to interact with staff in formal and informal situations, e.g. coffee mornings, regular staff meetings and professional development, staff working groups and shared interest groups.
- Staff attend after-school events such as sports fixtures, celebration evenings and performances. This provides teachers with the opportunity to interact with fellow teachers, pupils and parents/carers, building stronger relationships for all. It's also a great reminder of how special school communities actually are.

Being alert to indicators of social connectivity and positive social capital is important because it will help you to find a school for your ECT 1 year that is committed to improving relational quality. Developing relationships is the dual responsibility of the individual and the school and you need to find a school that will help you to feel like you belong and thrive as an Early Career Teacher.

The below recommendations can help you to increase your social capital in school:

1. Seek out opportunities to collaborate with staff within your department, e.g. co-plan lessons, help out with an enrichment activity or an after-school club. This will strengthen your mental model of different aspects of teaching and also enable you to foster a strong relationship with the teacher and pupils you are working with.
2. Seek out opportunities to work with staff outside of your department, e.g. volunteer to help out during a whole school event, e.g. a school performance, a charity event. This will help you to develop new skills, raise your profile in the school and enhance what you have to offer future employers.
3. Offer to go on trips or residentials. They are often a bonding experience and also a great way to get to know teachers and pupils outside of the classroom.
4. Plan or attend social events with colleagues in your school or your group of trainees. While teachers love to talk about teaching, conversations eventually move beyond this, and you'll not only develop a close network of support but also friends for life.

REFLECTION POINT

- Which of these recommendations are you going to prioritise? Why? You could think about the amount of time you'll have in different parts of your training, or your own talents, interests and experiences.
- What personal and/or professional barriers might you face? How could you overcome these barriers? What support might you need from your mentor?

By understanding how you can develop relatedness and increase your social capital, you can shape your teacher-learner identity so you know how to increase feelings of belonging and foster great relationships in any school you might work in for the rest of your teaching career. Learning does not occur in isolation and effective working relationships provide you with rich opportunities for personal and professional growth. While there are great benefits for the individual, effective working relationships also greatly benefit the school community and, ultimately, the pupils whom we serve.

YOUR TEACHER-LEARNER IDENTITY

In this chapter we have argued that you should develop an identity that puts your learning at the heart of what it means to be a teacher. We have also suggested some opportunities that will be presented to you, some ideas about how best to approach these, and some ideas about how to get over hurdles that you might face in your development. We want to conclude this chapter by reminding you that you are joining a profession, which means that part of your professional duty is to continue to seek out the opportunities for learning that your new career will present you with, because *every teacher needs to improve, not because they are not good enough, but because they can be even better* (Wiliam, 2019).

ASSIGNMENT LINKS

As part of your assignments during your training, you might be asked about:

1. How you have begun to develop a 'learning disposition' and how you see your identity as a teacher-learner
2. Specific moments where you were able to reflect on why experienced professionals had made the choice that they had (these might be described as 'crossroad moments')
3. How the theories you find in your reading of education literature are relevant to your own developing practice or placement contexts
4. How you are seeking and utilising opportunities to develop professional relationships.

LEARNING AND CONSOLIDATION ACTIVITIES

KEY THINGS TO LOOK OUT FOR DURING YOUR PLACEMENT

As you undertake your school placements, you might look out for and ask about:

- The ways in which experienced teachers continue to update their knowledge and understanding and develop their 'learner dispositions'. This is likely to be both at individual level and via group problem solving.
- The ways in which experienced teachers seek out and utilise the expertise of their colleagues. This will range from micro-moments to longer-term arrangements such as coaching or collaborative action research.
- Which sources of training, academic development, guidance, advice and support from beyond the school are utilised by teachers, and in what circumstances.

DISCUSSION POINTS FOR TUTORIALS AND SEMINARS

In your seminars and tutorials, you might get asked about:

- how you see yourself as a learner as well as a teacher;
- how you can make the most out of the opportunity of having a mentor;
- how you have prepared yourself to receive feedback, and then how you have reflected and acted upon it;
- how you might plan to expand your learning about education within and beyond the school.

It's important to note that these questions are not just summative 'place markers' in relation to that particular moment in your training but are posed to help establish habits of mind that will serve you well throughout your career.

IDEAS FOR GUIDED PRACTICE AND FEEDBACK

In order to implement the themes from this chapter into your own practice, you might now:

- Talk to your mentor, host teachers, staffroom colleagues and fellow trainees about practical strategies for maintaining a teacher-learner disposition.
- Find and bookmark websites and blogs relating to your phase and subject areas and sign up to newsletters or updates so that you will receive regular refreshers automatically.

- Speak to the school librarian about where to locate books and resources for staff continuing professional development. If there is no staff CPD library, you might be the person to nudge one into existence!
- Research opportunities in the local area or online for further qualifications/certification, e.g. university or college study while working, or online courses such as those provided by FutureLearn.org.uk. While you may find that you wish to wait until you have completed your early career years before pursuing further study, it is helpful to build awareness of your options.

CHAPTER SUMMARY

Now you have read this chapter, you will:

- understand that nurturing your learner identity will enhance your teacher identity throughout your career
- know that you should draw on the sources of knowledge available to you both within and beyond your school, in training and in employment
- identify ways in which you might strengthen your 'teacher-learner disposition' and, in doing so, strengthen your confidence in making a wider contribution in your workplace
- think of feedback as an opportunity and stimulus rather than as a threat
- revisit the importance of intentional work on social relationships with colleagues in order to gain from their explicit and hidden expertise and maintain positive wellbeing.

REFLECTION POINT

- What might be the potential barriers to maintaining a teacher-learner disposition? How might you overcome these barriers?
- What support exists within school for teachers-as-learners? This might take the form of people, resources, modelling or promotion of opportunities within and outside of the school.
- How do you feel about asking for help, ensuring you understand feedback fully, speaking up about knowledge and skill gaps, and articulating your learning needs and ambitions? Where have you noticed experienced colleagues doing this, and how did they go about it?
- What next steps might you take as you qualify and begin your career that will ensure that you avoid a 'progress plateau' and stay active as a learner?

FURTHER READING

McDonagh, C., Roche, M., Sullivan, B. and Glenn, M. (2020) *Enhancing Practice Through Classroom Research: A Teacher's Guide to Professional Development*. Routledge. This is a guide for teachers and by teachers about how to improve your own practice through a personal process of reflection, research and action. The 'self-study' approach outlined here reminds us that we don't need to wait for whole school CPD to work on deepening our learning.

Quigley, A. (2016) *The Confident Teacher*. Routledge. Alex Quigley talks honestly and with encouragement about facing his own fears in order to develop himself as a teacher, and the need to see change as an opportunity rather than a threat. You might also visit his website at theconfidentteacher.com for a range of thoughtful blogs on this theme.

Thom, J. (2018) *Slow Teaching: On Finding Calm, Clarity and Impact in the Classroom*. John Catt Publishing. In this clear and accessible book, Jamie Thom offers a range of practical ideas to help you and then your pupils take responsibility for developing learning.

REFERENCES

Adoniou, M. (2015) Teacher knowledge – a complex tapestry. *Asia-Pacific Journal of Teacher Education*, 43.

Ball, S.J. (2021) *The Education Debate*. Policy Press.

Beltman, S., Mansfield, C. and Price, A. (2011) Thriving not just surviving: a review of research on teacher resilience. *Educational Research Review*, 6(3): 185–207. DOI: 10.1016/j.edurev.2011.09.001

Brookfield, S. (1995) *Becoming a Critically Reflective Teacher*. San Francisco, CA: Jossey-Bass.

Deci, E. and Ryan, R. (2000) Self-determination theory and the facilitation of intrinsic motivation, social development, and well-being. *American Psychologist*, 55(1): 68–78. DOI: 10.1037/0003-066X.55.1.68

Cochran-Smith, M. and Lytle, S.L. (2009) *Inquiry as Stance: Practitioner Research for the Next Generation*. New York, NY: Teachers College Press.

Glackin, M. (2019) 'It's more than a prop': professional development session strategies as sources of teachers' self-efficacy and motivation to teach outside the classroom. *Professional Development in Education*, 45(3): 372–389. Routledge. DOI: 10.1080/19415257.2018.1490917

Hancock, C. (2016) Is the grass greener? Current and former music teachers' perceptions a year after moving to a different school or leaving the classroom. *Journal of Research in Music Education*, 63(4): 421–438. DOI: 10.1177/0022429415612191

Helsing, D. (2007) Regarding uncertainty in teachers and teaching. *Teaching and Teacher Education*, 23(8): 1317–1333. DOI: 10.1016/j.tate.2006.06.007

Kiechel, W. (2000) The new new capital thing. *Harvard Business Review*, *78*(4): 149–154. Available at: https://hbr.org/2000/07/the-new-new-capital-thing (accessed 29/7/22).

McCormick, K. (1992) Always already theorists: literary theory and theorising in the undergraduate curriculum, in M. Kecht (ed.) *Pedagogy is Politics*, pages 111–132. Illinois: University of Illinois Press.

Mccrea, P. (2018) *Expert Teaching: What It Is, and How Might We Develop It?* Institute for Teaching.

OECD (2015) *Frascati Manual 2015: Guidelines for Collecting and Reporting Data on Research and Experimental Development*, The Measurement of Scientific, Technological and Innovation Activities, OECD Publishing, Paris, DOI: 10.1787/9789264239012-en

Orchard, J. and Winch, C. (2015) What training do teachers need? Why theory is necessary to good teaching. *Impact, Nov 2015*(22): 1–43. DOI: 10.1111/2048-416X.2015.12002.x

Perry, J. (2022) English literature: what's the point? *Teaching English, Summer 2022*(29), NATE.

Putnam, R. (2000) *Bowling Alone: The Collapse and Renewal of American Community*. Simon and Schuster.

Schempp, P., Tan, S. and McCullick, B. (2002) The practices of expert teachers. *Teaching and Learning*, *23*(1): 99–106.

Udalowska, A. (2020) *Engaging Students with Asynchronous Online Tasks: Self-Determination Theory (SDT) Perspective*. Learning and Teaching Enhancement Unit, Aberystwyth University. Available at: https://wordpress.aber.ac.uk/e-learning/2020/10/05/engaging-students-with-asynchronous-online-tasks-self-determination-theory-sdt-perspective (accessed 1/11/21).

Vansteenkiste, M. (2020) Basic Psychological Needs. Center for Self-Determination Theory. Available at: https://selfdeterminationtheory.org/wp-content/uploads/2020/03/2020_VansteenkisteRyanSoenens_BPNSIntro_MOEM.pdf (accessed 4/3/22).

Wiliam, D. (2019) Teaching not a research-based profession. *Times Educational Supplement*, 30 May 2019.

Williams, J. (2004) *Great Minds: Education's Most Influential Philosophers* (A *Times Educational Supplement* Essential Guide).

3

PUPILS' SAFEGUARDING AND WELLBEING

ELIZABETH NASSEM AND NATASHA REYNOLDS

 **KEY WORDS**

- Emotional and physical safety
- Bullying and harassment
- Safeguarding
- Disclosure
- Cyber-bullying

CHAPTER OBJECTIVES

This chapter will introduce what we mean by safeguarding and wellbeing as well as highlighting the complexities around these terms. It is not possible to cover all possible interactions you will have with children in relation to their safety and wellbeing; however, we do outline how you can approach some challenging situations as they arise. As you read the chapter, you will be able to understand more about what is meant by the terms safeguarding and wellbeing as well as considering what constitutes different forms of abuse. We will outline and clarify expectations of your response to disclosure or suspected safeguarding issues, and in order to contextualise these, we will explore scenarios that might arise within your teaching career.

LINKS TO THE CORE CONTENT FRAMEWORK

All of the Core Content Framework themes are referred to and applied in this chapter, but the following are the most relevant:

Standard 1 – Set high expectations, particularly:

1. Teachers have the ability to affect and improve the wellbeing, motivation and behaviour of their pupils.
2. Teachers are key role models, who can influence the attitudes, values and behaviours of their pupils.

(Continued)

3. Setting clear expectations can help communicate shared values that improve classroom and school culture.

4. A culture of mutual trust and respect supports effective relationships.

Standard 7 – Manage behaviour effectively, particularly:

1. A predictable and secure environment benefits all pupils but is particularly valuable for pupils with special educational needs.

2. The ability to self-regulate one's emotions affects pupils' ability to learn, success in school and future lives.

3. Building effective relationships is easier when pupils believe that their feelings will be considered and understood.

Standard 8 – Fulfil wider professional responsibilities, particularly:

1. Teachers can make valuable contributions to the wider life of the school in a broad range of ways, including by supporting and developing effective professional relationships with colleagues.

2. Building effective relationships with parents, carers and families can improve pupils' motivation, behaviour and academic success.

INTRODUCTION

Safeguarding is the name given to the knowledge and processes that teachers and schools use to keep young people safe. In terms of permanent, high agenda responsibilities, safeguarding remains in number one position throughout your teaching career. This means that it has the potential to be one of the more daunting aspects of your role as teacher, but there is support, guidance and structures in place to enable you to manage this.

The greatest stories we hear are often reactive to situation; however, the focus for safeguarding is on preventative action to keep young people safe. This means that many of the 'worse case scenarios' you may fear having to deal with are prevented from taking place through the diligence of teachers and support staff. It is a broad term and often, when safeguarding is being discussed, you might also hear teachers talking about 'child protection'. Although both are linked, child protection issues have a slightly different focus. Safeguarding focuses on the prevention of harm, whereas child protection focuses on our (teachers and other appropriate agencies) response to harm. The wellbeing and safeguarding of all pupils is every teacher's responsibility, and the key roles assigned to colleagues in school will be introduced in this chapter. This chapter will cover the following topics: some of the different forms of abuse, eating disorders, the Prevent duty, bullying and sexual harassment. It will also outline what you need to do in the instance of you having safeguarding concerns.

HOW DO WE DEFINE SAFEGUARDING?

With this being such a key and broad area of our teaching responsibilities, it is important that we begin to think about what safeguarding actually means. There will be many nuanced discussions within schools around this, but as a starting point, safeguarding and promoting the welfare of children (those under 18 years of age) is defined by the government as:

- protecting children from maltreatment;
- preventing impairment of children's mental and physical health or development;
- ensuring that children grow up in circumstances consistent with the provision of safe and effective care;
- taking action to enable all children to have the best outcomes.

(DfE, 2018: 6–7)

There will be plenty of opportunity through your training and in any new school to become familiar with the safeguarding policy, key people and structures. It is worth starting to think about how you would aim to meet the demands of this definition as you develop as a trainee or ECT.

YOUR DUTY AS A TEACHER

The signs of risk and harm are not always visible, and as a teacher this emphasises why getting to know your pupils is not only beneficial to relationship building (See Chapters 2 and 5) but it also allows you to notice if their behaviour and attitudes change. Small strategies, such as standing by your classroom door to greet pupils as they enter your teaching space, are an important practice to establish because it offers teachers opportunity to check in with each pupil.

As you are probably aware, safeguarding is not a static role and is one which has updated guidance and support with some frequency. There are publications available to you as a teacher. You can keep yourself updated by reading the latest child protection and safeguarding updates from the Department for Education via www.gov.uk and organisations such as NSPCC. 'Keeping Children Safe in Education' is a key document available from www.gov.uk and is updated regularly. You may also sign up for weekly notifications from NSPCC through their Current Awareness Service for Policy, Practice and Research (CASPAR) briefing, as this will help you to keep yourself updated on safeguarding and child protection issues. You have a duty to ensure you are aware of the expectations on you with respect to safeguarding, so it is common to find that training days often have substantial elements of them dedicated to this topic. Due to the dynamic nature of safeguarding, we see additional policies and guidance emerging throughout our careers. Let's look, for example, at the Prevent duty.

The purpose of the Prevent duty in secondary schools is to prevent harm through radicalisation: to protect young people from radicalisation, as well as being drawn into terrorism. The Counter Terrorism and Security Act (July 2015) made it a legal requirement for schools, local authorities and other specified authorities and institutions to prevent people being drawn into terrorism. The Home Office (via gov.uk) offers online Prevent training which many schools and ITT providers use. Young people can be groomed and manipulated into radicalisation in the same way as they can with the forms of child abuse mentioned earlier in this chapter, and therefore, the risk of radicalisation or extremism should be taken as seriously as any other safeguarding concern. You would not be expected to investigate such a situation, but you would be expected to refer it to you your school's DSO, in the same way you would any other safeguarding concern.

WHAT CONSTITUTES ABUSE?

It is worth considering what we mean by abuse and how this can be identified. Abuse is maltreatment and can occur through causing or failing to prevent harm to a young person. Harm can take many forms, including mental as well as physical abuse such as domestic abuse and its effects on young people within the household. Abuse can take place in different settings, such as clubs and other organisations where young people may regularly attend. In more recent times, technology can play a major role in the progression of abuse, and it can be a platform to initiate offline abuse, and this is something we will pick up on later in the chapter. Some indicators of abuse and neglect are listed below as a starting point for your own thinking.

1. **Physical:** where a young person is physically harmed, and can include hitting, throwing, burning and any other action that may cause physical harm.
2. **Emotional:** where a young person's emotional development is impeded due to ongoing maltreatment and includes bullying.
3. **Sexual:** forcing or coercing a young person to participate in sexual activities, whether the child is aware or not of what is taking place. This can include physical and non-contact activities, such as grooming, in preparation for sexual abuse to take place.
4. **Neglect:** the serious impairment of a young person's health or development due to an ongoing failure to meet their physical and/or psychological needs.
5. **Child-on-child abuse:** there is a clear expectation that teachers in schools and colleges do not 'downplay' incidents of sexual harassment and bullying as 'banter' and 'part of growing up' as this can contribute to the abuse of young people being normalised.

MANAGING DISCLOSURES

Many new teachers have their first encounter with safeguarding issues through a 'disclosure' – meaning a pupil talks to you about a situation or incident where they or someone they know is at risk of harm or has been harmed. It is important that you follow your school's safeguarding policy, and to offer you further support, below is an outline of how you might respond if a pupil disclosed information to you that is a safeguarding concern. We will refer back to this box throughout the chapter as it forms the basis for good safeguarding protocol.

WHAT TO DO WITH A SAFEGUARDING CONCERN

1. **Reassure:** tell the pupils that they have done the right thing by talking to you about the situation.
2. **Listen silently:** listen without interrupting. Teachers do not decide what constitutes a legitimate concern; all claims must be taken seriously and reported in the appropriate way to the Designated Safeguarding Officer (DSO).
3. **Do not make promises of confidentiality:** it may be that the pupil asks that you do not tell anyone else about the information they have shared with you, or if you can keep this a secret, because of its sensitivity, for example. Please understand that you have a legal obligation to pass this information on to the DSO in your school.
4. **Write it up:** provide a detailed statement of the information given to you by the pupil, which should include dates, times, locations and names of the person/people involved.
5. **Inform the DSO immediately:** you should speak with the DSO to inform them of the situation immediately, or as soon as practically possible. The DSO will then contact appropriate agencies (such as the police or a local authority child protection agency). If you are a trainee on placement, you should also contact the DSO at your university and report the incident – this will often be your course lead.
6. **If the school DSO is unavailable:** you should report this to the DSO's deputy. If their deputy is unavailable, you could speak with a member of your school's Senior Leadership Team (head teacher, deputy and assistant head teachers), and you can directly refer the incident to the police or local authority child protection agency.
7. **Only discuss with appropriate colleagues:** you should not discuss/disclose information about this incident beyond the DSO (including their deputy), a member of your school's Senior Leadership Team (if DSO is unavailable), the police or local authority child protection agencies.
8. **What if you are personally affected by a safeguarding situation?** It can be worrying and upsetting when you encounter your first safeguarding incident and if you are affected by something arising from a safeguarding situation, you should speak about this with your school's DSO, who will further advise you. It may also be necessary for you to speak with your GP or another appropriate professional whose care you are under (e.g. a counsellor) about the situation in order to ensure your personal wellbeing is supported. You can also find approaches and strategies to help with your wellbeing and self-care in Chapter 5.

SAFEGUARDING AND YOUR LEARNING ENVIRONMENT

As a teacher, it is your responsibility to create a learning environment in which all pupils are physically and emotionally safe. You must establish expectations for and model the appropriate manner in which pupils should communicate with one another, be able to listen respectfully, along with general rules of conduct in your lesson. You can find more information about creating a positive learning environment and lesson planning in Chapter 6.

CASE STUDY

An eating disorder?

A pupil in your Year 9 form asks for your advice. She is worried about her friend, who she thinks is anorexic. She has noticed that she no longer eats lunch with them, exercises and walks excessively, and has talked about finding websites to help with avoiding food. Your pupil does not want to tell you the name of her friend; however, you are able to identify who she is talking about because you have noticed this pupil becoming more withdrawn and detached from form activity.

- What other signs of harm might you notice as a teacher of this pupil?
- Why are these kinds of harms so difficult to spot?
- What kinds of curricula experiences might highlight or expose related signs of harm?
- How would you respond to this pupil?

Among other reasons, eating disorders can develop as a stress response when a person feels they lack control in their lives. School-based triggers could be exams or other forms of assessments (performance-based activities, including sports events, can cause considerable stress for some young people) and changes in friendship groups. Triggers beyond school could include parental separation or loss of a parent or sibling, moving home, abuse and anxiety. Anxiety can often show itself as heightened worry during high-stakes periods, such as during exam/assessment periods or public-facing events such as sports day or other team events. Pupils can show this in a number of ways, such as becoming upset or tearful, being angry or aggressive, and also becoming withdrawn – and this is why getting to know your pupils is so important. By talking to your pupils on a regular basis – and not just in your lessons, for example, during form times, in the corridor, at break/lunch times – you will be able to build a rapport and notice changes in their behaviour. Your professional role as a teacher extends beyond the classroom walls. If you are teaching a subject that involves any work outside the classroom, be prepared that the less formal setting will allow for conversations that traditionally would not happen in the class. These are the greatest benefits of teaching in such spaces, but it shapes the nature of the relationship between teacher and pupil.

Always be ready to move into safeguarding situations, and remember the guidance set out above. You may sometimes feel that it is just a one-off or that the pupil has offered a plausible reason for certain behaviour. However, you may find that other colleagues in school have raised similar concerns with the DSO and this gives additional information for contact with specialist agencies, such as the police and local authority child services. Referring onwards is always the best policy. It is also worth noting that you would not be expected to talk to the pupil about how they have come to be in possession of such items. Questions of this nature could be interpreted as an accusation of theft and can result in a confrontational response.

During your time on placement, class teachers and form tutors should be present when you are teaching, to offer support and provide you with ongoing feedback for your subject and professional development. If you did notice a pupil you had concerns about, you should make the teacher or form tutor aware of this, who would support you in the process of referring this situation to the DSO. You should always be seeking advice from expert colleagues – the teachers and form tutors whose classes you are assigned to, your mentor and the DSO.

CASE STUDY

Racist comments or a Prevent referral?

During a lesson you are teaching, you overhear a pupil making a series of racist comments about a family described in the lesson resources and about another pupil in the class who comes from the same country as the family in the resource. The pupil tells the person sitting next to them that that pupil and her family are probably terrorists.

- What different ways could you deal with this situation? Ask your peers and tutors for more ideas.

- With your mentor or another appropriate colleague in school, investigate how your school policies are used to protect and support every young person in the school.

- Think about how you create a culture within your class that signals how to talk about these issues.

- As you respond to such instances, it is important that you maintain a calm manner.

1. It is essential that you write up the incident as a matter of urgency and make a referral to the Senior Leadership Team along with the appropriate pastoral lead, such as head of year. Even in jest, such comments are not acceptable.

2. The pupil's comments linking to terrorism mean that you are also required to report this as part of your school's response to the Prevent duty.

3 Pupils' safeguarding and wellbeing

BULLYING AND CYBERBULLYING

WHAT IS BULLYING?

A commonly discussed way that pupils can experience harm is from other pupils through being bullied. Schools have a legal duty to have measures in place to prevent bullying (DfE, 2017). What bullying is and when behaviour is considered bullying can be a challenge.

School bullying is usually defined as a specific form of aggression among pupils, tends to be repeated, is intentional and there is a clear imbalance of power between pupils (Olweus, 1993). However, this definition has been criticised. It is difficult for teachers to prove that maltreatment is intentional as many pupils say they 'didn't mean it'. There are cases when people can be just as harmed by one experience of aggression, and it can be difficult to identify a clear imbalance of power between pupils (Mishna, 2004; Lee, 2006).

Bullying can be overt, for example, through physical violence such as hitting, and it can be covert, for example, through individuals being ostracised. Overt bullying is more likely to be noticed and punished by teachers whereas covert bullying can be more difficult to recognise. It is helpful to understand bullying as a spectrum of maltreatment that can range from mild to severe such as teasing, ostracism and being kicked. However, interactions which might appear to be mild such as teasing can be associated with extreme distress for pupils. Pascoe (2013) argues that Olweus' (1993) definition does not consider how many of the aggressive interactions between children and young people can be associated with broader issues of inequality in society such as in gender and social class.

A prevalent feature of bullying is a sense of being trapped where pupils feel they cannot just stop their bullying, for example, by telling a teacher. Pupils who are victimised are often frightened, hurt and can develop a range of insecurities. One of the biggest signs that a child is being severely bullied is that they are significantly ostracised, persistently blamed for incidents and it becomes a peer group norm that they are segregated (Nassem, 2019). Pupils often find it difficult to report bullying to their teachers because they are frightened that it might make the bullying worse; for example, the perpetrator might become angry because they have been reported. Several children who are victimised can also feel ashamed and this can prevent them from reporting their abuse. Bullying is becoming increasingly spread online and what remains online can remain indefinitely (Kyriacou and Zuin, 2016). Although pupils who are bullied online do not always know their perpetrator, most pupils who are bullied online know their perpetrator and also get bullied by them in school (Wolke et al., 2017). This highlights how online bullying cannot always be clearly distinguished from bullying in school, which can add further complexities to tackling bullying.

> ### CASE STUDY
>
> **Bullying or Banter?**
>
> A girl named Melanie and a boy named Lee who are both in the same year group are talking to each other. Lee is telling Melanie about the new clothes and video games his mum has bought him. Lee asks Melanie, "What has your mum bought you lately?" and Melanie replies, "Nothing. You are just spoilt, aren't you?" and they both start laughing. In a class discussion about bullying, Melanie is the first to speak up and say, "There is no bullying. It's like that with Lee and I; we're always joking with each other."
>
> - Would you consider the interactions between Melanie and Lee bullying, and if so, who is bullying whom?
>
> - In your teaching practice, you could reflect on how broader issues of inequality, such as racism or gender, can contribute to experiences of bullying that children might have.

The example above has been taken from Nassem (2019) which demonstrates that, in some cases, it can be difficult to fully understand how individuals perceive their interactions and whether they are being harmed. Through facilitating dialogue with Melanie, it emerged that she was particularly upset by Lee's comments about his material possessions as she lives with just her mum in a caravan and doesn't have much money. It is important to understand the circumstances of the individuals involved and how they feel about their interactions when bullying is being investigated. This can be particularly complex if individuals who feel bullied laugh. However, some children don't want to show how upset they are, particularly if they are afraid that showing their upset could increase their bullying. It is important to examine beyond the surface of interactions where children are teasing each other and speak to children to find out more about their interactions. As a trainee teacher you need to explore these concerns with your host teachers and mentors. They are likely to have a more fully formed picture of any particular pupil's circumstances and help you in being supportive and taking the right next steps.

WHY DO PUPILS BULLY?

We often hear that the bully in a situation is often going through some period of challenge in their own life. This is not to excuse their behaviour, but it can be helpful to try to understand it. One of the main reasons children engage in bullying is to become popular and gain social approval and respect from their peers. Another reason children engage in bullying is because they are bored. Children who are bored can feel entrapped, and that they lack control and agency. Bullying can entertain children and provide a temporary release from boredom. Children also engage in bullying because they have been bullied. Researchers such as Wendt et al. (2019) have found that children who engage in bullying are a minority of individuals who lack empathy and are manipulative. However, Mishna et al. (2020) argue that bullying is entrenched within children's everyday experiences of school and has become normalised and minimised. Nassem (2017, 2019) interviewed over 90 children about bullying and none of them considered themselves as bullies. Instead, children attributed responsibility to other pupils, their teachers and inequalities in school.

TACKLING BULLYING

Read your school's anti-bullying policy and make sure that you follow your school's anti-bullying policy when you become aware of bullying. The Department for Education (DfE) (2017) recommends that schools evaluate and update their approach to new technology. It is useful to be aware of the ways that children are currently communicating with each other online as the platforms children can use for social networking can change rapidly. The online and digital world presents opportunities for inappropriate interaction between pupils that is not obvious to the teachers, parents or carers – and it is far more likely that this information will come to light through a disclosure by the bullied pupil or their friend. The spectrum of bullying may be similar to that in real life – groups or individuals ostracising through sharing of social events that someone wasn't invited to. It may be a more deliberate act of writing things that are offensive and hurtful or sharing these with others. It could be sharing of information or images that are of a sexual nature. This means that concerns about a pupil being bullied, or bullying others, might arise out of a pattern of things, and you should raise these worries just as you would for more obvious events.

There are different ways to deal with such matters, although the DfE (2017) advises that disciplinary cases should be fair and consistent. Punishment is often used in schools in England as a way to respond to bullying; for example, children who bully might be placed in isolation. However, punishments can contribute to children feeling angry and 'picked on' and this can further perpetuate bullying. A number of schools use restorative approaches as part of their anti-bullying policies and practices to tackle bullying (see Chapter 5). Restorative approaches focus on structured communication with individuals who are in conflict to discuss why the conflict has occurred and focuses on repairing relationships between individuals (Barter, 2011) However, restorative approaches might be traumatic for victims who could be concerned about being bullied if they have restorative meetings with their perpetrator (Littlechild and Sender, 2010; Song and Swearer, 2016). Restorative dialogue could be facilitated with the perpetrator and a teacher by asking questions such as: why did you respond the way you did? How might other children feel as a consequence? What are the alternative ways you could respond to other pupils you might be in conflict with? However, we reiterate that this would not be for you to take the lead on without support and direction from your more experienced colleagues in school.

> **■ ■ ■ — REFLECTION POINT**
>
> How does your school create and implement anti-bullying strategies? To what extent do you think your school substantially involves pupils in tackling bullying?

It is important that pupils connect to messages from school about bullying. Children can be disengaged by teacher-led assemblies about bullying and think that the messages are intended for the perpetrators of bullying and not them. Pupils could be involved in designing and implementing strategies to tackle bullying such as anti-bullying assemblies. This could include consultations with children about how pupils experience bullying, how they think pupils and teachers respond to bullying, and their ideas about how bullying should be addressed. Discussions could also be facilitated with pupils about their group norms, popularity and how pupils who are ostracised can be included.

SEXUAL HARASSMENT

In recent times, there has been an increased awareness about sexual harassment in schools. Again, this is a broad term and so we will define sexual harassment as *an all-encompassing term used to describe a spectrum of sexual behaviour* which is not wanted, agreed to or understood (Bovill et al., 2019: 1253). Forms of sexual harassment include catcalling, offensive sexual jokes, stalking and rape. The continuum of sexual harassment can range from mild (for example, offensive sexual jokes) to more severe (such as unwanted touching). Similarly to bullying, sexual harassment which appears to be mild, such as sexual comments, can be associated with serious distress for recipients.

Dahlqvist et al. (2021) argue that sexual harassment of pupils is a growing concern partly because there is an increase of sexualisation of girls, for example, in social media, and an increase in accessibility to violent pornography online. Furthermore, being in an environment where there is a risk of being exposed to sexual harassment can lead to a hostile environment even for non-exposed pupils. Ofsted (2021) recently published a report on sexual harassment and sexual abuse. They have found that sexual harassment and online abuse is commonplace in pupils' lives where children report that sexist name-calling happens a lot and girls have been rated out of ten for their looks and although research shows that sexual harassment is most often carried out by boys against girls, the NUT (2007) found that girls are increasingly directing abuse at other girls and boys. Stonewall (2017) have found that the majority of pupils hear the phrases 'that's so gay' or 'you're so gay' in school. It has also been found that both males and females reported being sexually 'touched up' against their will (Duncan, 1999; Bovill et al., 2019). Duncan (1999) argues that males can experience similarly sexually offensive language to girls. Schools are now required to listen more to the voices of children in relation to sexual harassment and abuse. Ofsted (2021) will be investigating how the system of safeguarding in school listens to the voices of children and what prevents children from reporting sexual abuse.

> ■ ■ ■ — **REFLECTION POINT**
>
> - When you were a pupil, were you aware of any forms of sexual harassment in school? If so, what were they?
> - Reflect on your current and/or previous placement/s. Did you notice any of the forms of sexual harassment discussed in this part of the chapter? If so, what were they?
> - Have you ever witnessed a teacher try to tackle sexual harassment, and if so, what strategies did they use?
> - To what extent do you think that the voices of pupils are listened to in relation to sexual harassment?

If you observe comments and behaviours from children which might be on the spectrum of sexual harassment, then make sure that you read and apply your school's safeguarding and behavioural policy. If you become aware that children are engaging in or experiencing harmful or illegal behaviour, then this should immediately be referred to the DSO. If your school is developing strategies to tackle sexual harassment and you would like to contribute to this, then you could ask your supervisor how you might get involved. Improving understanding of sexual harassment and communication about it can contribute to positive and proactive strategies to tackle it.

> ■ ■ ■ — **ASSIGNMENT LINKS**
>
> 1. As part of your Safeguarding and Child Protection training, your university may ask you to complete an assessment or online test after you have engaged with their teaching on this topic. The focus is on understanding the policy and responses required.
> 2. Observers might comment on how pupils interact with each other and the group dynamics, e.g. how pupils contribute to classroom discussions and how pupils interact in group work. Pupils who are abused might be reluctant to engage in classroom discussions. It is worthwhile to discuss the impact of bullying and deal with bullying in class when it arises. Reflect on how pupils interact with each other, how they articulate their voice and when they might be experiencing bullying.

KEY THINGS TO LOOK FOR WHEN OBSERVING

- Safeguarding, child protection and Prevent: be aware of how teachers weave signposting of how to report or talk about an incident into their lessons through topics or texts that they are teaching.

3 Pupils' safeguarding and wellbeing

- Notice how teachers respond to pupils when there are interactions with pupils that might be construed as bullying. Where possible, speak with a class teacher about their strategies for responding to bullying and how the school responds.

- Observe and notice the group dynamics in class, e.g. friendship groups, pupils' responses to each other. Is there a child who might sit on their own? Why might that be? Try to learn from children why they might be engaging in bullying. Find out if there are any issues which might be distracting children from their learning; there could be safeguarding concerns.

LEARNING AND CONSOLIDATION ACTIVITIES
DISCUSSING POINTS FOR TUTORIALS AND SEMINARS

- Watch the video, identify the types of abuse taking place (physical, emotional, sexual or neglect) and make notes on what the actions are from professional colleagues in response to each of these. https://youtu.be/MWB4dy_ObPE

- Using resources from the NSPCC YouTube channel to learn about specific aspects of safeguarding and child protection. www.youtube.com/c/NSPCCLearning/videos

- Read and follow your school's safeguarding policy. Read your school's anti-bullying policy and note down: how is bullying defined? Who should bullying be reported to? What happens when bullying is reported? What are the strengths and weaknesses of this policy? Additional activity: ask children to read their school's anti-bullying policy. Find out what children think about the policy and ask if they have any ideas for how the policy can be developed.

ACTIVITIES IN SCHOOL PLACEMENT

Access to your school's Safeguarding, Child Protection and Prevent policies should be made available to you as part of your formal induction to your school. If there are areas you do not understand, you should seek further clarification from your mentor and/or DSO.

Activity on school bullying: read your school's anti-bullying policy and note down: how is bullying defined? Who should bullying be reported to? What happens when bullying is reported? What are the strengths and weaknesses of this policy? Ask children what they think about their school's anti-bullying policy and how it can be developed.

CHAPTER SUMMARY

- Safeguarding, child protection and an understanding of the Prevent duty is every teacher's responsibility and you must understand policy and process relating to these areas.

(Continued)

- If a pupil discloses information to you, you cannot promise that the information they share will not be referred to a designated lead (such as Designated Safeguarding Lead, Designated Prevent Lead) or another appropriate colleague (including the head teacher). It is important to allow the pupils space to speak and you should make detailed notes.

- When dealing with bullying or racist behaviour in a whole-class situation, you should respond to pupils in a calm and objective manner, drawing upon your knowledge of your school's policies and the appropriate legislation.

- Schools can enhance understanding of safeguarding issues that harness pupil voice.

- Trainee teachers can also learn from the supervision and guidance of experienced teachers about safeguarding.

FURTHER READING

NSPCC (2020) How safe are our children? Available at: https://learning.nspcc.org.uk/research-resources/how-safe-are-our-children. Includes an overview of data about the abuse of adolescents.

Ofsted (2021) *Review of Sexual Abuse in Schools and Colleges*. Available at: www.gov.uk/government/publications/review-of-sexual-abuse-in-schools-and-colleges/review-of-sexual-abuse-in-schools-and-colleges. Provides an overview and up-to-date research findings about how pupils can experience sexual harassment in school.

Nassem, E. (2019) *The Teacher's Guide to Resolving School Bullying: Evidence Based Strategies and Pupil-Led Interventions*. Jessica Kingsley. This book delves into the complex nature of bullying at school in a clear and comprehensive way. It draws on cutting-edge research to help school practitioners understand children's perceptions and experiences of bullying and resolve bullying using pupil-led approaches.

REFERENCES

Barter, D. (March 2011) A restorative critique of restorative justice. Talk given at the Mediation and Restorative Justice Commission of the Rio Grande do Sul state branch of the Brazilian Lawyers Association, Porto Alegre, Brazil.

Barter, D. (2012) Walking toward conflict. *Tikkun*, 27: 21–70. DOI: 10.1215/08879982-2012-1010

Bovill, H., Waller, R. and McCartan, K. (2019) Discussing atypical sexual harassment as a controversial issue in bystander programmes: one UK campus study. *Sexuality and Culture*, 1–19. DOI: 10.1007/s12119-019-09682-8

Busher, J. and Jerome, L. (eds) (2020) *The Prevent Duty in Education: Impact, Enactment and Implications*. Cham, Switzerland: Palgrave Macmillan (Palgrave pivot).

Dahlqvist, H., Svensson, Å. and Gillander Gådin, K. (2022) Co-occurrence of online and offline bullying and sexual harassment among youth in Sweden: implications for studies on victimization and health a short communication. *International Journal of Circumpolar Health*, *81*(1), 2130362.

DfE (June 2015) *The Prevent Duty: Departmental Advice for Schools and Childcare Providers*. Available at: https://assets.publishing.service.gov.uk/government/uploads/system/uploads/attachment_data/file/439598/prevent-duty-departmental-advice-v6.pdf

DfE (2017) *Preventing and Tackling Bulling. Advice for Headteachers, Staff and Governing Bodies*. Department for Education.

DfE (July 2018) *Working Together to Safeguard Children*. Available at: https://assets.publishing.service.gov.uk/government/uploads/system/uploads/attachment_data/file/942454/Working_together_to_safeguard_children_inter_agency_guidance.pdf

DfE (September 2021) *Ofsted Safeguarding Policy*. Available at: www.gov.uk/government/publications/ofsted-safeguarding-policy/ofsted-safeguarding-policy

DfE (September 2022) *Keeping Children Safe in Education 2022*. Available at: https://assets.publishing.service.gov.uk/government/uploads/system/uploads/attachment_data/file/1101457/KCSIE_2022_Part_One.pdf

Duncan, N. (1999) *Sexual Bullying: Gender Conflict and Pupil Culture in Secondary Schools* (1st ed.). Routledge. DOI: 10.4324/9780203019108

HM Government (June 2011) The Prevent strategy review. Available at: https://assets.publishing.service.gov.uk/government/uploads/system/uploads/attachment_data/file/97976/prevent-strategy-review.pdf

Home Office (2021) Revise Prevent duty guidance for England and Wales. Available at: www.gov.uk/government/publications/prevent-duty-guidance/revised-prevent-duty-guidance-for-england-and-wales

Kyriacou, C. and Zuin, A. (2016) Cyberbullying and moral disengagement: an analysis based on a social pedagogy of pastoral care in schools. *Pastoral Care in Education*, *34*: 34–42. DOI: 10.1080/02643944.2015.1134631

Lee, C. (2006) Exploring teachers' definitions of bullying. *Emotional and Behavioural Difficulties*, *11*(1): 61–75. DOI: 10.1080/13632750500393342

Littlechild, B. and Sender, H. (2010) The introduction of restorative justice approaches in young people's residential units: a critical evaluation. Centre for Community Research, University of Hertfordshire.

Mishna, F. (2004) A qualitative study of bullying from multiple perspectives. *Children & Schools*, *26*(4): 234–247. DOI: 10.1093/cs/26.4.234

Mishna, F., Sanders, J.E., McNeil, S. Fearing, G. and Kalenteridis, K. (2020) "If somebody is different": a critical analysis of parent, teacher and student perspectives on bullying and cyberbullying. *Children and Youth Services Review*, *118*. DOI: 10.1016/j.childyouth.2020.105366

Nassem, E.M. (2017) The complexity of children's involvement in school bullying. *Journal of Children's Services*, *12*(4): 288–301. DOI: 10.1108/JCS-03-2017-0009

Nassem, E. (2019) *The Teacher's Guide to Resolving School Bullying: Evidence Based Strategies and Pupil-Led Interventions*. Jessica Kingsley.

National Union of Teachers (2007) NUT Policy Statement on Preventing Sexual Harassment and Bullying. NUT.

NSPCC (2020) How safe are our children? NSPCC. Available at: https://learning.nspcc.org.uk/research-resources/how-safe-are-our-children

Ofsted (2021) *Review of Sexual Abuse in Schools and Colleges*. Available at: www.gov.uk/government/publications/review-of-sexual-abuse-in-schools-and-colleges/review-of-sexual-abuse-in-schools-and-colleges

Olweus, D. (1993) *Bullying at School: What We Know and What We Can Do*. Malden, MA: Blackwell Publishing.

Pascoe, C. (2013) Notes on a sociology of bullying: young men's homophobia as gender socialization. *QED: A Journal in GLBTQ Worldmaking*, *1*: 87–103. DOI: 10.1353/qed.2013.0013

Song, S. and Swearer, S. (2016) The cart before the horse: the challenge and promise of restorative justice consultation in schools. *Journal of Educational and Psychological Consultation*, *26*(4): 313–324. DOI: 10.1080/10474412.2016.1246972

Stones, S. and Glazzard, J. (2020) *Relationships and Sex Education for Secondary Schools: A Practical Toolkit for Teachers*. St Albans: Critical Publishing (Practical Teaching).

Stonewall (2017) School Report. The experiences of lesbian, gay, bi and trans young people in schools in 2017. Stonewall.

Wendt, G.W., Appel-Silva, M. and Jones-Bartoli, A.P. (2019) Bullying involvement and psychopathic personality: disentangling the links among college students. *European Journal of Education and Psychology*, *12*(2): 125–137.

Wolke, D., Lee, K., Guy, A. (2017) Cyberbullying: a storm in a teacup? *European Child & Adolescent Psychiatry*, Aug, *26*(8): 899–908. DOI: 10.1007/s00787-017-0954-6

4

TEACHER WELLBEING

KATHRYN CAMERON AND IAN NEEDHAM

▬▬▬ KEY WORDS ▬▬▬

- Resilience
- Reflection
- Time management

- Wellbeing
- Relationships
- Critical incidents

CHAPTER OBJECTIVES

Teaching is an extremely rewarding career, quite unlike any other. However, it comes with many challenges that you need to be prepared for. You will already have seen media reports that teaching can be stressful. You may also know that one third of teachers leave within the first five years of qualifying (DfE, 2020). Retaining good staff represents a huge challenge for schools, and given the financial and emotional investment that you will have made in deciding to become a teacher, ITT providers and schools should help trainee teachers understand and deal with the inevitable stresses and pressures of the role.

This chapter will consider the academic and school-based issues and challenges typically faced during the PGCE year. Understanding strategies for maximising wellbeing and resilience are crucial and these will be discussed together with tools and techniques to help you recognise and deal with difficulties. Guidance on where to find additional support and guidance and further reading is provided.

▬▬▬ LINKS TO THE CORE CONTENT FRAMEWORK ▬▬▬

All of the Core Content Framework themes are referred to and applied in this chapter, but the following are the most relevant:

Standard 1 – Set high expectations, particularly:

1. Teachers are key role models, who can influence the attitudes, values and behaviours of their pupils.

(Continued)

4 Teacher wellbeing

Standard 7 – Manage behaviour effectively

1. The ability to self-regulate one's emotions affects pupils' ability to learn, success in school and future lives.

Standard 8 – Fulfil wider professional responsibilities

1. Effective professional development is likely to be sustained over time, involve expert support or coaching and opportunities for collaboration.
2. Reflective practice, supported by feedback from and observation of experienced colleagues, professional debate, and learning from educational research, is also likely to support improvement.
3. Teachers can make valuable contributions to the wider life of the school in a broad range of ways, including by supporting and developing effective professional relationships with colleagues.

━━ ■ ■ ■ ━━ **REFLECTION POINT** ━━

Working individually, in a pair or small group, spend five minutes discussing (as you feel comfortable) the following:

- What is wellbeing?
- What challenges do you think your wellbeing will face in your ITT year?
- What other life events can present a challenge to our wellbeing?

In a survey conducted by the authors in 2022, trainee teachers, at the end of their PGCE, associated wellbeing with a range of different feelings (see Figure 4.1).

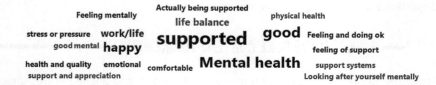

Figure 4.1 Survey results from trainee teachers in 2022

This word cloud demonstrates the importance of support and the networks you will need to develop to enhance and protect your wellbeing, as well as succeed in your course. It is clear that this support is mutual – while you will rely on support provided by others, you will similarly provide this for your peers and colleagues. There is more on this topic in this chapter, as well as in Chapter 2, about developing your teacher-learner identity.

WELLBEING AND RECOGNISING THREATS

Wellbeing is a much-discussed term yet can mean different things to different people. Holmes (2018: 5) defines wellbeing as *being in a comfortable or healthy state*. That said, wellbeing is a much more multi-faceted concept, such that: *Wellbeing can be understood as how people feel and how they function, both on a personal and a social level, and how they evaluate their lives as a whole* (New Economics Foundation, 2012).

Amid busy lives, we rarely take time out to self-evaluate our own wellbeing nor to recognise what is working well and what represents a threat. In contrast, we regularly look after the health of our car through servicing and an MOT.

Regardless of background, experience and belief system, all teachers experience a unique set of challenges that can, if allowed, negatively affect our wellbeing, or even become overwhelming (Holmes, 2018). Maintaining understanding of potential threats to your wellbeing is therefore vital. Research from Holmes (2018), Shields and Mullen (2020) and Bandura (1997) suggests that these threats can arise from:

- excessive stress and anxiety;
- burnout;
- excessive workload;
- difficult professional relationships;
- dealing with critical incidents.

As trainees, throughout your teaching journey, you will experience highs and lows. The key is to recognise and celebrate the highs and understand there may be times of feeling disheartened, overworked or undervalued. In these times we need to know how to select and utilise appropriate tools and techniques, access supportive networks, focus on what is important and recognise that any setback is only temporary. We will help you to do that by considering how you might:

- work with stress;
- develop habits and techniques of resilience;

- manage your time and workload;
- learn from negative feedback;
- deal with critical incidents.

WORKING WITH STRESS

In order to work positively with stress, we need to understand the difference between 'eustress', which means stress which is positive, and negative stress, which we will refer to as 'distress' (Holmes, 2018: 12).

EUSTRESS – HEALTHY CHALLENGES

We need to bear in mind that not all stress is damaging. Schools are exciting, dynamic environments where no two days are the same. Furthermore, teachers deal with a huge variety of personalities, potential barriers to learning and a myriad of external factors. Challenges and difficulties are therefore totally normal at every stage of a teacher's career. Although these challenges will compete for your time and energy, it is this complexity and variety that often makes teaching an attractive career. Many teachers will tell you that when barriers are overcome or a pupil's difficulties addressed, the sense of achievement is extremely rewarding. Eustress or positive stress can motivate us by demanding a higher level of performance, ultimately resulting in a stronger feeling of satisfaction (Holmes, 2018).

DISTRESS

Too much 'distress' causes biological and psychological responses. Over time these may lead to more serious reactions such as panic attacks, raised blood pressure or sleep disturbance. Too much distress can also cause demotivation and fatigue. It is crucial to be alert to these warning signs in ourselves and others, and to act to reduce the kinds of distress you are feeling.

When reactions or symptoms are noticed (by you or others), it is vital not to ignore but to act. This could simply mean taking a short break but if persistent should certainly involve consultation with a healthcare professional or GP. This should help to preserve positive mental health and to retain teachers to the profession.

You don't need to wait until you feel overwhelmed by stress and often we can plan ahead about identifiable stressful situations and reduce our emotional arousal to perceived threats (Bandura, 1997). You could discuss potential scenarios and options in school with your mentor or at university with your tutors and peers. This gives you an opportunity to practise responses in a non-threatening environment. We will look at this again in the section on dealing with critical incidents.

GETTING SUPPORT WITH STRESS

Asking for support is a sign of being human, and not weakness. Trainee teachers are surrounded by people equipped and willing to help and support. School-based mentors and co-ordinators or professional tutors, as well as your tutors at your training provider, will want to help you as much as they can. Trainees often use social media to keep in contact with their network of fellow trainees and use this to raise common issues, concerns and problems (although we must emphasise the importance of maintaining professional conduct within these). Just talking about worries and concerns to a close friend or partner can put them into perspective as well as help you think through some solutions.

You will also find that a great deal of academic support is also available. This may be particularly useful for those returning to a university from other industries, although more recent graduates may find the transition to a professional course daunting. Everyone brings with them different strengths and also challenges. Any trainees wanting help in developing their academic writing skills, and those with particular or special educational needs, will find that there is support available.

Despite the above, trainees might still experience difficulties coping. If this happens, further help is available through the education support charity (www.educationsupport.org.uk/). There is also a teacher support helpline (08000 562 561).

HABITS AND TECHNIQUES OF RESILIENCE?

Although some individuals may be naturally more resilient than others, you can develop habits and techniques that will help you feel more resilient. Research indicates that resilience is a major influence on a teacher's wellbeing, sense of purpose, motivation and job satisfaction, and so, unsurprisingly, resilience is a key factor when considering teacher retention beyond five years (Shields and Mullen, 2020).

An exact definition of teacher resilience is difficult to 'pin down'. Our ITT trainees defined resilience as: 'ability to keep going', 'put negative experiences behind you', 'determination to carry on through setbacks' and 'being able to take on any challenge you are faced with'. The Oxford English Dictionary defines resilience as *the capacity to recover quickly from difficulties; toughness* and Shields and Mullen (2020) define teacher resilience as *a process of adaption where teachers employ strategies to overcome adversity in their profession*. In this latter definition, resilience is not something you have, but a process – something you do. So that 'recovering quickly' from the knocks of professional life is something you can learn to do and get better at.

YOUR 'PURPOSE'

A good place to start is by recognising that you have already shown some important aspects of resilience. Shields and Mullen (2020) found that a sense of purpose, positive relationships and passion for teaching (Shields and Mullen, 2020) were key sources of resilience, enabling teachers to stay in the profession.

Most of those who embark upon an ITT course have invested a great deal to get to that point. Perhaps you have already worked in school or taken courses to develop your subject knowledge. You may also have saved money or be making sacrifices to train and therefore shown that you have the sense of purpose that can be a good foundation for resilience.

Throughout the training year, next steps targets and actions to achieve will be set that, with support, will help to develop expertise when achieved. As each new milestone is achieved, resilience strengthens as an identified difficulty has been overcome. Learning to be a teacher must be approached in incremental steps such that each time a hurdle is overcome, or target achieved, there will be another waiting to be solved. The key is to recognise this journey and accept that it is 'normal' at times to feel unsure or out of one's depth. Each new step and target can seem daunting but should be determined in conjunction with experienced others so that a sense of achievement is never far away. If things don't go as you hoped, you can take this as a learning opportunity as much as your successes, and the good news is that a bad lesson is over quickly, and you get a chance to try again tomorrow!

REFLECTION POINT

- On your own spend a few minutes completing the steps in this exercise:
- Think of something you had to work hard to achieve.
- What made this difficult?
- How did you avoid giving up? What made you keep trying?
- What support did you seek?
- What did you learn from this experience about tackling difficulty?
- Now compare your experiences with someone else, another trainee or your mentor.

KEYS TO RESILIENCE

So, what are the keys to resilience? Mansfield (2021: 29) has reviewed relevant literature and found that the research offers the following suggestions for developing your resilience.

DEVELOPING RELATIONSHIPS

During your training year, and afterwards, you will work with mentors, peers, and the wider teaching community and other support networks. Our survey of PGCE trainees found that their tutors and mentors were very important relationships. Their role is to guide, train and support as well as giving you feedback and completing your assessment on placement. Other teachers will remember the challenge of their early careers and will be able to help and offer guidance. Of course, everyone is busy in school, so you should always make good use of their time – Chapter 6 has some advice about how to do this. You can also expand your network by getting to your team room or staffroom for a chat during break, or by pitching in with group sessions at your training provider.

PREPARE FOR DIFFICULT SCENARIOS AND PRACTISE YOUR RESPONSES

The old adage 'forewarned is forearmed' is very true. Planning and preparation are fundamental skills for teachers. Trainees can expect to encounter many, varied and unexpected and often challenging situations. It is important to anticipate a number of these and discuss and rehearse responses with experienced others in order to be prepared for what may happen and how to respond. Critical instances, in particular, will be returned to later in this chapter.

ENGAGE YOUR EMOTIONAL INTELLIGENCE

Emotional intelligence is a vital attribute for anyone entering the teaching profession. Roberts (2022) defines emotional intelligence as … *being fluent in understanding what makes you tick and how you deal with your own and other's emotions*. Corcoran and Tormey (2012) argue that while positive emotions can anchor learning, negative emotion can prevent learning. Furthermore, Roberts (2022) suggests that pupils, and even some colleagues, may not have the capacity to understand or empathise. It is vital, therefore, that as teachers we strive to develop and recognise our own emotional intelligence.

Salovey and Mayer (1990) developed a skills framework encompassing four components, which are the ability to:

- Perceive emotions in self and others;
- Generate and use emotional states to facilitate different types of thinking;
- Analyse emotional information and understand emotional changes, blends and transitions;
- Regulate emotion in self and others.

Corcoran and Tormey (2012) argue that those teachers who are most skilled at regulating their emotions are more likely to prevent burnout. There is evidence that if you can control your level of emotional response to perceived threats, you can create a broader feeling of being in control and help de-escalate difficult situations (Bandura, 1997; Greer and Hollis, 2020) and this can enable you to think more clearly.

4 Teacher wellbeing

> ■■■ — **REFLECTION POINT**
>
> Reflect upon how you respond to situations you find challenging and stressful. What can you do to respond differently in the future? Conversely think about when you have met challenge and stress in a way that you have managed well. Think about how you can use these responses more.

RELAX AND TAKE A BREAK

Your mind and body both require a good deal of regular rest. It is very important to have a planned extended period away from work each and every week, for example by having a strict rule of not working on a Saturday or beyond 9 p.m. during the week. You might also find it useful to practise relaxation techniques such as meditation or 'square breathing'.

This is something that can even be utilised in the middle of a lesson to help calm the teacher, if needed. The method is as follows:

1. Breathe in through your nose while you count for four seconds.
2. Hold your breath for four seconds.
3. Breathe out through the mouth, again counting for four seconds.
4. Repeat these steps, 1–3, four times.

(adapted from Education Support, n.d.)

It is also really important to take your 'holidays' seriously – especially as you will sometimes need to use some of them to catch up on work or marking. Holidays must be used wisely. Taking several consecutive days off to 'unplug' without feeling guilty is a good strategy.

EXERCISE, SLEEP AND DIET

Exercise, sleep and diet can often be the first casualty when teachers are busy. Hydration is particularly important for a teacher as this maintains focus and protects your voice.

A disrupted sleep pattern will inevitably eventually cause problems, so being well rested and having sufficient sleep is imperative.

WORKLOAD AND TIME MANAGEMENT

> ■■■ — **CASE STUDY**
>
> **Time allocation**
>
> During her second placement, Sarah was given an increasing number of lessons to teach. This meant that she had to reduce the amount of time she spent planning

each lesson. As the time for a lesson approached, Sarah herself became more and more anxious and worried that reduced preparation time would negatively impact on pupils' learning.

After a number of sleepless nights, she spoke to her university tutor, who provided tips and advised her to discuss my concerns with her school mentor. Following a discussion with Sarah's mentor, she concentrated more on the end goal of objectives and their outcomes, with lessons focused on how to get pupils there. Sarah spent less time preparing to the nth degree for every possibility for each minute of every lesson, as much could be addressed during lessons when pupils encountered difficulties. She also used resources and presentations from departmental resources, adapting both for her own classes.

Her mentor also advised that she shouldn't spend more than 30 minutes on planning a lesson and to talk through ideas first, so that Sarah could be confident that she was planning along the right lines.

Consider your approach to time management:

- How much thought do you give to allocating time to tasks?
- Do you put things off for a later time or date?
- Do you ignore the difficult tasks and focus on completing the easy ones?

Having reflected on the questions above and considered how you work, think about the following points as a way of shaping your thinking.

Prioritisation is essential for managing workload. Greer and Hollis (2020), in their guide for Early Career Teachers, argue that everyone's attitude to workload is personal and influenced by the perceived importance of the task.

Time is a finite resource, and teaching is a busy job – it feels that there is never enough time to complete all required tasks to the highest possible quality. You will always be able to add more detail to lesson resources, or more marking and checking of pupil work. If you find yourself spending hours on the 'perfect' diagram, or polishing some feedback, then you might be spending time that could be spent to better effect on something else. Having a system to help you prioritise helps you get into a habit and gives you a feeling of control, so that when 30 or more children arrive at the classroom door, you are ready to teach them.

A common prioritisation approach is the Eisenhower matrix (Eisenhower, 1954). This approach divides tasks into four categories by assessing their relative urgency and importance (see Figure 4.2). This enables the user to prioritise tasks, focusing on those that are important but not yet urgent and so hopefully avoiding decision making while potentially experiencing time-constraint stress. Tasks and decision making to focus on now, which to schedule, which to delegate and which to delete can therefore be determined.

4 Teacher wellbeing

This sort of approach helps deal with an unhelpful trait, which is to put off work or procrastinate, by wasting time or doing something unrelated. Procrastination can lead to feelings of guilt (Laybourn, Frenzel and Fenzl, 2019) and, as such, if an email cannot be immediately responded to or a pile of marking isn't started straight away, you might not feel in control.

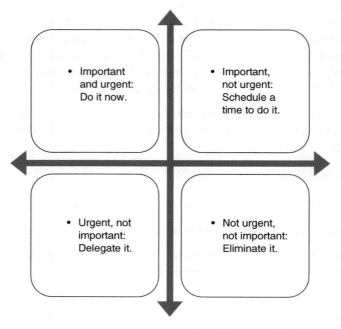

Figure 4.2 The Eisenhower matrix example

Greer and Hollis (2020) also suggest that when you need to, you should stop or take a break. Perhaps you could stand up and stretch after marking ten books, or stop and make a cup of tea having worked on a lesson plan for 30 minutes. Techniques like these, often called the Pomodoro method, might help you avoid procrastination and keep going if you have a number of things to do.

Teachers often use a planner or academic diary to keep a record of their timetable, tasks and classes. These planners usually have a section to record marking and class data collected in lessons. Using the planner wisely not only helps with knowing what the next task is, when it is due and spotting in advance pressure points of workload so that these can be tackled more manageably but is also a critical tool in ensuring maximum efficiency. Good uses of your planner include:

- Once a lesson has ended, make brief notes for the next lesson, for example, knowledge which should be returned to or moving 'chatty' pupils in the seating plan. This will help enormously in planning the next lesson and mitigate against making similar mistakes.

- During a 'free' period, plan one or two weeks in advance tasks to be completed.
- Make notes of when to submit lesson plans to your mentors or host teachers to allow for time to action any feedback.

USE IT TO HELP ORGANISE YOUR WORK

You can harness the power of IT to help reduce workload, keep you organised and look after the work you have created:

- **Keep all resources organised** – a well-planned folder structure for storing resources is essential and will save you time and anxiety for the whole of your career. You could organise this by year group and topic or whatever makes sense to you. What is important is that resources can be easily found now and in the future.
- **Be a magpie and don't be afraid to collect resources** – the most effective learning resources are those which you have used before and adapted to meet your pupils' needs. Often this is best achieved by re-using and adapting resources created by other colleagues or departmental resources. Few teachers reinvent the wheel, and neither should you.
- **Bookmark key websites** – every subject has key websites packed full of great resources and lesson activities; www.tes.com/teaching-resources is a good site to begin with, although some resources will require a small fee.
- **Make use of online activities** – many schools provide iPads for pupils or make use of a computing lab. There are many great self-guided learning websites for pupils that can be utilised or, alternatively, a flipped learning approach could be selected where, simplistically, the pupils conduct the research and the teacher's role is to assess this learning.
- **Self-marking assessments and tests** – this is a great way to save time and effort, having the added bonus that often someone else has already created a useful quiz or test. Common websites include Quizlet, Kahoot, Quizziz, Google Forms, Blooket or the create test/survey facility on Microsoft Teams can be used. These are great fun for starters and plenaries (although fun cannot be their only purpose) and take minutes to set up. The good news is that they can be used again and again to obtain crucial formative or summative assessment information yet require no marking on the part of the teacher.
- **Use the school VLE** – many schools have invested in virtual learning environments (VLEs) which provide access to resources, assignments and marking. Gaining confidence in navigating and using this should be an early objective of trainee teachers.
- **Find an IT buddy** – for trainees who are not confident in the use of IT, finding someone on the course who is willing to help is useful. Teaching is a collaborative profession and colleagues are usually happy to share knowledge and help each other.

Of course, the Covid pandemic opened up the world of online teaching using tools including, for example, Microsoft Teams and Zoom, although there are many more. This now means that when pupils are absent, and only when appropriate, work can be set online, or pupils can be invited into the class remotely. The other caveat with this is where you are using online or downloaded resources, ensure that you amend them so they are most fit for the purpose of the specific class you are teaching.

DEALING WITH NEGATIVE FEEDBACK

▪▪▪ CASE STUDY

Sam's lesson observation

Sam had been at their first placement school for seven weeks and settled in well. They had developed a good relationship with their mentor and felt well supported in the department.

They delivered a lesson period 3 on Tuesday, which their host teacher (not their mentor) observed. The feedback took Sam completely by surprise as he said their classroom management needed improving, with many pupils not making any progress because of this. Sam was also criticised for poor subject knowledge. This left them feeling downhearted and a little frustrated as they didn't think the lesson went too badly.

After discussing this with their mentor, they understood where the host teacher was coming from and set out some weekly targets and actions to specifically address these points. The following lesson with this class went better but, more importantly, Sam felt better able, with the support of their mentor, to objectively determine what could be improved further so that there could be focused discussion around strategies on how to achieve this.

- What steps did Sam take in order to learn from the feedback, even though it upset them?
- Consider a time when you have received feedback that left you feeling surprised or downhearted. How did you work through those feelings so that you still made progress?

Occasionally mentors will have to give negative but constructive feedback, and sometimes this feedback might be delivered quickly because mentors have lots of demands on their time. Sometimes you might be upset by this, particularly if you feel that some feedback has not been handled with much sensitivity. How you respond to this will directly affect the progress you make on placement.

Most mentors and trainees get along in a friendly manner. However, this is not always the case and indeed is not a requirement. What is a requirement is the need to retain a professional relationship that helps you make maximum use of the feedback you get, so that you can develop your knowledge and practice on placement.

4 Teacher wellbeing

Chapter 6 has more ideas about dealing with feedback and using this as part of your learning identity. Here we want to help you deal with the emotional aspects of negative feedback, with the following ideas:

- Resist the temptation of being too defensive (which comes across as arguing) with the host teachers or mentors about their perception of the teaching episode you are discussing.
- Try to look at the issue from the mentor or host teachers' perspective – consider the cues and events they refer to in the lesson to help you do this.
- If you are getting upset, it is probably better to make a few notes about what their concerns were so that you can reflect on these on your own or with someone else.
- Recognise that you feel upset, accept that this is natural when you get unexpectedly downbeat feedback, but also recognise that this feeling will change and you will get better at what you are doing.
- If you need to clear something up, or would like to know more about the concerns that have been raised, decide on some constructive questions you want to ask that person, or another person, to help you understand.

LEARNING FROM CRITICAL INCIDENTS

We want to finish this chapter by thinking about 'critical incidents'. These are the events that sometimes happen in school, or during your teaching, that are really important. Often these events might knock your confidence, but they can also become clear learning experiences, especially if you approach them with a reflective learning identity (see Chapter 2 for more).

Throughout a teacher's career, unexpected situations like these will arise. However, these incidents arise more frequently in the early days of a teacher's career and so we will start with a case study to give you an example of the kinds of event we want to discuss.

CASE STUDY

Unexpected change

After the Easter holidays some pupils from one of the Year 7 classes were taken out of Callum's Spanish class to have more literacy or numeracy with other teachers. Other pupils were then moved into his Spanish class, but they had not learnt Spanish before. Nobody notified him that this change was going to happen that day and his mentor was absent, so he had a cover teacher in the room with him.

(Continued)

Callum made all pupils stand and wait at the back of the classroom while he worked out a new seating plan, and he also explained the lesson might be a bit challenging for some of them. He made sure to tell pupils he would give them a sheet with all the vocabulary they had been working on so they could stick it in their books. Although not perfect, Callum did feel that he had made some mitigations to deal with this critical incident so that learning was not interrupted too much. He was then able to talk to his mentor about strategies for the next lesson before seeing the class again.

- Have you experienced any critical incidents or observed them during your school experience?
- What can you learn from them in order to deal most effectively with the next?

PREPARING FOR CRITICAL INCIDENTS

We started this chapter by recommending that you prepare for scenarios that you have not faced, perhaps by scripting possible responses, or even role playing through them. We have listed a series of critical incidents or challenges that you might face in your ITT year relating to:

- behaviour in lessons;
- teaching and school life;
- professional interaction with colleagues;
- external pressures;
- self-organisation.

Complete the reflective task at the end of this list of incidents and try to apply some of the ideas and approaches that we have outlined in this chapter. You could also talk some of these through with your mentor, as they will have faced similar challenges in their own teaching.

Behaviour management
A pupil refuses to hand over a mobile phone despite being asked repeatedly.
Pupils just won't be quiet or listen when you need them to.
Pupils are put into groups but then some start complaining about their group allocation. Comments such as "I can't work with her" are made to you.
A pupil becomes very confrontational when challenged.
You create a new seating plan but, after ten minutes, realise that some pupils are not in the correct seats.

Teaching, pedagogy and school life
Despite your detailed explanations, pupils still don't 'get it'.
During break a pupil becomes unwell. There are lots of children spectating and some trying to help, but all are potentially making a difficult situation worse.
You are becoming tired and irritated by pupils.
Pupils in a class say to you, "This is rubbish. When is Miss coming back?"
During a test, a child with autism becomes very upset and will not respond to requests to settle down.
Professional interaction with colleagues
You have spent hours planning a lesson and then 30 minutes before the lesson, the mentor says, "That won't work."
Following a very negative observation, you are asked, "Is teaching really for you?"
Your mentor is ill for the third time in a short period and misses your meeting again.
You feel you are not receiving enough feedback about your teaching as your mentor keeps cutting your feedback meetings short.
External pressures
A close family member is taken unwell, and you need to take time to care for them. You are likely to find it difficult to hand in lesson plans on time.
You find yourself without a car and the school placement will take a long time to get to on public transport.
Self-organisation
You are worried that some of your deadlines for university assignments might get missed.
A friend of yours on the course is still planning and refining lessons for the next day at 3 a.m.

▬■■■▬ REFLECTION POINT

This is best completed in pairs or small groups. Choose some of the critical incidents above and discuss the following:

- Have you encountered (or heard about) a similar incident?
- The reaction you would like to have.
- What can you do to prepare for such an incident?

4 Teacher wellbeing

■ ■ ■ — **ASSIGNMENT LINKS**

- The ideas and suggestions in this chapter should help you keep up with your workload and support you in completing your assignments.

LEARNING AND CONSOLIDATION ACTIVITIES

KEY THINGS TO LOOK FOR WHEN OBSERVING LESSONS OR TEACHING

- How do busy teachers manage their workload?
- In what ways do teachers reduce workload, for example, in setting and marking homework and in planning lessons and activities?
- How do teachers deal with confrontational situations and keep calm?
- How do teachers give and receive positive and negative feedback?

DISCUSSION POINTS FOR TUTORIALS AND SEMINARS

Trainees should discuss workload and how best to manage this with their mentor, making them aware of any concerns and gaining advice on how best to gather resources, plan lessons, mark assessments, etc. It is also important to use the Development Record/Reflective Journal to reflect on issues. This will help trainee teachers identify any issues that may affect wellbeing.

Understanding how to develop resilience and making use of the experiences of school-based colleagues.

Gradually trainees will increase their teaching load and the implications of this should be discussed with the school-based mentor.

IDEAS FOR GUIDED PRACTICE AND FEEDBACK

Monitor the daily routine, remove any time-wasting activity in pursuit of perfection and make decisions on what is working in terms of planning, marking, etc.

Make extensive use of a teacher planner.

Plan well in advance to allow for bumps in the road or unforeseen increases in your workload.

CHAPTER SUMMARY

It has been the intention of this chapter to help provide advice and tools to assist in surviving the challenging moments of the ITT year.

Through applying personal self-care and ensuring workload is managed, the trainee teacher will be ready to face whatever challenges they come across in the classroom.

As with all skills, wellbeing skills need to be continually practised and reviewed. Please do come back to some of the topics raised in this chapter if there is a need for some ideas. Please also investigate further into some of the ideas raised here through your own reading.

The following bullet points summarise the main points from the chapter:

- Be aware of your own wellbeing and understanding stress.
- Look to build resilience through developing contacts and networks.
- Prioritise tasks and manage time effectively.
- Understand the nature of feedback and use it to develop teacher identity.
- Plan for critical incidents and rehearse reactions to these.

Good luck and remember to look after yourself.

REFLECTION POINT

How will you look after yourself? Provide three things you do for yourself every day.

How will you allocate time to tasks, i.e. planning, marking, assignments, mentor meeting preparation, etc.?

How will you deal with negative feedback?

How will you deal with critical incidents as they arise in school?

FURTHER READING

1. Essential guides for Early Career Teachers: *Workload* by Greer and Hollis

This guide gives some practical hints and advice on how to manage your workload.

2. *A Practical Guide to Teacher Wellbeing by Holmes.*

This provides extended help on how to improve your wellbeing. Many of the ideas in this book have been shared here but in less depth.

3. *Cultivating Teacher Resilience by Mansfield.*

REFERENCES

Bandura, A. (1997) *Self-Efficacy: The Exercise of Control* (1st edn). Worth Publishers.

Corcoran, R. and Tormey, R. (2012) *Developing Emotionally Competent Teachers*. Oxford: Peter Lang.

DfE (2020) *School Workforce in England Report*. Available at: https://explore-education-statistics.service.gov.uk/find-statistics/school-workforce-in-england

Dickens, C. (1850) *David Copperfield*. London: Bradbury & Evans.

Education Support Charity (n.d.) Breathing exercises for beating stress and creating calm. Education Support. Available at: https://www.educationsupport.org.uk/resources/for-individuals/guides/breathing-exercises-for-beating-stress-and-creating-calm/?utm_source=twitter&utm_medium=social&utm_campaign=website-launch-resources (accessed 10/1/23).

Eisenhower (1954) The Eisenhower matrix. Available at: www.eisenhower.me/eisenhower-matrix/ (accessed 29/7/22).

Greer, J. and Hollis, E. (2020) *Workload*. Critical Publishing Ltd.

Holmes, E. (2018) *A Practical Guide to Teacher Wellbeing (Ready to Teach)* (1st edn). Learning Matters.

Laybourn, S., Frenzel, A. and Fenzl, T. (2019) Teacher procrastination, emotions, and stress: a qualitative study. *Frontiers In Psychology*, *10*. DOI: 10.3389/fpsyg.2019.02325

Lazarides, R. and Warner, L. (2020) Teacher self-efficacy. *Oxford Research Encyclopedia of Education*. Available at: https://oxfordre.com/education/view/10.1093/acrefore/9780190264093.001.0001/acrefore-9780190264093-e-890 (accessed 28/7/22).

Mansfield, C. (2021). *Cultivating Teacher Resilience*. [S.l.]: Springer Nature.

New Economics Foundation (2012) *Measuring Wellbeing: A Guide For Practitioners*. London: New Economics Foundation.

Rajkumar, L., Dubowy, C. and Khatib, A. (2021) Impact of practicing mindful breathing in class. *Teaching and Learning Excellence through Scholarship*, *1*(1).

Roberts, N.C. (2022). *The Emotionally Intelligent Teacher*. London: Bloomsbury.

Salovey, P. and Mayer, J. (1990) Emotional intelligence. *Imagination, Cognition And Personality*, *9*(3): 185–211. DOI: 10.2190/dugg-p24e-52wk-6cdg

SECED (2022) How to improve your workplace relationships. Available at: https://seced.mydigitalpublication.co.uk/publication/?m=65699&i=747154&view=articleBrowser&article_id=4270376&ver=html5 (accessed 26/7/22).

Shields, L. and Mullen, C. (2020) *Veteran Teacher Resilience*. Springer.

5

BEHAVIOUR IN SCHOOLS

NAZIYA O'REILLY AND SIOBHAN SIMMS

KEY WORDS

- Behaviour management
- Positive relationships
- Restorative practice
- Social and emotional learning
- Caring ethics

CHAPTER OBJECTIVES

Nearly all trainee teachers worry about behaviour in the classroom and about how they might manage challenging and disruptive behaviours. In this chapter you will be asked to think about how you can begin to understand behaviour management, what it is and what it means. It will introduce you to the rise of behaviourism, popular behavioural theories such as positive discipline and the draw towards a restorative approach to resolving difficult behaviours. Through case studies and a range of fundamental questions, a framework is given by which you can identify and develop a common set of preferred values and practices that can help you to work effectively with the most challenging of classes.

LINKS TO THE CORE CONTENT FRAMEWORK

All of the Core Content Framework themes are referred to and applied in this chapter, but the following are the most relevant:

Standard 7 – Manage behaviour effectively

(Continued)

1. Establishing and reinforcing routines, including through positive reinforcement, can help create an effective learning environment.
2. A predictable and secure environment benefits all pupils but is particularly valuable for pupils with special educational needs.
3. The ability to self-regulate one's emotions affects pupils' ability to learn, success in school and future lives.
4. Teachers can influence pupils' resilience and beliefs about their ability to succeed by ensuring all pupils have the opportunity to experience meaningful success.
5. Building effective relationships is easier when pupils believe that their feelings will be considered and understood.
6. Pupils are motivated by intrinsic factors (related to their identity and values) and extrinsic factors (related to reward); pupils' investment in learning is also driven by their prior experiences and perceptions of success and failure.

INTRODUCTION

WHAT DO WE MEAN WHEN WE TALK ABOUT BEHAVIOUR IN SCHOOLS?

What do you imagine when you think of behaviour in schools? It is very likely that the phrase good behaviour conjures an image of rows of pupils sitting attentively at their desks, books open, and with eyes fixed on the teacher at the front who is patiently explaining the finer points of the Industrial Revolution. If this sounds like a dream scenario, then it is most likely down to the constant TV tropes of bad behaviour that delight in showing us clusters of rowdy pupils sitting on desks, talking loudly or on their phones while a stressed and increasingly anxious adult tries to bring them to attention. That's without the fear of wider perceptions of anti-social behaviour such as bullying, vandalism, pupil assault and the more headline-grabbing acts of violent behaviour that may take place beyond the school gates. Teacher voice indicates a rise in violent and abusive behaviour. In 2013, 62 per cent of education professionals reported a rise in the number of pupils exhibiting emotional, behavioural or mental health problems over the last two years (ATL, 2013) with 55 per cent of teachers dealing with verbally aggressive pupils during a school year, and just over a fifth intervening in cases of physical aggression.

Almost certainly these deep-rooted challenges have been exacerbated by the impact of the Covid-19 pandemic, which has likely widened pre-existing opportunity and achievement gaps and adversely affected young people's mental health and wellbeing (Cowie and Myers, 2021). The office of the Children's Commissioner (2020) reported that the closure of schools as well as access to other services has been particularly detrimental on vulnerable teenagers who risk falling through the gaps. Preliminary findings also reveal that there will be a new wave of pupils (without previous mental health problems) experiencing increased feelings of anxiety and uncertainty and who will potentially struggle with concerns about their future, exams or relationships with others.

As you can see, apprehension around behaviour management can be very stressful at any stage of a teaching career and even more so when you are at the start of your career. Here are a few concerns from recent trainees that seem to sum up the fear around behaviour in schools.

"Will the pupils do what I ask them?"

"Is the behaviour policy clear?"

"How and when do I exercise authority?"

"What if I don't have the confidence to apply the policies?"

"What if the behaviour escalates?"

"How do I deal with a standoff?"

"What if they don't move seats or put their gum in the bin?"

"Who will support and listen to me?"

To help support trainees address these fears and develop their behaviour management skills, the Department for Education has produced a trainee teacher behavioural toolkit (DfE, 2019). This is a summary of points that sees behaviour management as a process, not merely reacting to misbehaviour when it occurs, but by proactively teaching and modelling for pupils precisely the behaviours that are expected of them. This is of importance to you since in order to achieve Qualified Teacher Status (QTS), you will be required to meet the competencies laid out by the ITT Core Content Framework, which are referenced at the beginning of this chapter. This can be summarised as understanding that without good behaviour from your pupils, your teaching and learning will be severely impeded. In 2016, the government adviser Tom Bennett produced a set of 'behaviour guidelines' about the areas that teachers should know to be classroom ready. These are around routines, responses and relationships and is a good place to start your training in the craft of classroom management. Likewise, you may also find Charlie Taylor's (2011) behaviour checklist to be helpful in looking at the basics of behaviour management and how you can adapt these for your own practice. Both are referenced at the end of this chapter.

However, there are other reasons why we all need to care about behaviour, and this is because we believe that as well as being able to manage pupil behaviour, we have an important role in shaping and nurturing them to become responsible citizens who can make informed choices in their lives. In the Special Educational Needs and Disability Code of Practice, children with challenging and disruptive behaviour also fall under the category of those with social, emotional and mental health problems (see Chapter 3).

5 Behaviour in schools

Although the toolkits presented here are of value, it is important to note that we are not advocating a 'one size fits all' approach to behaviour management as evidence shows this has a highly negative and exclusionary impact on Special Educational Needs and Disabilities (SEND) pupils (NEU, 2019).

As a trainee and new teacher, most of your day-to-day concerns with regard to behaviour will not present this level of challenge. Instead, a great deal of your time will be focused on low-level disruption of the kind with which we started this chapter. However, in supporting all children with challenging behaviour, it is vital that we take what Glazzard and Green (2022) calls 'a principled approach to behaviour management'. They are listed below:

- All children are inherently good.
- All behaviour is an attempt to communicate something.
- Adults in the classroom significantly affect the quality of the atmosphere for all pupils.
- Power and control are not effective ways to shape pupils' behaviour (Glazzard and Green, 2022).

Acquiring this sort of mindset is helpful because young people are very quick to pick up on whether they are being treated fairly and if the adult in question *actually likes them*. As a result, feeling mistreated or disempowered will only produce further poor behaviour and disengagement. Understanding how to manage individual behaviour, therefore, is as much about understanding how a range of factors – environmental and educational – have positively or negatively shaped the behaviours of your pupils. You may have learners with complex and chaotic home lives, learners who are unable to demonstrate the required academic achievements or learners who do not fit within the values communicated with the school system. In coming to understand the behaviour of these pupils, you are coming to understand their needs and how you might take on the responsibility of meeting them.

Finally, just as your pupils will know if you don't like them, they will know if you are kind, caring, respectful and, importantly, interested in them. For this reason, most of this chapter is devoted to exploring how it is possible to be invested in building positive and genuine relationships with your pupils as well as giving your pupils the necessary sound modelling and instruction that is a core part of your achievement for this standard. You will read in a number of the chapters the importance of establishing relationships with your pupils is a key to success in many of the areas of teaching.

With this in mind, this chapter takes you through some of the key issues inherent in thinking about behaviour in schools. It introduces you to significant research and influential policies that have shaped the way in which trainees are asked to conceptualise the teaching of good behaviour. As well as offering practical advice for difficult situations, guidance is offered to help you to nurture pro-social theories and to understand the links between dialogue, relationship and behaviour. Most importantly, using case studies, we invite you to engage in reflective thinking to help you to develop your own set of values and a principled approach to behaviour management.

BEHAVIOURAL THEORIES

It is tempting to think of behaviour management as solely a list of practical strategies to be deployed at the relevant moment to establish order, engage pupils or elicit co-operation. Take, for example, the DfE's stating of sanctions and rewards as an essential part of any behaviour management system. They state that teachers should use a combination of extrinsic (team points, certificates) and intrinsic rewards (targeted praise) together with pre-determined consequences in the form of sanctions (withdrawal of privilege, detentions) to assert what the norms or routines of the room (school) should be, even if they fall short.

The notion that pupils learn through reinforcement (operant conditioning) – constant feedback that tells them what they have done right or wrong – is known as behaviourism, a psychological theory invented by John Watson (1913), who believed that all behaviours are the result of experience. In educational theory, a behaviourist approach to learning occurs through teachers' rewards and punishments that lead to observable changes in pupil behaviour. In the same way that a scientist may systematically shape the behaviour of laboratory animals through stimulus and response, behaviourists believe that we can be trained into changing our behaviour through cause and effect. So, a pupil who is given consistent positive praise (stimulus) for completing work on time (response) is more likely to repeat that behaviour and a pupil who is given a detention is less likely. By giving a punishment we are trying to teach the child to voluntarily change their behaviour by making better choices in the future to avoid a punishment.

Today most teachers are familiar with behaviourism as to the reason why they must come up with a clear set of rules and rewards. Coming to prominence in the mid-1970s, through the work of American educators Lee and Marlene Canter (1992), 'assertive discipline' (AD) has long been considered 'the gold standard' in the field of behaviourism. Consisting in a three-part structured routine that consists in clearly visible and articulated classroom rules, verbal reinforcement and corrective action. The emphasis for AD rests on authority and consistency and the use of action or penalties that is imposed on a pupil for misbehaving or breaking a rule. In England particularly, these kinds of approaches have led to typically assertive, behaviourist ways of managing challenging behaviour where, in addition to recommending a reward and sanctions-based system to manage pupil behaviour, guidance also supports teachers' rights to search without consent, the power to use reasonable force, the use of seclusion or isolation rooms, and the ability to screen without consent.

Despite the proliferation of class charters (where children write their rules) and reward charts, how useful assertive discipline actually is remains a contestable issue. For instance, the use of rewards can result in children undertaking an activity showing less intrinsic interest than those who engage in an activity without expectation. Pupils do tend to act when threatened by coercion or promised rewards, and indeed they can modify unattractive behaviours based on their view of the motivational scales – establishing if changing is 'worth it'. Teachers might use certificates as rewards for good behaviour, Vivo Miles or simply resort to the store cupboard treat jar. However, the danger lies in the pupils' adoption of such behaviours due solely to the strength of the external motivation, and not from any personal judgement that the end goal is reasonable or valuable (Straughan, 1982). In this assessment, children do not follow rules because they are rules, instead learning to follow rules goes hand in hand with developing trust and confidence in the teacher.

Closely related to assertive discipline is positive discipline (PD), another practice of training or teaching a pupil to obey a code of behaviour or rules in both the short and long term. The difference between PD and AD is the focus on using techniques to develop pupil behaviour through self-control and making positive choices. This thinking is linked to the work of theorists Alfred Adler and Rudolph Dreikurs (see Nelson, 1996), who argued that many traditional disciplinary models treat discipline as synonymous with punishment. Positive discipline, however, looks for more effective ways to develop pupil behaviour. It encourages them to develop self-control, learn from their mistakes, and ultimately make positive decisions for themselves. Teachers should still use a reward system to encourage good behaviour in pupils who are misbehaving, but additionally incorporate techniques that will maintain a positive atmosphere and support an inclusive learning environment.

For example, if a pupil is unwilling to listen to a teacher's instructions and refusing to complete work, the teacher could ignore the unwanted behaviour and try instead to work the pupil into some sort of leadership role. This might be helping the teacher take the register, reading out questions, or writing the day's homework assignment on the whiteboard. The increased investment in personal relation, due to the specific teaching of interpersonal skills, results in less time dealing with problem behaviour.

Some positive discipline schools will use triangles of hierarchy about what happens if a pupil acts in a particular way. They may then be given sanctions like a verbal warning, name on the board, etc., building up to removal from the classroom to isolation. The aim here is to help pupils regulate their behaviour. In addition, it can be accompanied by a rewards system. Stamps can be used where the expectation is all pupils will receive a stamp for their behaviour in a lesson. This then builds so that some pupils will receive more stamps if they are working above the expected levels. In the long term these can build into bigger rewards. The motivating feature here is extrinsic rewards and this can create a good learning environment for some pupils.

Behaviour management policies are more effective when there is a whole school approach and when and if there are consistent systems in classrooms. It is almost a certainty that in your training or career you will be required to teach children using strategies based on AD or PD and there will often be strict policies in place.

5 Behaviour in schools

While following the school behaviour policy and strategy is key, don't fall into the trap of assuming that teachers can't make their own decisions about behaviour based on their understanding and relationship with their pupils. Given the emphasis on consistency, these deviations can make the teacher, or yourself, seem very inconsistent and you may worry what impact your actions may have on your training or even with your pupils. There are no clear answers to this dilemma. Your interaction with 'the rules' will always be about using your professional judgement and developing an informed and evidence-based response. In order to work on this, it is important to do your own research and to keep observing different teachers and teaching styles so you get a better sense of what works for you and your pupils.

CASE STUDY

Failure to follow school policies

George is often late to your lessons and when he does come in, he can cause disruption. It is not only your lesson he is late to but school in general. This pupil struggles to regulate his emotions when challenged.

- Think about your observations and experience in schools.
- How do the teachers challenge the lateness?
- How does the teacher follow the situation up?
- How do they deal with the problem if it escalates?
- How can you use engage, explain, expect to help resolve this situation restoratively?

One possible solution:

When George enters the classroom, give them the task straight away and don't challenge the failure to follow the school rules in front of the class.

When appropriate speak to George, explaining that it is good that he has come into the lesson and got on with the task but that his lateness has affected the lesson.

Explain that when he was late, it meant other children's learning had to slow down and that they didn't have the full content that they needed for the lesson. Listen to George's point of view. Say that you will need to meet up out of the lesson with a head of year to find a solution and to set some Specific, Measurable, Achievable, Relevant, Time-based (SMART) punctuality targets. Could George need support with organisation or are there other barriers that could be tackled?

Agree and explain the expectations that George continues to follow school policy. Ensure that he understands the expectations and that he has the support to achieve them.

5 Behaviour in schools

■■■ POSITIVE DISCIPLINE TECHNIQUES

- Positive instructions. These help pupils succeed because they tell them exactly what you want them to do. For example, say use your quiet voices instead of don't shout. This can increase the chances of pupils doing what you ask, because it gives them an action and a choice.
- Silent signals. When everyone in the classroom is raucous and excited, it can be tempting for the teacher to try and control the pupils by raising their own voice. Training pupils to recognise silent signals, such as finger on lips, means keeping the classroom calm and allowing pupils to quieten down quickly.
- Warm greetings. When pupils enter the classroom, give them a friendly greeting and ask them how they are. Make it known that you are happy that they are there and provide positive direction and guidance for the lesson.
- Classroom layout. Pupils sit in a horseshoe shape, creating a sense of openness. Rather than constructing a 'wall' between the teacher and pupils, this ensures a more democratic space.

■■■ CASE STUDY

Low-level behaviour

Fozia is very enthusiastic in your lesson. She joins in answering all questions asked to the whole class but shouts out each time. When you ask a question to a different child directly, Fozia interjects with the answer.

How would you approach dealing with this situation?

Ask or observe your teachers in school:

- how they challenge the behaviour but encourage learning and engagement
- how the teacher talks to the child about their behaviours
- how they speak to the whole class during the incident.

How can you use engage, explain, expect to help resolve this situation restoratively?

One possible solution:

Speak to Fozia, explaining that it is great she is so enthusiastic about her learning and keen to join in the lesson.

Explain that when she answers all the questions, it means other children don't get the opportunity to show what they know. It is also not good manners and makes others feel disheartened and frustrated. Listen to her point of view. Ask then to come up with a solution with you. Could she support by listening to the answers given by other children and showing whether they agree with the answer with a thumbs up or down? Work with Fozia to find a solution so that she can show what she knows and is able to answer questions while also letting other children learn and answer questions in class.

Agree and explain the expectations that Fozia continues to put her hand up to answer questions (this shows the teacher they have an answer) but that she does not shout out. If she shouts out, she will need to have a conversation at break to remind her again about why this is not appropriate.

GOOD RELATIONSHIPS MATTER

Recognition for establishing good teacher-pupil relationships through regular, effective communication is connected to further person-centred (or social) approaches to education that alter the idea of conditioned responses in order to shape behaviour. Instead, through encouraging dialogue-based techniques, pupils can be guided towards understanding a better social and emotional awareness of their own behaviour. Social and emotional awareness is understood as the ability to understand ourselves and other people, and to be aware about the emotional states of ourselves and others with competence. It includes the ability to understand, express and manage our own emotions, and respond to the emotions of others, in ways that are helpful to ourselves and others.

The implication of this social awareness broadens the individual focus on behaviour and is said to have more of an impact on pupils who may be unable to make the correlation between punishment and correction that are associated with consequence-based strategies. Glasser's Choice Theory (1988) encourages pupils to see the relationship between talking, thinking and learning as fundamental to not only their own learning, but in supporting the ways that they behave with each other. Here the choice is not about making a good decision or a bad one with regards to acceptable conduct but is based on the simple premise that every individual only has the power to control themselves and has limited power to control others.

Research suggests that having a sense of control over outcomes that are the result of our behaviours is related to several positive behaviour traits (see Galbraith and Alexander, 2005; Autry and Langenbach, 1985; Kremer, 1982). Pupils with a developed sense of their own locus of control learn to gain agency over their actions and in turn to take responsibility for them as well. Those who do not believe they have control, whose locus of control is poorly developed, display more negative behaviour traits. These pupils tend not to take responsibility for their actions. They will blame others as the cause for their poor behaviour or perhaps you for not being a good enough teacher; they will also engage in more destructive behaviour and environments. We have already seen how asking pupils to make choices is a powerful way of enabling them to think about their behaviour, but here thinking about choice goes one step further in that choice is closely related to understanding where the balance of power lies in the classroom. It invites you to take on board the notion that true agency is predicated on genuine choice and not the simulation of one. It even includes the notion that it may not be a choice that you yourself would make.

If that sounds uncomfortable, then let us reassure you that this is not about abandoning your values in favour of your pupils. We used the word *power* earlier in this chapter in connection with developing a principled approach to behaviour. In continuing to focus explicitly on the quality of relationships, considering who has power in the classroom will become more important. For now, let us state that we are not suggesting that trainees should give away their power as teachers, which is appropriate and necessary to perform the teacher role, but rather to offer what Drewery and Kecskemeti (2010) call a 'habitual stance' – meaning coming to terms with what you consider to be your dominant mode, or state of mind, or even your professional identity as a teacher. We will come back to this later, but for now we invite you to think about what your own 'habitual stance' is.

REFLECTION POINT

Classic theory: what does this look like in the classroom

Choice theory: in practice

1. Minimise coercion. Pupils aren't 'made' to behave using rewards and punishments. Instead, teachers build positive relationships with their pupils and manage them.

2. Teachers focus on quality. They expect mastery of concepts and encourage pupils to redo their work and try again until they have demonstrated competence and high-quality work. The emphasis is on deep learning through application.

3. Self-evaluation. Pupils are provided with helpful information and take ownership of their learning by evaluating their own performance. This promotes responsibility and helps pupils reach goals while becoming skilled decision-makers who are actively involved in their own education.

To what extent do you expect to work with your pupils on issues like these?

What are the advantages of giving pupils a say in all matters that affect them?

RESTORATIVE PRACTICE – BACKGROUND

Restorative practice (RP) – also referred to as restorative approaches or restorative measures – isn't drawn from a punitive lens, but a relational one. This is an understanding that sees wrongdoing not as a violation against the state but as harm done to a person and to the relationship with that person (Zehr, 2002).

In education, RP is argued to help manage behaviour in schools by actively teaching pupils how to resolve their conflicts not only with each other but also within the whole school community. It is a framework in which existing good practices are built on specific theories of relational pedagogy (Vaandering, 2015; Morrison and Vaandering, 2012). RP is described as based in 'constructivism' (Hansberry, 2016), a theory that says learners construct knowledge rather than passively take in information. Effective teachers look for new and better ways to interact with pupils in their classrooms, and to resolve an increasing range of difficult situations between teachers and pupils. RP, with its emphasis on relationship skills and a philosophy of restoration, offers both a basis for understanding and a process to put in place for conflict resolution.

Figure 5.1 explains how a relational pedagogy differentiates RP from other behavioural approaches mentioned in this chapter.

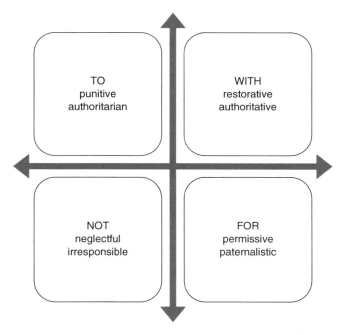

Figure 5.1 The Social Discipline Window

The four windows represent different combinations of high and low controlling and supporting behaviour strategies (McCold and Wachtel, 2002). A high control/low support approach, such as a punitive approach, characterises the use of strategies done to pupils; the person with authority deals a detention or suspension to whomever they believe caused the wrongdoing. While a neglectful teacher would do nothing at all (not likely), a permissive teacher shows care for the pupils.

In contrast, RP is not only high in control but also high in support since human beings are happier, more co-operative and productive, and more likely to make positive changes in their behaviour when those in positions of authority do things *with* them, rather than *to* them or *for* them. Thorsborne and Blood state there are four Guiding Principles in all examples of restorative conversations with pupils. These are: Connectedness (to the individual), Caring (about their problems), Value (their presence in community), Belief (that they can be better).

You can see straight away that RP is not a strategy that allows us to apply an arbitrary consequence to incidents of wrongdoing that occur in the classroom. It instead allows you to develop an approach that gives you space to understand the causes of children's behaviour that will ultimately have greater long-term benefits for both the pupil and their educational environment. However, it is important to take some time out here to consider the implications of this kind of intervention and ask yourself the following questions:

- Why might this approach be useful?
- Is it something that you have seen or experienced before in your own schooling or on placement?
- Who do you think should be the focus of attention in an incident that concerns wrongdoing?

One common announcement from experienced teachers who find out about RP strategies is that they were *already doing RP*. The ability to converse with your pupils over their issues, in effect to find out what's wrong, is part and parcel of developing your professional identity and, further, of being a decent human being. However, coming to understand RP as a behaviour approach is also to become familiar with a number of its key dialogic practices, which are outlined below.

RESTORATIVE ENQUIRY, CIRCLES AND CONFERENCES

Restorative enquiry can be used on a daily basis with all members of the school community. There are many situations in a school day where active non-judgemental listening and sharing of feelings can be used and you can see the case study below for an example. This is relatively easy if the people are not in conflict with each other but can also be used when conversations are difficult, and people see things differently. In this case, it is useful to change our language in order to use non-threatening, non-blaming conversations that are respectful but emotive ways of letting others know how their behaviour affects you.

A restorative conversation also describes a way of listening and responding to other people's points of view. It also involves the use of open body language, listening with empathy and listening for feelings and needs. The listener takes a neutral perspective and aims to help the other person identify what needs to be done in order to put things right or move on.

Restorative circles offer more open-ended opportunities to empower voice in marginalised young people since resilience is not a descriptor but the recognition of experience that an individual has. Already a popular strategy in schools, a circle-time structure can be used to air a problem or issue with a group of pupils while providing everyone within a community the opportunity to speak.

Restorative conferencing involves a group of people working together with a neutral facilitator to resolve conflict, repair relationships and move forward. It can follow a structured, scripted framework, within which everyone can express their thoughts and feelings about the issue being discussed and the impact it had on them.

CASE STUDY

Child-on-child fall-out

Charlotte and Zaha have been close friends, but when they come into school on a Monday, they have had a fall-out and have now started arguing with each other in your lesson.

On placement, speak to your mentor or host teachers or comment on it if you see a similar incident.

Ask them, has this ever happened to them?

- Ask how they dealt with it.
- What actions were taken at the time and what happened after?
- How was the relationship rebuilt between the children?
- How can you use engage, explain, expect to help resolve this situation restoratively?

One possible solution:

Explain to both the pupils that this is not the right time to have this conversation. Remind them of classroom expectations and encourage both of them to get on with their learning. If this fails, follow classroom procedures, which may require a time out, and ask for support if needed.

When appropriate, perhaps at the end of the lesson, ask both pupils to speak to you. Explain the impact their behaviour had on the lessons and offer them a chance to speak about how they feel. It is important that you don't interrupt or give solutions and make them be friends if that is not what they want.

Agree a time when both sides are ready to discuss solutions and how to move forward. Remember to ask for support from colleagues.

There is good evidence that restorative practice delivers a wide range of benefits for schools in the UK. Research suggests (see Bonell et al., 2018; Skinns et al., 2009; McCluskey et al., 2008; Bitel, 2005) that both teachers and pupils experience a calmer school atmosphere with more pupils showing positivity about their school's response to misbehaviour. RP is also found to directly impact the learning climate by allowing teachers to resolve behavioural issues in the long term, rather than dealing with the same day-to-day incidents of wrongdoing. Overall, there were fewer incidents of school bullying and aggression and an increase in pupils' mental health. Findings also indicated pupils appreciating a higher quality of school life and psychological wellbeing and lower psychological difficulties compared to pupils who were not involved with RP.

There are some very real implications here for the kind of behaviour management practice that we choose to engage with. RP is founded on taking responsibility, and for developing the skills of its community to solve problems and repair harm. How we manage incidents of conflict in school is important. How we develop a restorative culture in schools, making sure pupils have the ethical education they need to develop their voice, is critical.

If that is the case, then it is worth thinking about why policies or strategies that do not appear to support the building of these kinds of relationships are still courted with such favour and why many trainees struggle to interpret power and control in situations of conflict. Well, we think that such ideas still have purchase because teachers' lives are difficult. Teachers, especially trainee teachers, are frequently the victim of blame. If they accept responsibility, they are often in a no-win situation where the pupil, or management, has all the power, and the teacher has none. Often pupils must do things that are not necessarily fun but are still required for learning, such as keeping a classroom tidy or keeping to a routine. What happens when the teacher is constantly addressing interruptions to learning or other disturbances or yet again having to talk to a pupil over not handing coursework in?

Unsurprisingly RP, and other relationship-based strategies, make the headlines when there is a perceived breakdown of good behaviour, and this is often related to power. Given the need for teachers to support their own personal and professional agency, for many exerting power is seen as a shortcut to managing behaviour. For example, if I ask a pupil to complete this piece of coursework, and no coursework arrives, then I can think about this as being about compliance. To receive that coursework, meaning to turn non-compliance around, I need to apply a certain amount of pressure, such as a detention. How else, the trainee might argue, are they going to learn not to do it again?

In most cases, the detention *works*. The pupil never forgets or is late with their homework or whatever again. The trainee may well ask "Why do I need to take precious time 'to talk' with the pupil at all when I can simply assert the power I have been given? Particularly when I'm at risk of looking like I've lost control of the situation." It's far simpler for trainees to fall back on assertive systems since doing so not only communicates that you're in charge; it is also undeniably more effective, from a time-management point of view, than trying to navigate tricky human relationships. Time is of the essence, particularly given how short some teachers' working lives are and how quickly you must show that you have met the core competencies for this profession.

 **CASE STUDY**

Big aggressive flare-up

Rebecca comes into your lesson and seems to be in a bad mood and is slow to get onto task and is struggling with basic classroom exceptions. When you challenge the child, they start swearing at you and storm out after shouting across the whole class.

Ideas for guided practice and feedback

On placement, speak to your mentor or host teachers about explosive behaviour.

Ask them, has this ever happened to them?

Ask how it made them feel.

What actions were taken at the time and what happened after?

How can you use engage, explain, expect to help resolve this situation restoratively?

When Rebecca has walked out of the lesson follow the school policies and ask for support immediately to ensure that she is in a safe space.

One possible solution:

When the time is right, ask a colleague to help hold a restorative conversation. The time must be right so that both you and the pupil are at a point where both of you want to repair the relationship. In the conversation, go through the restorative question but also explain what happened and what impact it had on others. It is also important to not just see the conversation as a sorry without consequences; the pupil will need to know that what they have done should not have happened and they need to acknowledge this in line with the school policy.

With the help of the facilitator, try to come to a solution about how the relationship can be repaired.

A principled approach values the notion that it is your prerogative to support children to make good decisions and to establish an environment in which your pupil feels safe to do so. If this sounds improbably vague, then you can see the problem that many trainees have with putting relation-based strategies at the centre of their behaviour management skills.

There are no easy answers here, but one way to reframe this conversation is to rethink where power lies. In RP, everyone has power, including children. As we have said, sometimes this can be problematic, such as when a pupil is aware of their rights and uses this knowledge in a negative sense. That does not mean that pupils should not have rights or responsibilities but that you should consider the impact of power and control throughout communication. Is our pupil in this scenario difficult with a poor attitude to learning, or is there an underlying need that has affected their ability to hand in coursework on time?

5 Behaviour in schools

As we said earlier, thinking about behaviour in schools is not only limited to choosing which strategies you wish to use but also to engage in developing a principled approach based on your preferred values. Our focus on relation-based pedagogy in this chapter is to enable you to make some conscious decisions about your professional practice. RP's emphasis, for example, on facilitating productive dialogue and disagreement highlights the importance placed on how we can teach our pupils to have difficult conversations – a point which may resonate with you and which can be used to influence some of the practical strategies that other behavioural theories offer.

■■■ ASSIGNMENT LINKS

One of the most important points in developing your own set of principles is to keep communicating with colleagues who will help you to identify solutions to any specific behavioural issues that are currently concerning you. The following suggestions will support you with assignments that are linked to your professional studies.

1. Speak to your ITTC and ask how long their behaviour system has been in place and what the key principles behind it are. This will give you an understanding of the school's behaviour approaches and will allow you to investigate the research behind it.

2. With your mentor, pick a pupil who you will do a behaviour study on. Observe how they work in lessons – how they engage with tasks, how they relate to other pupils and to the staff. Look closely at how the teacher speaks to the pupils and deals with inappropriate behaviour. Discuss this in your mentor meeting.

3. Ask to shadow a year manager and observe how they communicate with pupils. Think about how they help build, maintain and repair relationships. Speak to them about why they took a particular action.

4. Reflecting on your own lesson practice, think about how you could deal more effectively with a barrier to learning. Try to use the engage, explain, expect model.

LEARNING AND CONSOLIDATION ACTIVITIES
KEY THINGS TO LOOK FOR WHEN OBSERVING LESSONS OR TEACHING

RP does not mean pupils simply saying sorry and moving on; it is a system where high support and high challenge is used to help regulate pupils' attitude to learning. One of the key ideas that can be used when working restoratively effectively is engage, explain, expect: a framework that has been developed at Carr Manor Community School that gives a format on how you can structure your thought process in your conversations with pupils.

Engage means speaking to the pupil and saying to them that you are going to have a conversation – it could be nonverbal as well. The point is the pupil will know that you are going to speak to them. Explain is the stage where you explain what the issue was and say how it caused a problem. At this point you can ask pupils to think about the effect that their action has had on other pupils and on their own learning. It is important to be calm and clear about the situation.

The expect phase is how you will help the pupil repair the situation and what that will look like. It could be clarity on behaviour for next lesson or an action that needs to be taken. It is even better if the pupil takes an active role in reaching the expectations. Look at how you can use the EEF framework to think through the following four scenarios.

DISCUSSION POINTS FOR TUTORIALS AND SEMINARS

Back in the seminar room

1. With fellow trainees, hold a general discussion about what behaviour practices are used in their placement schools. Think about the cohort, the school context and how effective you think the practices are.
2. In pairs, discuss a situation in which the behaviour, in your opinion, was not acceptable. Discuss what happened, your actions and what you might do differently next time.
3. On your own, write a short reflection about how a restorative approach might help you in your own classroom practices.

CHAPTER SUMMARY

Now you have read this chapter, you will:

- have an overview of different approaches to thinking about behaviour in the classroom
- understand the research behind relationship-based behaviour pedagogies
- have a framework to help think about becoming restorative in your approach
- understand that developing good behaviour management practices involves reflecting on experience
- seek advice and share openly and honestly with colleagues about how to build, repair and maintain relationships with the whole school community.

> ███ ── **REFLECTION POINT**
>
> - Having read and reflected on all the different theories, what would you like to take forward in your teaching practice?
> - Having read how important relationships are to children, how would you go about building professional and caring relationships?
> - Where do you personally feel you fit on a continuum between behaviourism and restorative approaches?
> - Why do you think a social discipline model of high challenge and high support is an effective and vital model for understanding behaviour in today's classroom?

FURTHER READING

Dix, P. (2017) *When the Adults change, Everything Changes*. Independent Thinking Press.

EEF (2020) Programmes to practices: identifying effective, evidence-based social and emotional learning strategies for teachers and schools: evidence review. Evidence reviews | EEF (educationendowmentfoundation.org.uk)

Hansberry, B. (2016) *A Practical Introduction to Restorative Practice in Schools*. Jessica Kingsley.

REFERENCES

Anti-Bullying Alliance (2016) Bullying and Wellbeing Report – Wave One Collection – March16 [Online]. Available at: https://anti-bullyingalliance.org.uk/sites/default/files/uploads/attachments/Bullying%20and%20Wellbeing%20Report%20-%20wave%20one%20collection%20-%20March16%20-%20FINAL%20%281%29_0.pdf

ATL (2013) Disruptive behaviour in schools and colleges rises alongside increase in children with behavioural and mental health problems. Association of Teachers and Lecturers Press Release, Liverpool, 24 March 2013.

Autry, L.B. and Langenbach, M. (1985) Locus of control and self-responsibility for behavior. *The Journal of Educational Research*, 79(2): 76–84.

Bitel, M. (2005) National Evaluation of the Restorative Justice in Schools Programme [Online]. Available at: www.gov.uk/government/organisations/youth-justice-board-for-england-and-wales (accessed 12/9/22).

Bonell, C., Allen, E., Warren, E., McGowan, J., Bevilacqua, L., ... Opondo, C. (2018) Effects of the Learning Together intervention on bullying and aggression in English secondary schools (INCLUSIVE): a cluster randomised controlled trial. *The Lancet*, 392(10163): 2452–2464. DOI: 10.1016/S0140-6736(18)31782-3

Canter, L. and Canter, M. (1992) *Lee Canter's Assertive Discipline: Positive Behaviour Management for Today's Classroom*. Canter and Associates.

Children's Commissioner (2020) Teenagers falling through the gaps. Available at: https://www.childrenscommissioner.gov.uk/report/teenagers-falling-through-the-gaps/

Cowie, H. and Myers, C. (2021) The impact of the COVID-19 pandemic on the mental health and well-being of children and young people. *Children & Society*, 35: 62–74.

DfE (2011) *Getting the Simple Things Right: Charlie Taylor's Behaviour Checklists*. Available at: https://dera.ioe.ac.uk//25115/

DfE (2019) *The Trainee Teacher Behavioural Toolkit: A Summary*. Available at: www.gov.uk/government/publications/initial-teacher-training-itt-core-content-framework/the-trainee-teacher-behavioural-toolkit-a-summary

Drewery, W. (2010) Restorative practice in schools: far reaching implications in restorative justice and practices in New Zealand, in G. Maxwell and J. Liu (eds) *Towards a Restorative Society*, pages 199–214. Eugene: Oegon.

Drewery, W. and Kecskemeti, M. (2010) Restorative practice and behaviour management in schools: discipline meets care. *Waikato Journal of Education*, 15(3): 101–113.

Galbraith, A. and Alexander, J. (2005) Literacy, self-esteem and locus of control. *Support for Learning*, 20(1): 28–34. DOI: 10.1111/j.0268-2141.2005.00357.x

Glasser, W. (1988) *Choice Theory in the Classroom*. Harper Collins.

Glazzard, J. and Green, M. (2022) *Learning to be a Primary Teacher: Core Knowledge and Understanding*. Critical Publishing.

Hansberry, B. (2016) *A Practical Introduction to Restorative Practice in Schools*. Paul Chapman.

Kremer, L. (1982) Locus of control, attitudes toward education, and teaching behaviors. *Scandinavian Journal of Educational Research*, 26(1): 1–11.

McCluskey, G., Lloyd, G., Kane, J., Riddell, S., Stead, J. and Weedon, E. (2008) Can restorative practice in schools make a difference. *Educational Review*, 60(4): 405–417.

McCold, P. and Wachtel, T. (2002) Restorative justice theory and validation, in G. Elmar and K. Hans-Jürgen (eds) *Restorative Justice: Theoretical Foundations*, pages 110–142. Devon: Willan Publishing.

Morrison, B. and Vaandering, D. (2012) Restorative justice: pedagogy, praxis, and discipline. *Journal of School Violence*, 11(2) 138–155.

National Education Union (2019) SEND Building inclusion in schools and colleges. Available at: www.neu.org.uk/send

Nelson. J. (1996) *Positive Discipline: The Classic Guide to Helping Children Develop Self-Discipline, Responsibility, Cooperation, and Problem-Solving Skills*. Random House Publishing.

Skinns, L., Du Rose, N. and Hough, M. (2009) An Evaluation of Bristol RAiS Project Report [Online]. Available at: www.restorativejustice.org.uk/resources/restorativeapproaches-schools-bristol-rais-evaluation (accessed 22/6/17).

Straughan, R. (1982) *Can We Teach Children to Be Good?* London: Allen and Unwin.

Taylor, C. (2011) Getting the simple things right: Charlie Taylor's behaviour checklist. DfE.

Thorsborne, M. and Blood, P. (2013) *Implementing Restorative Practices in Schools: A Practical Guide to Transforming Schools and Communities*. London: Jessica Kingsley.

Vaandering, D. (2015) Relational restorative justice pedagogy in educator professional development. *Curriculum Inquiry*, *44*(4) 508–530.

Watson, J. (1913) Psychology as the behaviorist views it. *Psychological Review*, *20*(2): 158–177.

Zehr, H. (1990) *Changing Lenses*. Scottdale, PA: Herald Press.

Zehr, H. (2002) *The Little Book of Restorative Justice*. New York: Good Books.

6

PLANNING YOUR TEACHING

CHRISTINA TURNER AND ALISON MANSFIELD

KEY WORDS

- Preparation
- Planning
- Memory
- Practice
- Modelling
- Reflection

CHAPTER OBJECTIVES

Planning forms a significant part of your teaching in both training and the early years of your career. To help you to see why planning is important, regardless of your school context, and to support you in undertaking this task, this chapter will provide you with some possible steps to use when planning. We will give you an overview of some key learning theories that will help to make sense of your planning and offer ideas on how to incorporate meaningful dialogue in lessons. The content will also prompt your thinking around risk-taking in lessons, and to help contextualise the information, we will provide scenarios to reflect on alongside activities to complete with your mentor.

LINKS TO THE CORE CONTENT FRAMEWORK

All of the Core Content Framework themes are referred to and applied in this chapter, but the following are the most relevant:

Standard 3 – Demonstrate good subject and curriculum knowledge

3. Ensuring pupils master foundational concepts and knowledge before moving on is likely to build pupils' confidence and help them succeed.

(Continued)

6 Planning your teaching

> 4. Anticipating common misconceptions within particular subjects is also an important aspect of curricular knowledge; working closely with colleagues to develop an understanding of likely misconceptions is valuable.
>
> 5. Explicitly teaching pupils the knowledge and skills they need to succeed within particular subject areas is beneficial.
>
> Standard 4 – Plan and teach well-structured lessons – the whole of this standard is the particular focus of this chapter.

Planning lessons is a craft that evolves over the length of a teaching career. There is no 'one right way' to plan a lesson, and so the aim of this chapter is to give you some steps that you can follow when starting out. As you become more confident, you might find that you incorporate these steps in a more flexible manner throughout a whole sequence of learning, rather than by simply following a 'lesson by lesson' approach.

WHY IS PLANNING IMPORTANT?

> ### ■ ■ ■ — CASE STUDY
>
> **Sumera and pre-planned lessons**
>
> Sumera is training to become a maths teacher and is towards the end of her first school placement. The maths department has a bank of lesson plans and resources, used by all members of the team. Prior to the lesson, Sumera went through the lesson slides carefully and considered how to link the resources to the model examples. During the lesson, the pupils copied down the examples and started completing the activity. She felt as though she had thought of everything and was sure of impressing her mentor.
>
> Sumera has just been observed by her mentor and is disappointed with the feedback. Her mentor questioned the *purpose* of the specific examples that she had modelled and suggested that pupils couldn't express *why* they were undertaking each step and how this linked to the *goal* of the lesson. She also questioned the *way* in which Sumera had modelled these. Sumera started to feel defensive and told her mentor that she had used the centralised lesson materials.
>
> What do you think the mentor was trying to uncover in her post-lesson review questions? Is there anything that Sumera had forgotten to think about before delivering the lesson? Is planning a lesson still important if there are pre-prepared lessons ready for you to use? What do you think about Sumera's response to her mentor's feedback?

You might be questioning the point of planning, especially if the teachers in your placement school don't seem to plan lessons, or if they use pre-prepared lesson slides and activities. It is important to recognise that more experienced teachers have a wealth of knowledge originating from the hours of practice that they have already had in the classroom. They often unconsciously apply this knowledge to lesson planning, without needing a step-by-step plan. Knowing that these teachers have been honing their craft over years highlights a crucial point: all teachers are also learners. If we are to learn something, then there will be a starting point for us.

In the context of lesson planning, this starting point is to explicitly think about each element of a lesson so that we can begin to establish those positive habits of mind, ultimately freeing up our attention for the next steps in our teaching journey. This is the same if the lesson activities have already been created for you. So you can understand *why* an activity or example is being used, and *how* to use it well. Furthermore, practising these activities or explanations can help you to identify pitfalls that might occur, and how to adapt your teaching for the needs of your pupils (see Chapters 8 and 9 for more on this).

GETTING TO GRIPS WITH PLANNING

It is tempting to grapple with your presentation, or get resources from the department's shared files, before thinking about the lesson as a whole. You will get better at planning learning much more quickly if you work through the steps outlined in this chapter. Along the way we will also think about our understanding of how pupils learn, and how you can use this to help your planning.

- Step 1 – see the whole journey
- Step 2 – clear objectives
- Step 3 – planning the delivery, resources and timings
- Step 4 – working out if pupils are learning
- Step 5 – script and practise
- Step 6 – evaluate the impact

STEP 1 – SEEING THE WHOLE JOURNEY

Before writing a lesson plan, you will need to prepare yourself by considering the following questions and issues. Invest time here, as it will enable you to efficiently plan a lesson that is more likely to be effective.

6 Planning your teaching

> **REFLECTION POINT**
>
> Questions to ask about the lesson or sequence of lessons you are planning
>
> - What am I teaching?
>   - What do I want the pupils to learn?
>   - What do the pupils already know?
>   - What will they go on to learn next, with this new knowledge?
>   - Is *my* knowledge of this secure?
>   - What are the common misconceptions?
>   - How does this learning objective connect to other areas of the subject curriculum?
> - Who am I teaching?
>   - What do they know already?
>   - What might they find difficult or confusing?
>   - Are there specific needs in the group which I will need to address?
> - Where can I find ideas for lessons? Where can I find resources?
> - What strategies can I use to assess progress?

You will be able to find many of the answers in your department's medium-term sequences of learning (sometimes called 'schemes of work'). It is always a good idea to check with your mentor that you have understood the answers to these questions. They can also help in other ways – perhaps they can tell you about resources that you can use to strengthen your knowledge, or explain decisions made when the planning was initially created.

STEP 2 – LEARNING OBJECTIVES – SETTING GOALS THAT CHALLENGE AND STRETCH PUPILS

When planning your lesson, think about what you want your pupils to be able to do by the end of the lesson. Lemov (2014) calls this 'beginning with the end' and proposes that you start by defining the objective, rather than by choosing your lesson activities. A good learning objective therefore provides clarity.

Often objectives might need to be broken down into a series of smaller steps, because a cumbersome lesson objective can also place too high a demand on pupils cognitively

(Sweller et al., 2019). For example, the objective 'be able to add fractions' can be broken down into the following smaller steps:

- Add unit fractions with the same denominator.
- Understand and use equivalent fractions.
- Add fractions where denominators share a simple common multiple.
- Add fractions with any denominator.
- Add improper fractions and mixed numbers.

In some subjects, writing objectives as key questions can clarify learning goals for the pupils. For example, if we know that we want our pupils to be able to explain the principle of 'energy transfer', we can we break this down into a sequence of key questions.

- What is the law of conservation of energy?
- Why are there not different *types* of energy but rather different *ways* in which energy is stored?
- What are the different mechanisms in which energy is carried between stores?
- Is money (in the bank, purse …) a good analogy to energy transfer?

The aim is to focus on these key questions during a lesson or sequence of lessons, checking on pupil knowledge and understanding so that progression is secured towards the overarching goal.

A good learning objective is also at the core of formative assessment. If the learning objective is *challenging* with respect to the pupils' current skills and knowledge, it provides opportunities for *strategy-focused* feedback (rather than comfort-focused words such as 'well done'), which not only supports pupils on the learning journey but increases motivation (Rattan et al., 2012). See Chapter 10 for more on formative assessment.

CASE STUDY

Eric's lesson objectives

Eric is training to become a history teacher. During his first placement he teaches a Year 8 mixed attainment class. Eric categorises the pupils of the class into low, middle and high ability to make planning easier. He writes a lesson objective aimed at each group of pupils. Eric then adapts an activity for each group and colour codes these: red (low), yellow (middle) and green (high). The 'green' activity provides opportunities for the

(Continued)

pupils to *analyse, evaluate and judge interpretations of the historical event*, while the 'red' activity is focused on *demonstration of knowledge*. In the lesson he allows pupils to choose the activity that they feel most confident in completing. Eric is surprised during feedback to learn that his mentor has some reservations about this approach.

- How have Eric's beliefs are about the 'abilities' of the pupils in his class influenced the learning objectives?
- Why might writing separate objectives restrict learning for some pupils?
- What are the practical issues of developing activities in this way for every lesson?

■■■ CASE STUDY

Eric's lesson objectives

When Eric set a separate learning objective for each of his defined group of pupils, he was setting out his own expectations for their learning. Rosenthal and Jacobson (1968) demonstrate that these preconceived beliefs about pupils' capacity for learning leads to a self-fulfilling prophecy. Pupils who are believed to be 'high ability' are given further learning opportunities and more feedback than those who are believed to be 'low ability'. Pupils internalise these interactions and begin to believe that they are indeed 'low ability' and act accordingly. So of course, when Eric then offers pupils the choice of activities based on levels of difficulty, pupils are likely to choose the activity that they believe matches the label they have been given. Thus, the self-fulfilling prophecy becomes established. Chapter 8 can help you with thinking about adapting teaching more effectively.

- Check your learning objective with your mentor. Is it challenging for the pupils in your class?
- Can you, or might you need to break it down into a series of smaller steps?
- Would it help to write the learning objective as a list of questions?
- Will there be a space in the classroom where you can display an objective?

TURNING AIMS INTO LEARNING OUTCOMES AND SUCCESS CRITERIA

In all subjects, pupils need to know what success looks like. A common misconception is that success is, for example, completing the activity or doing ten questions. The problem is that pupils being busy or engaged is a poor proxy for learning (Coe et al., 2014). Learning outcomes express what the pupil will achieve by the end of the lesson (for example, in technology, it might be 'to produce an electrical schematic'). They form the evidence that allows you to reflect on the extent to which the lesson has been successful. As such, the learning outcomes could be tangible, such as work in books, but also intangible, such as discussions, statements or role plays.

Success criteria define what is required for the learning outcome to be judged a success. The way in which you use learning outcomes and success criteria in practice can depend on the nature of your subject. The success criteria act a bit like a mark scheme, defining what it is about the pupil's response that makes it 'good'. It is very important to avoid pupils merely mimicking the success criteria. Asking pupils to explain their thinking to each other and including questions in a variety of formats so that the depth of understanding can be assessed is a good way of preventing this.

For example, if you are teaching maths and the learning objective is 'to be able to solve equations with unknowns on each side', the outcome could be to solve several examples, by following a worked example, while the success criteria would be to complete a correct example using the 'balance method' set out in that example.

This modelled solution gives a visual indication of the success criteria (refer to Figure 6.1). This example could remain on display as an example of what's expected when pupils complete an activity.

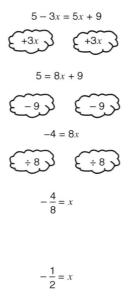

Figure 6.1 Modelled solution – a worked example of the 'balance method' of solving equations

6 Planning your teaching

> ▀ ▀ ▀ ── **REFLECTION POINT**
>
> Think about the lesson that you are planning.
>
> - What will the outcomes of the lesson be?
> - What will success look like?
> - How will the pupils know this?

WHAT IS LEARNING? HOW DO WE LEARN?

To be able to take the next step in planning, you need to have some knowledge of what learning is, and how we learn. Recent research on the relationship between memory and learning has suggested that learning is *a change in long-term memory* (Kirschner et al., 2006), or that *understanding is memory in disguise* (Willingham, 2009). There are lots of excellent books and papers on how memory works. These often focus on the limited capacity of *Working Memory* and the need for pupils to instead retrieve important knowledge from their much more efficient *Long-Term Memory* (Lovell, 2020).

One prominent example is Cognitive Load Theory (CLT) (Sweller et al., 2019), which suggests that it is very important not to overload pupils' working memory, which can only hold a very limited amount of information. CLT describes two different kinds of loads that are helpful to consider when planning how we manage new learning:

Intrinsic cognitive load refers to the difficulty of the subject content being taught.

Extrinsic cognitive load is the load from processing other information in the environment. This kind of cognitive load detracts from the learning objective, adding to working memory load, and so is unhelpful.

As well as thinking about the presentation of *new* material, we need to consider how we can help pupils move *previously experienced* information to their Long-Term Memory, from where they can retrieve it without overwhelming their Working Memory. Some really crucial concepts about this transfer include:

Encoding: encoding information (explaining, processing, understanding and categorising it) is an important element of the process of transferring information from Working Memory to Long-Term Memory (Craik and Lockhart, 1972).

Schemata: the brain organises the information into schemata (networks of information). New information is more likely to be stored if it can be connected to prior knowledge in an existing schema. For example, I am more likely to remember that 48 is a multiple of 2 if I can tether it to my pre-existing schema involving even numbers and the 2 times table. Activating this prior knowledge in the first place supports pupils to make these connections, helping them to 'tether' new information to a pre-existing schema.

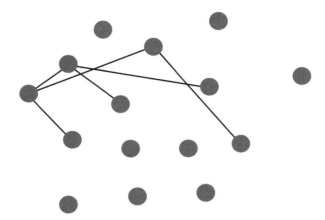

Figure 6.2 Schema model

The more interconnected a schema is, the easier it becomes for pupils to understand next steps and to integrate them within their schema. An *interconnected schema* supports the transfer of information from short-term to long-term memory.

Misconceptions: sometimes, a schema can contain incorrect information. For example, a pupil might think that all prime numbers are odd numbers, so 2 cannot possibly be a prime number. This is a misconception and probably has been formed because all prime numbers are odd, except for the number 2. A mistake and a misconception are different things. A mistake is generally a 'one-off' event where a pupil has a good understanding but makes an error (for example, due to a distraction). A misconception is where a pupil believes something to be correct when it is actually incorrect). Later in this chapter we will look at dealing with misconceptions.

Retrieval: there is no point in storing information in long-term memory if it cannot be retrieved. By practising retrieval of information, it becomes easier to recall it. Furthermore, allowing memory to decay and then retrieving information can strengthen long-term learning (Bjork, 1975).

In the next section we will look at the implications of these theories for how we plan lessons and series of lessons.

UNCOVERING MISCONCEPTIONS

Knowing the common misconceptions pupils hold regarding the topic that you are teaching is very useful, but also harder than it sounds! The more experience you have in teaching a topic, the more familiar you become with different misconceptions.

6 Planning your teaching

Therefore, we advise that you speak to experienced colleagues in your placement schools before teaching a new topic, to explore the misconceptions that they have encountered.

Diagnostic questions can help you find out what a pupil is thinking and can expose misconceptions, especially if used with mini whiteboards for quickly assessing pupil responses. You can find out more about any misconceptions by asking pupils to *explain their reasoning* for their choice of answer.

CASE STUDY

Diagnostic Questions

Consider this diagnostic question used by a maths teacher.

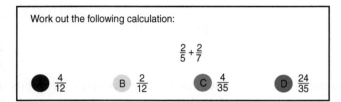

Work out the following calculation:

$$\frac{2}{5} + \frac{2}{7}$$

A) $\frac{4}{12}$ B) $\frac{2}{12}$ C) $\frac{4}{35}$ D) $\frac{24}{35}$

Figure 6.3 Diagnostic question example

The correct answer is D. Here the pupil has correctly calculated the equivalent fractions using a common denominator:

$$\frac{2}{5} + \frac{2}{7} = \frac{14}{35} + \frac{10}{35} = \frac{24}{35}$$

Figure 6.4 Calculating equivalent fractions

The teacher purposefully selected the answers for the other choices.

Answer	Common misconception
A	The pupil falsely believes that to add fractions, you add the numerators together and then you add the denominators together.
B	The pupil falsely believes that you need to add the denominators together (because they are different numbers) and not the numerators (because they are the same number).
C	The pupil understands that a common denominator is required but doesn't understand how this relates to equivalent fractions.

With your mentor, write a diagnostic question that could help you uncover misconceptions for the topic that you are teaching. While you're reading the next section, consider when in the lesson you might use this diagnostic question.

STEP 3 – PLANNING THE DELIVERY, RESOURCES AND TIMING

Now that you have clarity about *what* you are teaching, you can turn to *how* you will do this.

When you first start, you'll think a lot about what you are doing as the teacher. However, it is just as important to think about what the pupils will be doing during each phase of the lesson. By doing this, you will begin to 'see' the lesson from the perspective of the pupil, which will help you to consider whether your planning is meeting their learning needs. Most lesson plans will have a space for you to add in this information.

Think back to Sumera's experiences in our first case study in this chapter. She needed to think about all the things in this section, even if the materials and activities were already prepared. In other schools you might be given more options about how you teach a lesson or topic, but the same thinking still needs to be done. Many schools have expectations on the structure of lessons, designed so that pupils experience consistency. You will need to find out about these, from your mentor and through observing teachers in the school teach, so that you can include these expectations and routines in your planning.

STARTERS, RETRIEVAL AND ACTIVATING PRIOR KNOWLEDGE

A good example of these policies is the common expectation that pupils will arrive at the lesson and complete a 'starter', so that they can settle, and so the teacher can take the register. Starters are also ideal for reviewing previously taught information, in a way that makes it easy for you to check answers quickly.

For example:

- in religious studies pupils might label a plan of a mosque;
- in science pupils might write down three key points about photosynthesis;
- in geography pupils might summarise pros and cons of a renewable energy source in a table;
- in physical education pupils create a mind map connecting the structure and functions of the skeleton.

These starters are examples of 'retrieval' activities. The aim of retrieval is to allow for skills to be practised, or knowledge to be recalled, to the point where they become automatic. Note that there is no point in trying to retrieve information that has not been well rehearsed in the first place. Retrieval activities should focus on practising recall of knowledge that is (or should be) already relatively secure, and to use the outcomes of the activity to inform your next steps as a teacher.

6 Planning your teaching

▄■■ — CASE STUDY

Low-Stakes Quizzing

Let's look at an example of a 'low-stakes quiz' used to start a French lesson, where pupils are asked to retrieve information that has been 'stored' over different periods of time.

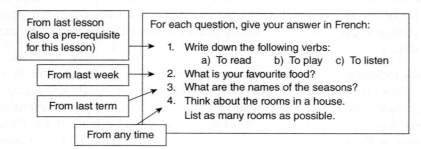

Figure 6.5 Example low-stakes quiz

You can see that the activity is designed so that pupils can do it independently, without need for teacher explanation. The more open-ended question at the end of the activity means that pupils can't 'finish' the task until the teacher is ready to move on. It is also a good idea to ensure that at least one of the questions tests the prior knowledge required for the main learning objective in the upcoming lesson.

▄■■ — REFLECTION POINT

Think about the lesson that you are planning.

- How will you activate the knowledge that pupils already know, but will need to use in this lesson?
- How will you assess it?
- How will you address any 'gaps' in the prior knowledge?

PLANNING LESSON ACTIVITIES AND TASKS, AND MANAGING COGNITIVE LOAD

Now you will need to decide what the pupils will hear, read, examine, practise and do in the lesson. What information will you need to give as direct instruction and explanation? What do pupils do while you give the direct instruction? Are they copying what you do? Watching and following? Making their own notes? What questions do you need to ask to help you check their understanding? If there are materials for the pupils to read, how will you approach this? Who will read, you or the pupils? What will you need to model?

6 Planning your teaching

The cognitive load on the pupils throughout your delivery should be considered. It is worth noting that our understanding of cognitive science (which seeks to understand how the brain thinks and learns) and CLT is still developing. We are still learning about how to translate theories into classroom practice. Perry et al. (2021) highlight problems that can occur when the theory is misinterpreted. However, there is no doubt that when carefully considered, CLT provides the basis for some excellent advice on managing cognitive load when explaining or when modelling techniques, skills or procedures in your subject.

- Direct instruction and dual coding – put simply, working memory has two 'input' streams, the visual and verbal. By sharing the load between the two streams, we can make more efficient use of limited working memory capacity. If we can utilise both streams (for example, provide a verbal explanation alongside a relevant image), then these can work together. This dual coding of information aids retrieval from long-term memory. This effect is nuanced and must be applied with careful thought. If, for example, there are too many complicated diagrams, or diagrams accompanied by too much text, or indeed, if there is a muddled explanation accompanying a diagram, then the effect is lost.

- Worked example effect – when learning something new, learning through problem solving is less effective than studying a worked example (Sweller et al., 1998). A worked example goes through a skill or technique in a step-by-step manner to reduce the burden on working memory and focus attention on each step. To maximise the impact of a worked example, you might consider a 'think aloud' approach, where you talk through your decision-making process in each step, outlining what you are doing and why. This models metacognition (planning, monitoring and evaluating learning), which supports pupils to become more independent (Quigley et al., 2018).

- Guidance fading – fading is a method of removing guidance steps (starting by removing the last step) to help pupils transition to more independence (Renkl and Atkinson, 2003). As pupil confidence grows, more steps can be removed until they are able to complete a whole example on their own. The removal of steps could vary between pupils depending on whether they are ready to 'go solo'.

- Mistakes in worked examples – making a mistake in a worked example allows you to model how to overcome a mistake (and show that mistakes are a part of the learning journey). Being able to explain why a mistake has occurred also strengthens understanding. This can be a highly effective strategy but only if used at the right time in the learning process. If used too early on, it can lead to confusion and/or the development of misconceptions.

Finally, you may want to include concrete and/or pictorial models instead of providing solely abstract models, as research suggests that this supports learning (Bruner, 1966). For example, using double-sided counters in maths might help pupils understand the concept of zero pairs. Science teachers might use molecular diagrams to support their teaching of symbolic equations.

TIMINGS

Getting the timings of the lesson right is one of the hardest aspects of teaching to master. Planning your timings will help with this. It is likely that the lesson will have been planned so that pupils complete work of increasing depth and complexity, so the sections of the lesson need to reflect this. Your initial timings should identify the number of minutes that you will spend on each section of the lesson. It is helpful before delivering the lesson to convert these into specific times. For example, if the lesson begins at 8.45 a.m. and you have allocated seven minutes to your first task, then write 8.45 a.m.– 8.52 a.m. on your lesson plan. This reduces your cognitive load in the classroom by enabling you to track your delivery against a clock or watch.

> ### ▀▀▀ — REFLECTION POINT
>
> Alongside your mentor, design the explaining and modelling aspects of your lesson, thinking particularly about the individual small steps that you will need to outline. Once this is designed, practise modelling this new learning, ensuring that you explain your thinking as you move from one step to the next.
>
> Check that you have considered the following questions:
>
> - How can you best model the new learning in your next lesson? Will you use concrete manipulatives or a concrete example to support understanding? Will you use a diagram or picture?
> - How will you ensure that these modes of delivery won't overload working memory?
> - What are the individual steps needed?
> - How much of the lesson time will you spend on modelling?
> - How will you gradually facilitate pupils to become more independent?
> - When will you introduce further challenge?

STEP 4 – WORKING OUT IF PUPILS ARE LEARNING

Whether we are learning how to divide fractions, play an instrument, or how to read and analyse poetry, we need to practise. Giving pupils the opportunity to practise techniques and use the knowledge you have been teaching also gives teachers opportunities to see if the pupils have learned what has been taught. However, not all practice is the same in terms of effectiveness. Mindless repetition, especially if it takes up a substantial proportion of the lesson, without any teacher input, can have a negative impact on learning. You might want to think about splitting practice activity into phases, perhaps with discussion points or further teacher instruction in between.

Ericsson et al. (1993) defined set conditions for improving performance, and specific features of this can guide the planning of pupil practice. Make sure that:

- Pupils understand the goals of the practice;
- Skills are isolated and sequenced carefully in the practice, such that goals are achieved in a chosen order;
- Pupils can perform the task independently (supported in the initial stages by clear teacher instruction and guidance);
- Pupils receive immediate feedback, allowing them to adjust as necessary.

By the end of the process, pupils should be able to work fully independently, achieving the goal and meeting the success criteria set. You'll need to think carefully about all these things – and in particular how you are going to evaluate and give feedback to pupils on their work or performance. You could:

- Circulate the room – spot when pupils need a prompt to make the next step, or a prompt that provides extra challenge.
- Assessment points – when planning your lesson, think about adding in three more formal assessment points. You might use short or True/False questions to check on pupil thinking. Mini whiteboards can help with this.
- Use model answers or pieces of work – pupils can quickly see if they are on track, or if they need to check their understanding with either their peer or teacher.
- Collaboration – activating pupils to support each other can enhance opportunities for feedback, but be careful that misconceptions aren't being shared or strengthened.

DEALING WITH MISCONCEPTIONS

Dealing with misconceptions is not easy. Recall the misconception that 2 is not a prime number because it is an even number. Just telling the pupil that '2 is a prime number' will probably not correct the schema on which the misconception is based, as this doesn't affect the misunderstanding in the pupil's underlying schema (that prime numbers are always odd).

One strategy that can be used to tackle misconceptions is *cognitive conflict*. Cognitive conflict is triggered when pupils are shown clearly *why* their beliefs and understanding are incorrect. Pupils are then more likely to engage with the new information, and to apply effort to adjust their existing beliefs and understanding. Sherrington and Caviglioli (2020) suggest the following steps:

INTRODUCE THE MISCONCEPTION EXPLICITLY

Ensure that all pupils know what mistakes have been made and why. This is likely to involve whole class explanation and discussion.

REINFORCE WITH THE CORRECT MODEL

Now ensure that all pupils are aware of what is correct and why. Have a full, correct model and explanation ready so that you can fully challenge the misconceptions. While it's helpful to highlight where a misconception might have formed and why it's wrong, make sure you are emphasising the correct model (we don't want the misconception to stick in their memory!).

CHECK FOR UNDERSTANDING OF BOTH THE ERROR AND THE CORRECTION

During the lesson and/or unit of work, you might consider using further strategies for checking understanding. Providing pupils with a challenging question or prompt that probes understanding is one way of doing this.

PRACTISE THE CORRECT METHOD/VERSION

To ensure that the correct method or version is established, pupils need time to practise. This practice should test the misconception, and so any activity must link directly to this (Sherrington and Caviglioli, 2020: 86–87).

HOW ARE YOU GOING TO END THE LESSON?

The end of a lesson can be very quickly lost in finishing an activity, packing away and simply waiting to leave. Don't allow this to happen! Make sure that the ending is powerful so that pupils leave with a clear sense of what they have achieved. Here are some ideas for lesson endings:

- Use an 'exit ticket' – this is a short set of questions based on the lesson objective. Some teachers collect the exit tickets as pupils leave the room. In your next lesson, you can focus on any misunderstandings, or build on the current understanding of the pupils, based on these tickets.
- Ask pupils to complete guided reflection on their learning, using the Learning Objectives as a guide. You can give opportunities to discuss it with partners and/or ask individuals for feedback.

- Some teachers use mind maps to collect and organise new information and ask pupils to add to this at the end of a lesson.

CONTINGENCY PLANNING FOR DURING THE TEACHING

Of course you will make sure you have your resources, and that the IT is working, but what will you do if the whole class is struggling to understand your explanation? Think about how you can break the concept down further (perhaps increasing the number of steps) or by having a different model ready. It's a good idea to have 'enabling' questions or prompts prepared so that you have these to hand if pupils are struggling. Similarly, ensure that you have planned at least one 'stretch' question or prompt, which you can use in response to pupils who demonstrate a good understanding of the learning objective.

STEP 5 – SCRIPT AND PRACTISE

Once you have completed these planning processes, you should practise your delivery. This is a crucial step which is often overlooked. If you start your career by scripting your explanations and content, and then by practising your delivery (particularly as there is time to do this while you are training), then your efficacy in the classroom is likely to be higher and pupil outcomes will improve as a result. Instead of your explanation being spontaneous and perhaps not logically sequenced for pupils (who, in this context, are the guinea pigs for your untested explanation), your explanation is tested, tweaked and has greater clarity. Thus, the pupils are beneficiaries of higher-quality instructions. Some options for practice are:

- Focus on points in the lesson where you need to give crucial information, direct instruction or explanations.

- Script and role play the way in which you are going to deliver your teaching. This would ideally be in a classroom with the teaching tools you will be using, along with the resources.

- Practise your delivery, reflect on it with your mentor and practise again. You may have several iterations of this before you are happy. If there is a gap between your practice and the classroom delivery, perhaps write down your script to practise or take a recording to watch again before the lesson.

- Practise with another trainee (acting as the pupil) – check whether they fully understood your explanations.

- Use technology – record your explanations and listen back, reflecting on its clarity and coherence. Then refine it and have another go.

- Complete yourself the tasks that you will ask pupils to do. You will spot difficulties and be able to prepare explanations or help.

In most subjects, practising reading aloud the texts that you are going to use will be important. Reading through the texts in advance will help you pace the reading and practise any difficult terminology, for example in history saying 'worms' (invertebrates) instead of 'Worms' (a German city).

STEP 6 – EVALUATE THE IMPACT

Finally, a well-prepared teacher is one who systematically reflects on the lessons that they teach. These reflections empower you to develop your classroom practice in a structured manner, thinking about what worked and what you might change. Reflecting on what the pupils now know, and what they are still confused on, also gives you the opportunity to crystallise starting points for the next lesson. In this way, preparing for a lesson becomes a developmental process that builds on what you have done.

LEARNING ABOUT PLANNING – IN CONTEXT

As a final thought we want to recognise that the context of the school and department you are teaching in will determine the action steps you need to take, and how much room for movement you have in planning lessons. In some schools there will be an expectation to use the already prepared materials as they are presented to you. In others you will have much more freedom to adapt these – perhaps with choices or suggested activities. All schools will have medium-term plans that you will need to make sure you are addressing in your planning and teaching.

The more freedom you have, the more important it is to keep objectives in mind throughout the planning process. You should also keep questioning yourself as to whether the inclusion of a specific aspect is necessary, is crucial. It can be very easy to get overexcited at this stage and want to impart lots of information on a topic you are passionate about!

In schools which offer you more choice, there is also the risk that you can spend hours trying to plan the perfect lesson or fall into an internet wormhole surrounded by more resources than you can imagine and without a clear idea of what to use. This is why keeping an eye on your objectives is so important. Often searching for resources or spending hours working out 'what to do' will either lead to task-driven lessons (rather than learning-focused) or waste a huge amount of your time and cause you to feel swamped.

We have also seen that you cannot just pick up a pre-planned lesson, and its resources, walk into a classroom and teach it. If you rely too heavily on materials you have not written and don't fully understand, delivery in the classroom will not be as effective as it could be. Going through the steps outlined here – whether you're adapting a lesson plan or creating it yourself – will help you stay on track.

> ### ASSIGNMENT LINKS
>
> This chapter can support you with the following big ideas in professional studies:
>
> - Memory and learning
> - Strategies underpinned by cognitive science and Cognitive Load Theory (and some debates on effectiveness)
> - Identifying and dealing with misconceptions
> - Structuring an objective-led lesson
> - Planning sequences of lessons.

LEARNING AND CONSOLIDATION ACTIVITIES

KEY THINGS TO LOOK FOR WHEN OBSERVING LESSONS OR TEACHING

- How are prior knowledge and skills reviewed?
- How is knowledge required for the lesson activated?
- How do teachers set learning objectives? Are they posed as questions? Are they reviewed during the lesson? How? When?
- How do pupils know what success looks like?
- How is the learning objective reflected in both modelling and independent practice?
- What types of modelling does the teacher use? How is the learning objective broken down into smaller steps? What is the impact of the modelling on the pupils?
- How does the teacher gradually release responsibility for applying the new knowledge or skill to the pupils?
- What are the pupils doing at each point in the lesson?
- How does the teacher assess the learning?

DISCUSSION POINTS FOR TUTORIALS AND SEMINARS

- What are the challenges in transferring theories of learning into classroom practice?
- How robust is the education evidence base?
- Where can good evidence-based strategies be found?
- Can my own practice be considered research? In what ways?

IDEAS FOR GUIDED PRACTICE AND FEEDBACK

- Observe expert teachers in your placement department, focusing on specific phases of the lesson. What do they do in each phase that impacts positively on learning?

- Choose three pupils within a lesson to observe. Focus only on what these three pupils are doing and learning throughout the lesson. What have you learnt from this experience?

- Observe a pupil throughout every lesson during a day. What is their overall learning experience like? What did they learn? What strategies can you add to your own toolkit as a result?

- Ensure that you co-plan at least one lesson with each host teacher and your mentor.

- Together with your mentor, review a departmental sequence of learning. How are key concepts revisited? What can pupils now do, and what do they now know compared to their starting point? How is this reflected in the activities and tasks they undertake as the sequence develops?

CHAPTER SUMMARY

Now you have read this chapter, you will:

- know more about what learning is, and how we learn
- know more about memory and its relationship with learning
- know the key elements of a lesson and the reasons for these
- be able to structure a learning-focused lesson
- be able to plan lessons and sequences of lessons in different types of school contexts.

REFLECTION POINT

- How do you think lesson *preparation* changes with experience?
- How can you ensure smooth transitions between the different phases of the lesson?
- What are the challenges in transferring theories of learning into classroom practice?
- Think about risk-taking and what that means to you in the context of teaching. What would you like to 'try out' in the classroom? How do you think this will impact on learning?

FURTHER READING

Clowes, G. (2011) *The Essential 5: A Starting Point for Kagan Cooperative Learning.* San Clemente, CA: Kagan Publishing. *Kagan Online Magazine*, Spring 2011. Available at: www.kaganonline.com/free_articles/research_and_rationale/330/The-Essential-5-A-Starting-Point-for-Kagan-Cooperative-Learning

Coe, R., Rauch, C.J., Kime, S. and Singleton, D. (2020) *Great Teaching Toolkit Evidence Review.* Evidence Based Education in partnership with Cambridge Assessment International Education.

Quigley, A., Muijs, D. and Stringer, E. (2018) *Metacognition and Self-Regulated Learning.* Education Endowment Foundation.

Rosenshine, B. (2012) Principles of instruction: research-based strategies that all teachers should know. *American Educator, 36*(1): 12–39.

REFERENCES

Bjork, R.A. (1975) Retrieval as a memory modifier, in R.L. Sols (ed.) *Information Processing and Cognition: The Loyola Symposium*, pages 123–144. L. Erlbaum Associates.

Bruner, J.S. (1966) *Toward a Theory of Instruction.* Harvard University Press.

Coe, R., Aloisi, C., Higgins, S. and Major, L.E. (2014) *What Makes Great Teaching? Review of the Underpinning Research.* Sutton Trust.

Craik, F.I.M. and Lockhart, R.S. (1972) Levels of processing: a framework for memory research. *Journal of Verbal Learning and Verbal behavior, 11*(6): 671–684.

Didau, D. (2015) *What if Everything You Knew About Education Was Wrong?* (1st edn). Carmarthen: Crown House Publishing.

Ericsson, K.A., Krampe, R.T. and Tesch-Römer, C. (1993) The role of deliberate practice in the acquisition of expert performance. *Psychological Review, 100*: 363–406. DOI: 10.1037/0033-295X.87.3.215

Jay, T., Willis, B., Thomas, P., Taylor, R., Moore, N., Burnett, C., Merchant, G. and Stevens, A. (2017) *Dialogic Teaching: Evaluation Report and Executive Summary.* Education Endowment Foundation.

Kirschner, P.A., Sweller, J. and Clark, R.E. (2006) Why minimal guidance during instruction does not work: an analysis of the failure of constructivist discovery, problem-based, experiential, and inquiry-based teaching. *Educational Psychologist, 4*(2): 75–86. DOI: 10.1207/s15326985ep4102_1

Lemov, D. (2014) *Teach Like a Champion 2.0.* John Wiley & Sons.

Lovell, O. (2020) *Sweller's Cognitive Load Theory in Action.* John Catt.

Orru, G. and Longo, L. (2019) The evolution of cognitive load theory and the measurement of its intrinsic, extraneous and germane loads: a review, in L. Longo and M. Leva (eds) *Human Mental Workload: Models and Applications. H-WORKLOAD 2018. Communications in Computer and Information Science*, vol *1012*. Springer, Cham. DOI: 10.1007/978-3-030-14273-5_3

Perry, T., Lea, R., Jorgensen, C.R., Cordingley, P., Shapiro, K. and Youdell, D. (2021) *Cognitive Science Approaches in the Classroom: A Review of the Evidence*. Education Endowment Foundation.

Quigley, A., Muijs, D. and Stringer, E. (2018) *Metacognition and Self-Regulated Learning*. Education Endowment Foundation.

Rattan, A., Good, C. and Dweck, C. (2012) "It's ok – not everyone can be good at math": instructors with an entity theory comfort (and demotivate) students. *Journal of Experimental Social Psychology, 48*(3): 731–737. DOI: 10.1016/j.jesp.2011.12.012

Renkl, A. and Atkinson, R.K. (2003) Structuring the transition from example study to problem solving in cognitive skill acquisition: a cognitive load perspective. *Educational Psychologist, 38*(1): 15–22. DOI: 10.1207/S15326985EP3801_3

Rosenshine, B. (2012) Principles of instruction: research-based strategies that all teachers should know. *American Educator, 36*(1): 12–39.

Rosenthal, R. and Jacobson, L. (1968) Pygmalion in the classroom. *The Urban Review, 3*(1): 16–20.

Schnotz, W. and Kürschner, C. (2007) A reconsideration of cognitive load theory. *Educational Psychology Review, 19*: 469–508.

Sherrington, T. and Caviglioli, O. (2020). *Walkthrus – Five Step Guides to Instructional Coaching*. London: John Catt Educational Ltd.

Sherrington, T. and Stafford, S. (2018) *Schema and Misconceptions*. Chartered College of Teachers. Available at: Schema-and-Misconceptions-1.pdf (chartered.college)

Sweller, J., van Merriënboer, J.J.G. and Paas, F. (1998) Cognitive architecture and instructional design. *Educational Psychology Review, 10*(3): 251–296. DOI: 10.1023/a:1022193728205

Sweller, J., van Merriënboer, J.J.G. and Paas, F. (2019) Cognitive architecture and instructional design: 20 years later. *Educational Psychology Review, 31*(2): 261–292. DOI: 10.1007/s10648-019-09465-5

Willingham, D.T. (2009) *Why Don't Students Like School? A Cognitive Scientist Answers Questions About How The Mind Works and What It Means For Your Classroom*. San Francisco, California: Jossey-Bass.

7

THE CURRICULUM AND THE TEACHER

HEENA DAVE AND SOPHIE WILSON

 **KEY WORDS**

- Curriculum
- Knowledge
- Content
- Sequencing
- Pedagogical content knowledge
- Inclusion

CHAPTER OBJECTIVES

In this chapter you will explore some of the 'big ideas' around the concept and meaning of a curriculum. Before developing a curriculum, you will consider your school's wider purpose of education and how that curriculum intends to bring that to life. You will also learn that a curriculum has many dimensions and should adhere to national guidance and frameworks as well as explicitly lay out the knowledge, content and sequencing of learning and respond to the misconceptions that a learner may hold. Finally, an effective curriculum is one that provides windows and mirrors for all learners. You will also consider the evidence for developing a curriculum that is inclusive. What is important is realising that the curriculum is not static but there to be engaged with as a teacher.

LINKS TO THE ITT CORE CONTENT FRAMEWORK

All of the Core Content Framework themes are referred to and applied in this chapter, but the following are the most obviously relevant:

Standard 1 - Set high expectations, particularly:

(Continued)

7 The curriculum and the teacher

> 3. Teacher expectations can affect pupil outcomes; setting goals that challenge and stretch pupils is essential.
> 4. Setting clear expectations can help communicate shared values that improve classroom and school culture.
>
> Standard 2 - Promote good progress
>
> 2. Prior knowledge plays an important role in how pupils learn; committing some key facts to their long-term memory is likely to help pupils learn more complex ideas.
> 6. Where prior knowledge is weak, pupils are more likely to develop misconceptions, particularly if new ideas are introduced too quickly.
>
> Standard 3 - Demonstrate good subject and curriculum knowledge
>
> 1. A school's curriculum enables it to set out its vision for the knowledge, skills and values that its pupils will learn, encompassing the National Curriculum within a coherent wider vision for successful learning.
> 3. Ensuring pupils master foundational concepts and knowledge before moving on is likely to build pupils' confidence and help them succeed.
>
> Standard 4 - Plan and teach well-structured lessons
>
> 2. Effective teachers introduce new material in steps, explicitly linking new ideas to what has been previously studied and learned.
> 4. Guides, scaffolds and worked examples can help pupils apply new ideas but should be gradually removed as pupil expertise increases.

THE PURPOSE(S) OF EDUCATION AND CURRICULUM

WHAT DO WE MEAN BY CURRICULUM?

Despite being a very common word, the meaning of curriculum is contested. Elements of the debates around curriculum will unfold throughout this chapter as we examine the complexity of its roles and functions in school, and your own day-to-day teaching.

The word 'curriculum' stems from the Latin verb 'currere', which means 'to run'. Curriculum can also be translated as 'racecourse' (Leyendecker, 2012). These words conjure up images of a pre-set course that learners engage with and finish. In practice, ideas about curriculum are more complex. Most concepts of curriculum include some element of planning. Tyler (1957), for instance, defines curriculum as *all the learning experiences planned and directed by the school to attain its educational goals*. Similarly, Wheeler (1967) describes curriculum as the *planned experiences offered to the learner under guidance of the school*.

Others write about the way that school experiences teach things to pupils in an unplanned 'hidden curriculum'. This is because pupils learn more than is directly taught during school. They learn about the world through how we teach, as well as through what we teach (Biesta, 2020). For instance, schooling passes on ideas about their place in society, how conflicts are dealt with, what people value in friendship, among many other things (Jackson, 1968; Biddulph et al., 2020). The school curriculum can therefore be seen as the total learning experience, by which students are helped to 'make meaning' through a variety of 'lenses on the world' (Ashbee, 2021).

For many years the focus of education policy and regulation was on pedagogy – the way that things are taught – however, the focus of policy makers and regulators is now firmly on the issue of curriculum. For instance, Ofsted have re-emphasised the importance of curriculum in the most recent Schools Inspection Framework (Ofsted, 2019), which they use to inspect and make judgements about the quality of schools. The SIF defines curriculum as *The framework for setting out the aims of a programme of education, including the knowledge and skills to be gained at each stage.* You will hear this referred to as the school's 'intent'. This definition suggests that for Ofsted the focus is on the idea of curriculum as a plan. The SIF also covers the way that this plan is enacted by subject departments and teachers (referred to as 'implementation'), and the impact that this has on pupils' learning and knowledge (called 'impact'). The ITT Core Content Framework (CCF) (DfE, 2019b) defines the function of a school's curriculum as to *set out its vision for the knowledge, skills and values that its pupils will learn, encompassing the national curriculum within a coherent wider vision for successful learning.*

So, for the purposes of this chapter, we will refer to the school curriculum mostly in the sense of planned learning experiences and goals. However, as you will see, we will also refer to the other 'hidden curriculum' at times – those important aspects of the world and society that our schools teach, sometimes without realising.

REFLECTION POINT

- What do teachers and school leaders in your context mean when they use the word curriculum?
- To what extent does this align to the DfE's (2019) guidance and Ofsted's (2019) inspection framework?
- What does the word curriculum mean to you?

WHAT ARE SCHOOLS FOR?

Secondary schooling used to be a luxury. Until the late nineteenth century only the wealthy could usually send their children to school. Private and public schools taught the children of the wealthy an elite cultural curriculum, based on classical languages such as Latin and Greek. Even when education became compulsory in 1870, the school leaving age was just 11 years old, compared with 18 today. Only well-off children got anything more than a basic elementary education in reading and writing. It is also only relatively recently that it has become an accepted ambition of modern society to study at university, with just 3 per cent of the population gaining a degree qualification in the 1950s compared to 50 per cent today. Furthermore, according to OEDC, this is still only an aspiration for one in five school-aged children across the world.

Each of these different purposes of schooling would imply a very different form of curriculum. As we start to think about curriculum, we should consider what schools are for. Schools are frequently criticised for being too examination led or asked to cure major problems of inequality in society, both economic and social. Schools are often described as 'preparing students for life', or for new jobs in a changing world. Biesta (2016) encourages teachers to consider these foundational issues – to think about the purpose for which their curriculum is developed. Biesta argues, like Wiliam (2013) and Turner (2016), that teachers should question, reflect on, and understand the aims of education within their context. Biesta (2016) suggests that education performs three main functions:

- Qualification: providing learners with the knowledge, skills and understanding to gain qualifications.
- Socialisation: the ways in which, through education, learners become members of and part of particular social, cultural and political orders.
- Subjectification: the ways in which education impacts and enhances an individual's learning to enable independence of thought from others.

Biesta argues that a good education will involve all three of these purposes. Some schools may favour one over the other, while other schools may wish to achieve a balance of all three. For Biesta, this balance will always be shifting, even from lesson to lesson. These decisions in turn should guide the development of the curriculum and allow teachers to shift their focus from 'How can we introduce these new ideas in the classroom?' to 'Why are we introducing these new ideas in the classroom?' (Biesta, 2016).

Thinking about curriculum through the lens of 'purpose' should help inform our decisions about curriculum content or knowledge, develop our understanding and interpretation of national guidance and frameworks, resourcing a curriculum, exploring sequencing, misconceptions and literacy requirements. Critically, considering the why of the curriculum also enables you to reflect more deeply on the needs of the learners within your context and the extent to which the curriculum meets their needs.

This kind of thinking about curriculum has a long tradition. Tyler (1949), for instance, challenged teachers to reflect on four fundamental questions about *what* they were teaching pupils:

- What educational purposes does your school seek to attain?
- What learning experiences can you select to achieve these purposes?
- How can you effectively organise these experiences to best achieve your purposes?
- How can you evaluate the effectiveness of these experiences?

Examining your current curriculum based on these questions will enable you to understand the decisions made about what content has been included and how that content is taught. Tyler's (1949) questions may also act as a scaffold in supporting you to plan your lessons, and when you have more experience and responsibility, to review and improve the curriculum you teach.

REFLECTION POINT

- To what extent do you discuss questions about the purpose of education with colleagues?
- What is the purpose of education within your context?
- How is your curriculum structured and designed to enact those purposes?

THE IMPORTANCE OF YOUR CURRICULUM THINKING

A school's curriculum is important because it creates a shared understanding about what knowledge, skills and values will be taught to a learner, why it should be taught and when it will be taught. Curriculum planning is therefore like a good *road map: it shows the final destination and (hopefully) the best way to get there* (Judd, 2018 in Myatt, n.d.).

The argument is that a high-quality and well thought out curriculum, as Coe et al. (2020) emphasise, is an integral part of maintaining the quality of teaching, and the quality of teaching is a hugely important factor in securing positive outcomes for children and young people. Part of that quality teaching is understanding what you are teaching, and why you are teaching it. With the pressures of a training year, and your ECT years, you will be focused on learning how to teach high-quality lessons. Because of this pressure it might be tempting to take a scheme of work or a lesson plan and learn the pedagogic techniques to deliver it in isolation, without fully considering the wider purpose behind it, or its relation to the rest of the curriculum. Often what remains unresolved are questions like what impact does this curriculum aim to have? Or how will it improve the lives of my learners? Wiliam (2013) and Turner (2016) argue that before considering the content to be taught, teachers should reflect on the purposes of the curriculum, and we argue that this also means thinking about how your teaching relates to the broader purposes of education.

We'll come back to the issue of knowledge, what you know, and what you might want your pupils to know later in the chapter. In the next section we will find out about how all these expectations about schools' curriculum and teaching are evaluated by bodies such as Ofsted.

THE REGULATORY FRAMEWORK

Policy guidance: the benchmark for high-quality curricula:

National organisations, standards, and frameworks

Curriculum used to be called 'the secret garden' of teacher's autonomy because, until the 1970s and 1980s, governments did not intrude by regulating which content was taught. Since 1988 the National Curriculum has sought to set out guidelines (sometimes strict, sometimes more relaxed) about what schools should teach. We therefore need to understand curriculum development through a national lens. There are a range of organisations, various frameworks and different standards that regulate the design, delivery and evaluation of a school's curriculum. This national landscape is complex and can often seem confusing. It is important that you understand the mechanisms that are designed to keep Multi-Academy Trusts (MATs) and schools focused on particular ways of improving pupil outcomes. The main organisations, standards and frameworks are summarised below.

ORGANISATIONS
THE DEPARTMENT FOR EDUCATION (DFE)

Is responsible for children's services and education, including early years, schools, higher and further education policy, apprenticeships and wider skills in England.

OFSTED

Is the Office for Standards in Education, Children's Services and Skills. They inspect services providing education and skills for learners of all ages. They also inspect and regulate services that care for children and young people.

STANDARDS
NATIONAL CURRICULUM (DFE, 2014)

Is a set of subjects and standards used by primary and secondary schools, so children learn the same things. It covers what subjects are taught and the standards children should reach in each subject. The National Curriculum should be seen as a minimum entitlement and state-funded schools must be able to demonstrate that they are meeting, if not exceeding, the requirements of the National Curriculum (DfE, 2014).

TEACHERS' STANDARDS (DFE, 2021)

Define the minimum level of practice expected of trainees and teachers from the point of being awarded Qualified Teacher Status (QTS). They are used to assess all trainees working towards QTS, and all those completing their statutory induction period. The standards emphasise the importance of curriculum by stating that teachers should:

- promote good progress and outcomes by pupils;
- demonstrate good subject and curriculum knowledge;
- plan and teach well-structured lessons.

Head teachers' Standards (DfE, 2020):

The Head teachers' Standards for curriculum and assessment outline that a school must:

- ensure a broad, structured and coherent curriculum entitlement that sets out the knowledge, skills and values that will be taught;
- establish effective curricular leadership, developing subject leaders with high levels of relevant expertise with access to professional networks and communities;
- ensure valid, reliable and proportionate approaches are used when assessing pupils' knowledge and understanding of the curriculum.

FRAMEWORKS

CORE CONTENT FRAMEWORK (CCF) FOR INITIAL TEACHER TRAINING (DFE, 2019B) AND EARLY CAREER FRAMEWORK (ECF) FOR EARLY CAREERS TEACHERS (DFE, 2019A)

These frameworks have been designed to support trainee development in five core areas – behaviour management, pedagogy, curriculum, assessment and professional behaviours. The CCF and ECF set out two types of content. Within each area, key evidence statements ('Learn that …') and practice statements ('Learn how to …') have been informed by high-quality evidence and expertise.

NATIONAL PROFESSIONAL QUALIFICATIONS FRAMEWORKS (DFE, 2022)

National Professional Qualifications (NPQs) are designed to support the professional development of teachers and leaders. NPQs are designed to provide training and support for teachers and school leaders at all levels and aim to deliver improved outcomes for young people. The NPQs mirror the CCF and ECF by outlining the key evidence statements ('Learn that ...') and practice statements ('Learn how to ...') in relation to curriculum and assessment.

THE OFSTED INSPECTION FRAMEWORK (2019)

Ofsted is the regulating body that inspects schools and details the various areas that are judged as part of their inspection. These areas include:

- quality of education;
- behaviour and attitudes;
- leadership and management;
- personal development.

The 'quality of education' judgement encompasses:

Curriculum intent: the construction of a curriculum that is ambitious for all learners and is coherently planned and sequenced towards cumulatively sufficient knowledge and skills for future learning and employment.

Curriculum implementation: all teachers have good knowledge of the subject(s) and courses they teach. Teachers present subject matter clearly, promoting appropriate discussion about the subject matter they are teaching. They check learners' understanding, identify misconceptions accurately and provide clear, direct feedback.

Curriculum impact: learners develop detailed knowledge and skills across the curriculum and, as a result, achieve well. Where relevant, this is reflected in results from national tests and examinations that meet government expectations, or in the qualifications obtained.

■■■ — REFLECTION POINT

- Which of these organisations and frameworks will be uppermost in the minds of the following people who work in schools and MATs?
- What do you think the concerns of classroom teachers will most focus on?

ACCOUNTABILITY AND THE CURRICULUM

You can see that there are many frameworks, documents, and different measures of success and quality to become familiar with. Sometimes these different aspects of accountability are in tension with each other. Head teachers are accountable to the school's wider community, to their governors as well as to Ofsted, which is in turn governed by a set of standards laid out by the Department for Education. We have already seen that the Ofsted SIF has been developed out of a concern that some schools have been 'teaching to the test' or 'gaming' which qualifications they put some pupils through. Amanda Spielman, Chief Inspector for Ofsted, made a speech in 2019, which argued that this gaming led to a narrowing of pupils' curriculum experience, and an urgent need for reforms that would lead to a more 'ambitious curriculum' (Spielman, 2020). The new framework therefore emphasises the quality of the curriculum. But it also still requires that the 'impact' on pupils is that they do well in their exams. Schools' results are published in local league tables, and an Ofsted grade can make a big difference to how a school attracts pupils and teachers to work there.

So, it seems that a school's curriculum takes on different of roles, some of which might be in tension with others. A curriculum needs to meet the needs of learners, fulfil national accountability measures and standards, and be enacted by teachers. It also needs to be judged 'ambitious' and coherent enough to be well-received by Ofsted in an inspection. One of the key issues in deciding whether a curriculum is 'ambitious' is the way that it deals with knowledge. In the next section we will focus on the role and status of knowledge in curriculum.

■■■ — REFLECTION POINT

- To what extent do you understand the role of national actors and frameworks and guidance in relation to the curriculum?
- How does this system support you in developing your expertise in relation to curriculum?
- How has your curriculum supported positive outcomes for learners in your context?

THE ROLE OF KNOWLEDGE

As Coe et al. (2020) remind us, the fundamental goal of everyone who works in education is to improve children's lives and life chances. Wiliam (2018) argues that raising the quality of teaching is probably the single most effective thing we could do to promote both overall attainment and equity. You should by now understand that our key argument is that a good curriculum is one of the most important resources that contributes to high-quality teaching.

7 The curriculum and the teacher

However, the curriculum is only one part of the process and actions that make up great teaching. In other words the curriculum has to be *taught*. Now we have a good overview of some of the ideas and debates around the meaning and importance of curriculum, you are ready to consider your own role in enacting it. Let's start by thinking about your knowledge. In their review of evidence of 'great teaching', Coe et al. (2020) concluded that your understanding of the content that is being taught and how it is learnt is crucial to great teaching.

▩▢▢ REFLECTION POINT

Pick a lesson that you taught recently, or one you are about teach. To what extent do you agree with the following statements about that lesson:

- 'I have a deep and fluent knowledge and flexible understanding of the content.'
- 'I understand what knowledge the pupils are building on, and what they will go on to learn about next in the sequence.'
- 'I know what the tasks, assessments and activities are supposed to achieve, and what they're supposed to tell me about how well the pupils understand and are learning.'
- 'I can come up with a variety of explanations and multiple analogies or examples for the content I am teaching.'
- 'I know about common student strategies, misconceptions, and sticking points in relation to the content I am teaching.'

Depending on the topic and how much teaching you have done, you will feel much more confident about some of these questions than others. Discussing your answers with people on your training programme will give you an idea about what affects their confidence about these things. You will also find that your confidence changes as your training and ECT years go on – because you will develop the experience and knowledge that you need to teach a really broad range of topics in your subject. However, one of the great things about teaching is that you will always be finding out about new things. Each year there will be new topics in the curriculum, new ways of teaching or assessing it, and new ways of thinking about why some topics are harder to learn than others. In this section we will think about these different aspects of 'knowledge' – yours, your pupils' and what knowledge is set out in the curriculum you teach.

> ### ■■■ CASE STUDY
>
> **What does the curriculum mean to you?**
>
> Lehka has recently started her second school experience in a different school. In the first placement she was given the topic to teach and shown where there were resources to support her if she wanted to use them. In this second placement she is given very detailed instructions and resources that she has to deliver to. She compares the two approaches and sees there are aspects of value in both.
>
> Think about how you have been able to engage with the curriculum on your school experiences. The questions below might help you evaluate the differences. Thinking about how the school curriculum is set is something that is worth considering as you find future teaching posts.
>
> - Where have you experienced the impact of a high-quality curriculum in improving outcomes for learners?
> - To what extent do you have a deep and fluent understanding of the content you are teaching?
> - How does your curriculum set high expectations for all your learners?

THE AMBITIOUS CURRICULUM AND 'POWERFUL KNOWLEDGE'

Policy makers have always been concerned with all three parts of Biesta's account of the purposes of education, but they have tended to emphasise 'qualification' as the education system's main role. As we have seen, recent policy and regulation has tended to focus on the knowledge aspect of qualification; the importance of pupils *knowing more and remembering more* (Ofsted, 2018). Mark Enser (2019) (now Geography subject lead at Ofsted) describes this passing on of our knowledge of the world as, 'our children's inheritance'. This perspective builds on the view of educational sociologists such as Michael F.D. Young (2007), who argues that the curriculum should pass on 'powerful knowledge'.

Young et al. (2014) define 'powerful knowledge' as knowledge derived from academic disciplines, which pupils could not encounter in their day-to-day lives. Their view is that this knowledge has power because it has been developed, tested and improved by the processes and expertise of academics working in that discipline. In this view the school curriculum should combine each subject discipline's continuously developing body of knowledge and unique lens on the world – each discipline's way of thinking. This idea also emphasises the power of disciplinary knowledge in helping pupils become useful and informed citizens, capable of interpreting the world. Finally, for Young this kind of knowledge also has a role in maintaining a sustainable and just democracy, while also instilling respect for authority, and the ability to engage in societal debate. Some even argue that this kind of knowledge supports pupils' learning cognitively – because it allows them to make meaningful links in their long-term memory (see Chapter 6 on planning for more about this idea of building schema) (Ashbee, 2021; Christodoulou, 2014).

The idea of powerful knowledge is not straightforward. The idea that school subjects can merely re-contextualise knowledge obtained from the disciplines is not universally accepted. Even if we take a highly structured way of looking at the world, such as physics, what is powerful about school physics does not directly map onto the current development of the discipline. Neither does the discipline of physics offer straightforward ideas about how to construct a curriculum, in terms of sequencing knowledge that children will build on and develop as they progress through school (Yates and Millar, 2016).

In other less structured subjects, such as history or geography, there is a tendency, as Young himself has outlined, for 'powerful knowledge', in the hands of policy makers, to become traditional knowledge, or knowledge of the powerful (Duoblys, 2022). A traditional curriculum that emphasises Victorian English writers and makes less room for modern authors or authors with roots and literary heritage from outside Britain might make it much more difficult for teachers to make a curriculum that acts as a mirror and as a window. In other words, we need to think carefully about what makes our subject powerful.

TENSIONS IN THE CURRICULUM

Biesta's model of the purposes of education argues that we can never have a perfect curriculum, because the different purposes for education are always in tension with each other – that teachers and curriculum planners are always balancing and adjusting the curriculum to address several layers of need. In considering how those layers are created, Turner (2016) reminds us that there are many approaches a teacher may take when thinking about the content of their curriculum. Some of these approaches are:

Hirsch (1988): makes the argument for a broad but shallow approach to curriculum that prioritises the importance of shared cultural, and usually national core knowledge that must be learned for pupils to be able to live well and contribute to a democratic society.

Dewey (1938): in contrast questions the dominance of knowledge within the curriculum and places a stronger emphasis on the experiences that learners are provided with. Arguing that these experiences must be expansive in developing a learner's understanding of the subject matter.

Style (1996): brings the focus of a curriculum back to the needs of learners and argues that learning does takes place in a vacuum but is contextual. Style suggests the curriculum should function both as window and as mirror. The knowledge within the curriculum needs to enable the learner to look through window frames to see the realities of others and into mirrors to see their own reality reflected.

This fleeting overview of the role of knowledge cannot provide a detailed critique of any one approach, and neither does it provide an exhaustive list of these approaches. It does, however, seek to highlight the debate and conversations teachers may engage in when considering the development of their curriculum. If a school takes a knowledge-rich approach, which may favour qualification as a core purpose for education, this will influence the nature and focus of its curriculum. Similarly, more inclusive efforts to provide windows and mirrors for all learners will have to be carefully achieved, so that there is still important and powerful knowledge within the curriculum.

DISCIPLINES, SUBJECTS AND RECONTEXTUALISATION

Understanding how these decisions affect curriculum is a critical inflection point for teachers and will help you to understand the role that your subject teaching plays in meeting the school's aims. Not all subjects are the same, and different subjects bring different concerns and traditions to the curriculum. Each subject presents a different way of viewing, explaining and understanding the world. The kind of knowledge and ways of working that each promotes will therefore also be different. The powerful knowledge paradigm might be more applicable to some than others.

Subject associations, such as the National Association of Teachers of English (NATE) or the Association for Science Education (ASE), and grass-roots teacher groups like #TeachMeetHistoryIcons or #CogSciSci can help you think carefully about your subject. Teacher-authors can also offer ideas. Mary Myatt (2018) suggests we can think about our subjects by comparing famous quotations about some of them. For instance:

- Design and technology: *Good buildings come from good people, and all problems are solved by good design* – Stephen Gardiner, Bishop of the Church of England from the fifteenth century

- English: *When I read great literature, great drama, or sermons, I feel that the human mind has not achieved anything greater than the ability to share feelings and thoughts through language* – James Earl Jones, Actor

- Science: *It is important to view knowledge as sort of a semantic tree — make sure you understand the fundamental principles, i.e. the trunk and big branches, before you get into the leaves/details or there is nothing for them to hang on to* – Elon Musk

(adapted from Myatt, 2018)

7 The curriculum and the teacher

> ### ▪▫▫ — CASE STUDY
>
> **Does choice matter?**
>
> Sarah and Piotr are talking during lunchtime. They do their training together through the same university, although Sarah teaches maths and Piotr teaches geography. The conversation turns to the number of pupils that each teach through their Year 11 contact. Sarah argues that as everyone has to study maths through GCSE, she has more of a challenge with some in terms of engagement and behaviour. She feels that Piotr has pupils who have deliberately chosen to be there. They turn to thinking about the curriculum more widely and what they would make compulsory if they had the power to, including aspects traditionally seen as 'extra-curricular'.
>
> Think about how you would design a curriculum and on what basis do you make these decisions? Think about the quotations adapted from Myatt above ...
>
> How helpful are quotes like this for thinking about what makes your subject or discipline a source of powerful knowledge for your pupils?
>
> What do your own experiences of your discipline suggest might represent powerful knowledge in your subject?

Bernstein (1999) points out that school subjects, despite being a 'co-dependent field' of the university discipline where they are produced, are not the same as that discipline. Subjects are recontextualised by the processes of curriculum planning and, as we will see, of 'curriculum making' (Lambert and Morgan, 2010). This process changes discipline into subject and curricula into lesson plans, making the discipline more suitable for schools, and for the classes that you teach. We want to outline the kinds of knowledge about your subject that you will bring to this process of recontextualisation.

Pedagogic content knowledge – Shulman (1986) described this form of knowledge as associated with *the most regularly taught topics in one's subject area*. It includes representations of knowledge (analogies, illustrations, examples, explanations and demonstrations) and difficulties or misconceptions about a topic, and strategies to deal with them. PCK is something that teachers learn from each other. They can do this from practice, from reflecting on what they are teaching or by engaging in planning or evaluating teaching with other teachers and their wider subject community. In your training you will be learning this kind of knowledge from your subject tutors and from your mentor. Eventually this will become part of your tacit knowledge of your practice. See Chapter 2 on your learning identity for more ideas about how to develop your approach to learning in this way.

Misconceptions and sticking points – whenever we learn something new, we use our prior knowledge to help make sense of the new information (Bransford et al., 1999).

However, when our prior knowledge is inaccurate, we are more likely to misinterpret, misunderstand or even disregard new information. Inaccurate prior knowledge – or misconceptions – can be a significant barrier to new learning. Experienced teachers have a great deal of knowledge about what pupils might find hard, misunderstand or get wrong. They design their presentations and learning activities to anticipate and address these misconceptions directly and explicitly, both by exposing and challenging the misconception and by presenting the correct conception clearly and directly (Coe et al., 2020). See Chapter 6 on planning lessons for more on how to approach misconceptions.

Discipline-specific curriculum – we are not only teaching pupils knowledge derived from disciplines, but also about the specific processes and ways of thinking that our subject disciplines use to explore the world. Disciplinary knowledge helps pupils understand how each discipline works, its degree of certainty and how it continues to be revised by scholars, artists or professional practice. This is that part of the subject where pupils understand each discipline as a distinctive tradition of inquiry: whether through empirical testing in science, argumentation in philosophy/history, logic in mathematics or aesthetic and emotional responses in the arts (Counsell, 2018). This means that we need to think about the kinds of things that artists, historians, chemists, geographers, literary critics or writers *do*, and use pedagogies and resources that allow pupils to enter into these disciplinary practices. This disciplinary knowledge should be chosen so that it helps pupils understand the substantive knowledge they are learning. For example, exploring and setting up a mini greenhouse to explore and understand the greenhouse effect in chemistry. Generic pedagogies, such as those that are being explored and developed through cognitive science, also have to be adapted for specific subjects (Perry et al., 2021) to reflect these disciplinary approaches.

DEVELOPING CURRICULUM / CURRICULUM SEQUENCING

THE 'STORY' IN THE CURRICULUM

We can think of knowledge as the facts or information acquired about a specific subject. Building this knowledge over time helps to develop a learner's skills, which can be thought of as having the expertise to carry out a subject-specific activity effectively through practice. From this perspective, it can be argued that knowledge and skills are inextricably linked and their inclusion within a curriculum should be considered carefully. However, a curriculum is not just a list of knowledge and a schedule of skills and practice. A good curriculum has multiple layers and will:

- tell a compelling story about the subject;

- bring the knowledge and skills of the subject to life for learners;

- be a map through which both teacher and learner will navigate the knowledge and skills of the subject;

- provide pathways through and around the barriers learners may face;
- champion and achieve the school's purpose for education.

In this section we will look at the processes of sequencing curriculum in order to address these aims, then we will turn to your role in the classroom, where a sequence is brought to life and enacted for the pupils you are teaching.

CURRICULUM SEQUENCING – HOW DO YOU PLAN A CURRICULUM?

Coe et al. highlight how knowledge is crucial in understanding how to sequence knowledge. When considering this, Wiggins and McTighe (2011) suggest 'backward design' as a way of designing a curriculum. Backward design involves three stages:

Stage 1: identify desired results. At this stage you are answering big questions, such as 'What should students know, understand, and be able to do?' and 'What content is worthy of understanding?' In Stage 1 we consider our goals, examine established content standards (national, state, district) and review curriculum expectations. Because typically we have more content than we can reasonably address within the available time, we must make choices.

Stage 2: determine acceptable evidence. How will we know if students have achieved the desired results? What will we accept as evidence of student understanding and proficiency? The backward design orientation suggests that we think about a unit or course in terms of the collected assessment evidence needed to document and validate that the desired learning has been achieved, not simply as content to be covered or as a series of learning activities. This approach encourages teachers and curriculum planners to first 'think like an assessor' before designing specific units and lessons, and thus to consider up front how they will determine if students have attained the desired understandings.

Stage 3: plan learning experiences and instruction. At this stage, several key questions become important:

- What enabling knowledge (facts, concepts, principles) and skills (processes, procedures, strategies) will students need in order to perform effectively and achieve desired results?
- What activities will equip students with the needed knowledge and skills?
- What will need to be taught and coached, and how should it best be taught, in light of performance goals?
- What materials and resources are best suited to accomplish these goals?

In all subject areas, pupils learn new ideas by linking those ideas to existing knowledge, organising this knowledge into increasingly complex mental models (or 'schemata');

carefully sequencing teaching to facilitate this process is important. Harlen and James (1997) suggest that when planning and sequencing pupils' learning experiences, teacher should ensure it:

- Progressively develops in terms of 'big ideas' within a subject or discipline;
- Is constructed on the basis of prior knowledge and previous teaching;
- Provides opportunities to apply knowledge in contexts other than those in which it was originally taught;
- Is owned by the pupil and becomes a fundamental part of the way they understand the world – not simply knowledge that may be memorised for recall in examinations and subsequently forgotten.

You might recognise this kind of thinking from the first pages of this chapter. Tyler (1949) was writing in similar ways back in the 1950s, so there is a long tradition of starting out by keeping the end in mind. The chapter on planning lessons in this book (Chapter 6) takes a similar approach.

These processes happen at a number of different levels (Thijs and van den Akker, 2009; Priestley et al., 2021), with different people and organisations:

- 'Supra transnational' organisations like the Organisation for Economic Co-operation and Development (OECD), the World Bank and the Programme for International Student Assessment (PISA) league tables and other sources of big ideas (M.F.D. Young's ideas of 'powerful knowledge' (Young and Muller, 2013) and E.D. Hirsch's concept of cultural literacy (Hirsch et al., 1988) for instance) influence policy makers.
- 'Macro' policy layer produces national guidelines and regulation, which we have encountered in the form of things like the National Curriculum and Ofsted frameworks.
- 'Meso' layer develops and enacts these policies through bodies such as multi-academy trusts, subject associations and lobby groups or government-funded organisations such as the Education Endowment Foundation (EEF).
- At the 'Micro' level schools get involved, turning the policy, frameworks and regulation into policy and guidance in the school.
- Finally, as a classroom teacher you are usually working at the 'Nano' level – where 'curriculum making' takes place (Lambert and Morgan, 2010).

Within the Micro level, schools will also work at several levels of their own. A head teacher and School Leadership Team (SLT) will want to ensure that the whole school curriculum meets the vision for education that the school has developed, and that it will be evaluated positively by Ofsted. Department heads will need to think about the requirements of the National Curriculum and the GSCE or A level specifications they are

7 The curriculum and the teacher

teaching, as well as the resources, money, skills and interests of their team members. At the Nano level, teachers (and that means you too) will be thinking about how to make this curriculum work for their classes – using their knowledge of the topic, of how to teach it, and of their pupils in the process. It is this stage that we will look at next, but first let's look at one sequence or scheme of work from our own subject areas.

> **■ ■ ■ — REFLECTION POINT**
>
> Review a curriculum plan from your subject in your placement school and look for the following features:
>
> - What are the aims of this sequence - what new knowledge and skills will the pupils have acquired and practised by the end?
> - What kinds of resources and teaching skills are used by this sequence of lessons?
> - How does the plan set out forms of assessment (see Chapter 10)?
> - What happens at the end of the sequence?

CURRICULUM MAKING – WHAT WE KNOW ABOUT OUR PUPILS AND HOW TO USE IT

Chapter 6 on planning lessons sets out the kinds of things you might do, and some of the things that you might think about, when planning individual lessons or sequences of lessons. Lambert and Morgan (2010) call this 'curriculum making'. They describe it as *in between work* (page 51) that teachers do in translating curriculum plans into learning activities, resources and lesson plans. In a later piece Lambert and Biddulph (2015) have developed this idea, arguing that curriculum making is how teachers fulfil their *moral responsibility to re-present the curriculum ... in ways that bring meaning and critical insight to their [pupils]* (page 215). They suggest that 'curriculum making' involves using three different kinds of teacher knowledge:

- knowledge about the subject and about the specific topics and content being taught;
- knowledge about which pedagogical techniques relate to that subject knowledge;
- knowledge about the pupils, their needs, experiences and prior knowledge.

This pushes us to think about what is being taught, how it is being taught and to whom it is being taught, and where all three overlap is where we find the curriculum 'sweet spot'.

We can relate the first and second of these types of knowledge to 'discipline-specific subject knowledge', and the second to 'pedagogical content knowledge', which we have already discussed. In this last section we want to focus on the third kind of knowledge. We will relate it to your thinking about the other two forms of teacher knowledge and consider the ways in which our curricula can give pupils 'mirrors and windows' in their relationships with the world.

PUPILS' RELATIONSHIPS WITH YOUR SUBJECT

We have briefly discussed the need for teachers to understand how misconceptions form, and to know about the important or common misconceptions that pupils might have. This is a vital aspect of thinking about what pupils bring to their own learning, but it is not the only aspect. We need to find ways to help pupils relate to and engage meaningfully with the knowledge, skills and practices that we are teaching. In the context of geography teaching, Firth and Biddulph (2009) have developed some ideas about how this might be achieved. We think these might also have relevance for other subjects:

- acknowledging pupils' experiences, using these and important and relevant issues to create 'hooks' that help pupils connect with new knowledge;

- valuing conversation between teachers and pupils and between pupils and their peers, to explore perspectives;

- valuing ideas and diverse perspectives – recognising that new ideas are important for knowledge building, and that ideas are improvable;

- using disciplinary knowledge and processes to help build knowledge;

- advancing knowledge through enquiry about subject and using subject-disciplinary procedures – giving pupils agency and responsibility in knowledge building.

(adapted from Firth and Biddulph (2009) and Lambert and Biddulph (2015))

A PUPIL'S VIEW ON THE WORLD – WINDOWS AND MIRRORS

Another way of thinking about how pupils will connect with and relate to the curriculum we are teaching is to consider the extent to which our plans create both 'windows' and 'mirrors' for all our learners. Emily Styles (1996) put forward the idea that the curriculum should enable students to see themselves in the world, but also give them a standpoint from which to see new things – to look at the world in new ways. Chapter 11 on social justice also discusses the various ways in which some pupils are disadvantaged by and in the education system. We want you to consider how our choices as teachers and curriculum makers enable pupils to see themselves and connect with the world.

Think back to the start of this chapter. We discussed how Biesta's purposes of education, as well as 'qualification' (knowledge, results, qualification), also include 'socialisation' (learning to live and work with and understand others) and 'subjectification' (learning about yourself and your individual place in the world). We can perhaps see how this might lead us to take seriously Styles' concerns about the *copious blind spots of the traditional curriculum*, and how it creates experiences in which pupils from some backgrounds and with some experiences find it much easier to see themselves reflected. On the other hand, some pupils struggle to see connections between their lives and what they are taught in school. Similarly, Vincent (2022) develops an idea of 'national belonging' for pupils, which goes beyond the possession of formal rights, and that it depends also on *affective bonds* and *mutual recognition from others*. Nick Dennis (2021) suggests that the stories we tell about ourselves need to reflect the complexity and diversity of our pupils' lives, and that telling stories that reflect only traditional ways of understanding our subjects is selling our pupils short. Elliott (2020) exemplifies the lack of mirrors within the English literature curriculum, highlighting that 82 per cent of pupils responding did not recall ever studying a text by a Black, Asian or minority ethnic author.

WHAT KIND OF DIVERSITY DO WE NEED TO REFLECT?

There are several ways of looking at this issue. We could take the Equalities Act (2010) as a starting point. This sets out nine 'protected characteristics' that should not be discriminated against:

- age;
- disability;
- gender reassignment;
- marriage and civil partnership;
- pregnancy and maternity;
- race;
- religion or belief;
- sex;
- sexual orientation.

We might also think about ways in which pupils or their families are marginalised – socio-economic status is an important factor in how well pupils achieve at school, for instance (as we can see from Chapter 11). Another way might be to consider the diversity in our school populations. This last one is important, but it would be wrong to think that pupils only need to find out about diversity if they live in diverse ethnic communities. If powerful knowledge means anything, it means that all students benefit from learning about and celebrating the diversity of the world as it really is (Maylor, 2021). Especially in the United Kingdom, we could find that using a decolonialising lens on our school curriculum helps us recognise that knowledge is created, transmitted and promoted in a framework built on Britain's imperial past. This in turn might help us to understand the diversity of our population, but also the reasons why some knowledge and perspectives aren't promoted or amplified by the curriculum.

There are several ways in which we can better achieve a curriculum in which pupils are able to see themselves and get a better view on the world. In these ideas we address issues of race, but many of these can also be applied to the other forms of diversity that reflect pupils' lives:

Teacher knowledge. Evidence suggests that many teachers don't feel confident in approaching issues of diversity, and one reason seems to be that they need to know more (Maylor, 2021; Elliott, 2020). For instance, understanding 'racial literacy' could help teachers better understand issues related to racial discrimination, and give them more knowledge and confidence about how to address it in their teaching (Joseph-Salisbury, 2021). Finding good sources of information and places to talk about these issues can be difficult. One place to start might be websites such as www.diverseeducators.co.uk, which is a collection of advice, reading lists and examples of diverse education, run by teachers.

Connecting with pupils' experiences and the wider world. Meetoo (2020) notices that some teachers are able to incorporate aspects of and issues relating to pupils' home lives or backgrounds when exemplifying or illustrating aspects of the lessons being taught. Maylor (2021) suggests that valuing cultural differences as an asset to understanding and finding opportunities to discuss diverse perspectives can help with this.

Considering where the knowledge comes from. Gandolfi, who worked with science teachers in building a decolonialised science curriculum, helped them to teach pupils about how knowledge is generated across the world, so that science is not seen as an exclusively 'western' form of knowledge (Gandolfi, 2021).

Getting pupils to consider where knowledge comes from. Dennis suggests we can use questions about how knowledge is made to help us complicate the simple stories that pupils are told. He uses Trouillot's (1995) framework to do this, with its focus on several important 'moments' in which these stories are made, or given significance:

- moment of fact creation – making of sources;
- moment of fact assembly – the making of archives;
- moment of fact retrieval – the moment of fact retrieval – the making of narratives;
- moment of retrospective significance – the moment of teaching?

7 The curriculum and the teacher

> ■■■ — **REFLECTION POINT**
>
> - How do you create windows and mirrors within your curriculum?
> - To what extent does your curriculum create a sense of belonging?
> - How does your curriculum reflect the backgrounds and identity of your pupils?
> - What are your needs for professional development in ensuring your curriculum meets the needs of all your learners?

CONCLUSION

This chapter presents curriculum as being far from something that is fixed. It is there to be interacted with, to be shaped and moulded in a way that enables you as a teacher to translate it into something that is meaningful for your pupils. There are challenging and 'big' ideas presented within this chapter, some of which will be challenging in the early stages of your training and teaching career; however, it is important that as professional teachers we recognise that there is scope to 'work' the curriculum and not just have this blindly imposed on us. Dealing with the curriculum in isolation is also difficult – it is intrinsically linked with pedagogy – and so often it can be daunting when we first start to delve into what curriculum means and sets out to achieve. We hope, however, that this chapter has highlighted how it can positively influence the learning experience for your pupils if you engage with the curriculum you are teaching on a deeper level.

> ■■■ — **CHAPTER SUMMARY**
>
> Now you have read this chapter, you will:
>
> - have a greater understanding of the nature of curricula and how it is translated into teaching and learning within the classroom
> - have thought about the ways in which you can engage with the curriculum
> - have considered the curriculum as a means of positioning subject-specific knowledge through your teaching
> - recognise that the curriculum can be used as an approach to challenging issues around lack of diversity and also to enable the pupils to 'see themselves' in your subject.

▰▰▰— ASSIGNMENT LINKS

You might be asked as part of your studies to outline a sequence of learning within your teaching or unpick something about the specifics of your subject in relation to what is taught and how. This chapter will allow you to do this through a critical lens.

You might be asked to consider how your subject can support diversification of the curriculum.

LEARNING AND CONSOLIDATION ACTIVITIES

When you are observing lessons, think about the ways in which curriculum statements and content are translated into teaching in the classroom. Discuss with your mentor and class teachers why they chose *that* way to teach the content.

Look for examples where the diversity of the class is represented in the examples used. For example, in science when famous scientists are referred to, are there also contemporary examples used or from a range of ethnicities?

▰▰▰— REFLECTION POINT

How important to you is the extent to which you can interact with and shape the curriculum you teach?

What principles of curricula are most important to you and will inform how you plan and teach your subject?

What is the 'curriculum story' for your subject?

FURTHER READING

Ashbee, R. (2021) *Curriculum: Theory, Culture and the Subject Specialisms*. London: Routledge.

This book provides an overview of curriculum theories and how the school subjects are organised. It clearly identifies the important contribution that the different subject lenses make for deepening understanding and making meaning of the world.

Biesta, G. (2016) *Good Education in an Age of Measurement: Ethics, Politics, Democracy*. London: Routledge.

This book questions the purpose of education and presents an insightful debate about the impact of measuring the quality of education is having.

Myatt, M. (2018) *The Curriculum: Gallimaufry to Coherence*. Woodbridge: John Catt Educational Ltd.

Increasingly, in schools, people are talking about knowledge and curriculum. In this book, Mary Myatt argues that overcoming barriers to achievement lies in understanding the curriculum deeply and in what children should know.

REFERENCES

Allison, S., Tharby, A. and Lemov, D. (2015) *Making Every Lesson Count: Six Principles to Support Great Teaching and Learning*. Carmarthen: Crown House Publishing.

Armstrong, A.L. (2021) *The Representation of Social Groups in U. S. Educational Materials and Why it Matters*. [online] New America. Available at: www.newamerica.org/education-policy/reports/the-representation-of-social-groups-in-u-s-educational-materials-and-why-it-matter/ (accessed 9/10/22).

Ashbee, R. (2021) *Curriculum: Theory, Culture and the Subject Specialisms*. London: Routledge.

Bernstein, B. (1999) Vertical and horizontal discourse: an essay. *British Journal of Sociology of Education*, *20*(2): 157–173.

Biddulph et al. (2020) Teaching powerful geographical knowledge – a matter of social justice: Initial findings from the GeoCapabilities 3 project. *International Research in Geographical and Environmental Education*, *29*(3): 260–274. DOI: 10.1080/10382046.2020.1749756

Biesta, G. (2016) *Good Education in an Age of Measurement: Ethics, Politics, Democracy*. London: Routledge.

Biesta, G. (2020) *Educational Research: An Unorthodox Introduction*. Bloomsbury Academic.

Blatchford, R. (2019) *The Secondary Curriculum Leader's Handbook*. Melton, Woodbridge: John Catt Educational Ltd.

Bransford, J.D., Brown, A.L. and Cocking, R.R. (eds) (1999) *How People Learn: Brain, Mind, Experience, and School*. National Academy Press.

Christodoulou, D. (2014) *Seven Myths about Education*. London: Taylor & Francis Group.

Coe, R., Rauch, C., Kime, S. and Singleton, D. (2020) *Evidence Review Great Teaching Toolkit*. [online] Available at: https://assets.website-files.com/5ee28729f7b4a5fa99bef2b3/5ee9f507021911ae35ac6c4d_EBE_GTT_EVIDENCE%20REVIEW_DIGITAL.pdf?utm_referrer=https%3A%2F%2Fwww.greatteaching.com%2F. (accessed 9/10/22).

Counsell, C. (2018) Taking curriculum seriously. *Impact Magazine*. Chartered College of Teaching. Available at: https://impact.chartered.college/wp-content/uploads/2018/03/Christine-Counsell-article.pdf (accessed 9/10/22).

Cuthbert, A.S. and Standish, A. (2021) What should schools teach? Disciplines, subjects and the pursuit of truth. *UCL Press, Open Access PDF*. Available at: www.uclpress.co.uk/products/165025 (accessed 8/22).

Dennis, N. (2021) The stories we tell ourselves: history teaching, powerful knowledge and the importance of context, in *Knowing History in Schools: Powerful Knowledge and the Powers of Knowledge*, pages 216–333.

Dewey, J. (1938) *Experience and Education*. New York: Free Press.

DfE (2014) *National Curriculum*. [online] gov.uk. Available at: www.gov.uk/government/collections/national-curriculum

DfE (2019a) *Early Career Framework*. [online] Available at: https://assets.publishing.service.gov.uk/government/uploads/system/uploads/attachment_data/file/978358/Early-Career_Framework_April_2021.pdf (accessed 9/10/22).

DfE (2019b) *ITT Core Content Framework*. [online] gov.uk. Available at: https://assets.publishing.service.gov.uk/government/uploads/system/uploads/attachment_data/file/974307/ITT_core_content_framework_.pdf

DfE (2020) *Headteachers' Standards 2020*. [online] Available at: www.gov.uk/government/publications/national-standards-of-excellence-for-headteachers/headteachers-standards-2020 (accessed 9/10/22).

DfE (2021) *Teachers' Standards Guidance for School Leaders, School Staff and Governing Bodies*. [online] gov.uk. Available at: https://assets.publishing.service.gov.uk/government/uploads/system/uploads/attachment_data/file/1040274/Teachers__Standards_Dec_2021.pdf (accessed 9/10/22).

DfE (2022) *National Professional Qualifications (NPQs) Reforms*. [online] Available at: www.gov.uk/government/publications/national-professional-qualifications-npqs-reforms/national-professional-qualifications-npqs-reforms (accessed 9/10/22).

Duoblys, G. (2022) Michael Young: What we've got wrong about knowledge and curriculum. *TES*. Available at: https://www.tes.com/magazine/teaching-learning/general/michael-young-powerful-knowledge-curriculum

Elliott, V. (2020) *Knowledge in English: Canon, Curriculum and Cultural Literacy*. Taylor & Francis. DOI: 10.4324/9780429331275

Elliott, V., Nelson-Addy, L., Chantiluke, R. and Courtney, M. (n.d.) *Diversity in Literature in English Schools*. [online] Available at: https://assets.website-files.com/61488f992b58e687f1108c7c/61d6fc0b4a6b8786bd88d10b_Lit-in-Colour-research-report-min.pdf (accessed 9/10/22).

Enser, M. (2019) *Teach Like Nobody's Watching: The Essential Guide to Effective and Efficient Teaching*. Carmarthen: Crown House Publishing.

Firth, R. and Biddulph, M. (2009). Young people's geographies. *34*. 32–34.

Gandolfi, H.E. (2021) Decolonising the science curriculum in England: bringing decolonial science and technology studies to secondary education. *The Curriculum Journal*, *32*(3): 510–532.

Glare, P.G.W. (ed.) (2000) *Oxford Latin Dictionary*. Oxford: Oxford University Press.

Harlen, W. and James, M. (1997) Assessment and learning: differences and relationships between formative and summative assessment. *Assessment in Education: Principles, Policy & Practice*, [online] *4*(3): 365–379. DOI: 10.1080/0969594970040304.

Hirsch, E.D., Kett, J.F. and Trefil, J. (1988) *Cultural Literacy: What Every American Needs to Know*. New York: Vintage Books.

Jackson, P. (1968) *Life in Classrooms*. New York: Holt, Rinehart & Winston.

Joseph-Salisbury, R., and Wallace, D. (2021) How, still, is the Black Caribbean child made educationally subnormal in the English school system?. *Ethnic and Racial Studies 45*(8): 1426–1452. DOI: 10.1080/01419870.2021.1981969

Kelly, A.V. (2009) *The Curriculum: Theory and Practice* (6th edn). London: Sage.

Lambert, D. and Biddulph, M. (2015) The dialogic space offered by curriculum-making in the process of learning to teach, and the creation of a progressive knowledge-led curriculum. *Asia-Pacific Journal of Teacher Education*, *43*(3): 210–224. DOI: 10.1080/1359866X.2014.934197

Lambert, D. and Morgan, J. (2010) *Teaching Geography 11–18: A Conceptual Approach*. New York: McGraw-Hill Education.

Lemov, D. (2021) *Teach Like a Champion 3.0: 63 Techniques That Put Students on the Path to College*. San Francisco: Jossey-Bass.

Leyendecker, R. (2012) Curriculum and learning, in N.M. Seel (ed.) *Encyclopedia of the Sciences of Learning*. Boston, MA: Springer. DOI: 10.1007/978-1-4419-1428-6_1617

Lilienfeld, S.O. (2010) Confronting psychological misconceptions in the classroom. *APS Observer*, [online] 23. Available at: www.psychologicalscience.org/observer/confronting-psychological-misconceptions-in-the-classroom (accessed 9/10/22).

Maylor, U. (2021) Curriculum diversity and social justice education: from New Labour to Conservative government control of education in England, in A. Ross (ed.) *Educational Research for Social Justice. Education Science, Evidence, and the Public Good*, vol *1*. Springer, Cham. DOI: 10.1007/978-3-030-62572-6_11

Meetoo, V. (2020). Negotiating the diversity of 'everyday' multiculturalism: teachers' enactments in an inner city secondary school. *Race Ethnicity and Education*, *23*(2); 261–279.

Myatt, M. (n.d.) Some principles for planning. *Mary Myatt*. Available at: https://www.marymyatt.com/blog/some-principles-for-planning (accessed 10/1/23).

Myatt, M. (2018) *The Curriculum: Gallimaufry to Coherence*. Woodbridge: John Catt Educational Ltd.

Myatt, M. (2020) *Back on Track: Fewer Things, Greater Depth*. Woodbridge: John Catt Educational Ltd.

OECD Pisa rankings (2015) Available at: www.oecd.org/pisa/pisa-2015-results-in-focus.pdf (accessed 7/22).

Ofsted (2018) *Assessment – What Are Inspectors Looking At?* Available at: https://education-inspection.blog.gov.uk/2018/04/23/assessment-what-are-inspectors-looking-at/ (accessed 7/11/22).

Ofsted (2019) *Education Inspection Framework*. [online] gov.uk. Available at: www.gov.uk/government/publications/education-inspection-framework/education-inspection-framework (accessed 9/10/22).

Oreskes, N. (2019) *Why Trust Science?* Princeton, New Jersey: Princeton University Press.

Perry, T. et al. (2021) *Cognitive Science in the Classroom*. London: Education Endowment Foundation (EEF).

Priestley, M., Philippou, S., Alvunger, D. and Soini, T. (2021) Curriculum making: a conceptual framing, in M. Priestley, D. Alvunger, S. Philippou and T. Soini (eds) *Curriculum Making in Europe: Policy and Practice within and Across Diverse Contexts*, pages 1–28. Bingley: Emerald Publishing Limited. DOI: 10.1108/978-1-83867-735-020211002

Rosenshine, B. (2012) Principles of instruction. *American Educator* (Spring).

Sherrington, T. (2017) *The Learning Rainforest: Great Teaching in Real Classrooms*. Woodbridge: John Catt Educational.

Sherrington, T. (2019) *Rosenshine's Principles in Action*. Melton, Woodbridge: John Catt Educational.

Shulman, L. (1986) Those who understand: Knowledge growth in teaching. *Educational Researcher*, 15(2): 4–14.

Spielman, A. (1 December 2020). *Launch of Annual Report* [Lecture]. Ofsted. Available at: https://www.gov.uk/government/speeches/amanda-spielman-launches-ofsteds-annual-report-201920

Style, E. (1996) *First published in Listening for All Voices*. [online] *Oak Knoll School monograph*. Available at: https://nationalseedproject.org/images/documents/Curriculum_As_Window_and_Mirror.pdf (accessed 9/10/22).

Tharby, A. (2018) *How to Explain Absolutely Anything to Absolutely Anyone: The Art and Science of Teacher Explanation*. Carmarthen: Crown House Publishing.

Thijs, A. and van den Akker, J. (eds) (2009) *Curriculum in Development*. Enschede: SLO.

Trouillot, M. (2015) *Silencing the Past (20th Anniversary Edition): Power and the Production of History*. United States: Beacon Press.

Trouillot, M. (1995) *Silencing the Past: Power and the Production of History.* Boston: Beacon Press. DOI: 10.1086/ahr/102.2.426

Turner, S. (2016) *Bloomsbury CPD Library: Secondary Curriculum Design and Assessment.* London: Bloomsbury Publishing.

Tyler, R.W. (1949) *Basic Principles of Curriculum and Instruction.* Chicago: University of Chicago Press.

Tyler, R.W. (1957) *The curriculum then and now*, in Proceedings of the 1956 Invitational Conference on Testing Problems, Educational Testing Service, Princeton, 79.

Vincent, C. (2022) Belonging in England today: Schools, race, class and policy. *Journal of Sociology, 58*(3): 324–341.

Wheeler, D.K. (1967) *Curriculum Process.* London: University of London Press.

Wiggins, G. and McTighe, J. (2011) *The Understanding by Design Guide to Creating High-quality Units.* ASCD, Alexandria.

Wiliam, D. (2013) *Redesigning Schooling – 3 Principled Curriculum Design.* [online] Available at: https://webcontent.ssatuk.co.uk/wp-content/uploads/2013/09/Dylan-Wiliam-Principled-curriculum-design-chapter-1.pdf (accessed 9/10/22).

Wiliam, D. (2018) *Creating the Schools Our Children Need: Why What We're Doing Now Won't Help Much (And What We Can Do Instead).* Learning Sciences International.

Yates, L. and Millar, V. (2016) 'Powerful knowledge' curriculum theories and the case of physics. *The Curriculum Journal, 27*: 298–312. DOI: 10.1080/09585176.2016.1174141

Young, M. (2007) *Bringing Knowledge Back In. From Social Constructivism to Social Realism in the Sociology of Education.* London: Routledge.

Young, M. (ed.) (2018) Designing a curriculum: delivering strategies to support access to knowledge. *Impact 4* (Autumn).

Young, M.F.D., Lambert, D., Roberts, C.R. and Roberts, M. (2014) *Knowledge and the Future School: Curriculum and Social Justice.* London; New York: Bloomsbury Academic.

Young, M. and Muller, J. (2013) On the powers of powerful knowledge. *Review of Education, 1*(3): 229–250. DOI: 10.1002/rev3.3017

8

ADAPTIVE TEACHING

AMY THOMPSON AND LEIGH HOATH

KEY WORDS

- Responsive teaching
- Individual needs
- Planning in action

CHAPTER OBJECTIVES

This chapter considers how strategies in the classroom can best support your teaching and learning in ways that meet the individual needs of the pupils you teach. More discussion around inclusion is seen in Chapter 9; however, this chapter will help you to develop approaches within lessons.

By the end of this chapter, you will have a greater understanding of what adaptive teaching is and looks like within the classroom as well as been introduced to a range of strategies to try with the pupils in your class. We will also highlight the interrelationships between adaptive teaching and assessment, planning and high expectations for your pupils.

LINKS TO THE CORE CONTENT FRAMEWORK

All of the Core Content Framework themes are referred to and applied in this chapter, but the following are the most relevant:

Standard 1 – Set high expectations, with a focus on:

1. Teacher expectations can affect pupil outcomes; setting goals that challenge and stretch pupils is essential.

(Continued)

8 Adaptive teaching

Standard 4 - Plan and teach well-structured lessons, with a focus on:

1. Effective teachers introduce new material in steps, explicitly linking new ideas to what has been previously studied and learned.
2. Modelling helps pupils understand new processes and ideas; good models make abstract ideas concrete and accessible.
3. Guides, scaffolds and worked examples can help pupils apply new ideas, but should be gradually removed as pupil expertise increases.

Standard 5 - Adapt teaching, with a focus on:

1. Seeking to understand pupils' differences, including their different levels of prior knowledge and potential barriers to learning, is an essential part of teaching.
2. Adapting teaching in a responsive way, including by providing targeted support to pupils who are struggling, is likely to increase pupil success.
3. Adaptive teaching is less likely to be valuable if it causes the teacher to artificially create distinct tasks for different groups of pupils or to set lower expectations for particular pupils.

WHAT IS 'ADAPTIVE' TEACHING?

Imagine you are leading a mountain expedition with a group of climbers. Within your preparations, you will assess the needs of the team and judicious adjustment to your generic plan, taking into account their strengths and weaknesses. After all, you are responsible for the group as a whole and each of the individual climbers. You will, as a worthy leader, visualise the path ahead and make contingencies for when the weather changes or an obstacle befalls the group. You would do everything possible to foresee the unforeseen.

Once on the path to the summit, however, only a leader steeped in hubris would fail to continue making adjustments. When a team member takes a minor injury, you might lighten his pack to give him the time to recover fully. When one of the group shows a previously unknown aptitude to scout ahead, you give her the space to do so and add another skilled pathfinder to the group. All the while you would maintain the expectation that all would reach the summit, but that all would need your help differently in achieving this. Each of these adjustments would be underpinned by your wisdom and experience, knowing the ultimate goal is to get everyone to the summit.

Adaptive teaching is the approach where we work towards a common learning outcome but take into account the different needs and aptitudes of the class, rather than assuming all will move as one (Smart and Marshall, 2013). All pupils can encounter barriers to their learning and progress and while many of these barriers are temporary, some are long lasting. All pupils acquire knowledge and know-how (skills) at a slightly different rate. Similarly (and importantly), they forget and retrieve knowledge and know-how differently. In the classroom, just as on the mountain trail, your ability to plan ahead and the dexterity to make adaptations is critical to your eventual success.

Research suggests that expert instruction, and attention to details within explanations and giving of instructions, powerfully simplifies difficult concepts, making them more clear and accessible. Similarly, well-crafted and judicious retrieval practice helps pupils to retain and retrieve their prior learning with more efficacy. In turn, this allows them to learn more and remember more over time. The more responsive and adaptive you can be to the individual needs within your classroom, the more resilient they will be to challenges and barriers to their learning and the more progress your pupils will make in the long term (Quigley et al., 2018). Consequently, investing in your pedagogical practice will improve your technical dexterity as a teacher and your ability to be adaptive and responsive in the classroom.

Writing this in the summer of 2022, as we continue to regenerate our schools following the pandemic, the power and importance of adaptive teaching is especially important. Every child had a different experience of and response to the years disrupted by Covid-19. Not just the 'lockdowns' in 2020 and 2021, which resulted in home learning for many, but the challenging reality of what schools were like the rest of the time that Covid-19 restrictions were in place. School staff worked tirelessly (and innovatively) to mitigate the impact of all of this on pupils, but there was an impact that we will be unpicking for years to come. Now, more than ever, our profession needs to flex its adaptive skills within the classroom for the benefit of all pupils.

DANGER: PITFALLS AHEAD!

As an established adaptive teacher, you will think carefully about the needs and knowledge of pupils in your class and then make judicious adjustments to your delivery plan in order to meet these needs. Along the way, however, you may need to contend with some difficulties.

Crucially, adaptive and responsive teaching are about detecting and dismantling barriers to students gaining knowledge and know-how. It is vital that this is not achieved by diminishing the high expectations of your curriculum or your practice. Again and again, pupils are supported by a 'dumbing down' of the experience and the offer. This is especially true of adaptations made for those with SEND or from disadvantaged backgrounds. They are given less than their peers. Read that again. Completely unacceptable, correct? Your adaptiveness must hold fast to the highest of expectations for all (Murdock-Perriera and Sedlacek, 2018).

There are many unhelpful approaches to being adaptive. Some are grounded in outdated/debunked theories and practice that still pervade the profession (Dekker et al., 2012). For a long time, educators were encouraged to adapt delivery to take into account each pupil's learning style, which has now been challenged and debunked. As a Newly Qualified Teacher (NQT) when this approach was still very much in vogue, I can remember being told that using Punctuation Kung Fu would assist my kinaesthetic learners in grappling with the ever-elusive semicolon. This was the process of assigning a 'Kung Fu' move to each form of punctuation and the class completing these moves while being read a piece of text. Almost always, confusion and carnage would ensue. No one would be any clearer about how to use a semicolon.

Other unhelpful strategies create drudgery for the classroom practitioner. For example, generating multiple worksheets and distinct activities (often on different coloured paper) for different abilities within the classroom. This approach is burdensome, unhelpful for your practice and rarely beneficial for the pupils' long-term progress.

Responsivity and adaptive teaching are rooted in dexterity as a practitioner. Thus, the more confidence and agility you have in utilising different delivery strategies, the more responsive and adaptive you can be. For example, one of the greatest responsive tools you have as a teacher is your questioning and I would make this your top priority when considering where next to strengthen your practice (see also Chapter 6 on planning and Chapter 10 on assessment). Even the most expert and experienced of teachers benefits from a questioning refresher! As you become more fluent in your questioning, learning how to probe and to clarify and help pupils to enhance and extend their answers and address misconceptions, the more adaptive you can be to the needs of your learners (Alexander, 2018). It is also an extremely low workload approach to adaptation – always a winner!

As a trainee or ECT practitioner, it may feel that the task of adaptation is burdensome. Do not become disheartened. As an established adaptive teacher, you will think carefully about the needs and abilities of your class and then make judicious adjustments to your delivery plan in order to meet these needs. As time goes on, especially as you work with specific pupils and curricula in the long term, you will make these adaptations and adjustments almost without thinking. Never underestimate the degree to which continuing to enhance your subject knowledge will benefit your adaptive skills. Invest the time in expanding your subject expertise and this will enable you to find alternative routes through the material that will benefit your pupils.

My advice would be to focus on doing a small number of adaptations well and doing them consistently.

WHERE TO START?

When you are planning or reflecting on your adaptive practice, ask yourself to finish these statements:

'To be at their best, the class need …'

'To be at his/her best, XX needs …'

8 Adaptive teaching

KNOWING YOUR PUPILS WELL

Adaptive teaching requires you to know your pupils very well and make use of a range of 'data' that is already available. Schools are data-rich environments – but data isn't just about attainment levels and test scores (see also Chapter 10 on assessment). Think of this as 'hard data' – examples include: test scores, KS1/2 outcomes, mock exam grades, formative assessment scores, attendance, number of fixed term exclusions. Hard data can encourage prejudice, so guard against prior data overruling what your own eyes are telling you about a pupil. For example, a low prior attaining pupil may not be a low-ability pupil now – much can change from one key stage to the next.

Just as powerful for your practice are the 'soft' qualitative rather than quantitative data sets. This might be the pupil's response to challenge, their personal organisation, how comfortable they are asking for help. It really helps to also know this about a pupil in order to effectively adapt teaching to meet their needs.

In effect what you are doing is gathering intelligence on *how* to deliver the next phase of the curriculum sequence; the more you know, the more effective your plans can be. This may mean taking into account different starting points, more or less secure prior learning, cognitive or sensory support needs, behaviour/attitudinal support requirements or even something as mundane as this being the first lesson back after a long break.

Here are some good places to start for gathering useful intelligence:

Table 8.1 Formative data gathered through your 'in-flight' active assessment of the class.

Formative data gathered through your 'in-flight' active assessment of the class.		
Teaching sequences/schemes of work from earlier in the curriculum.	Prior attainment data on your class.	SEND passports or learning plans for pupils on the SEND register.
Available data on reading language and communications, especially reading ages.	If you have English as an Additional Language (EAL) pupils in the early stages of language acquisition, they may also have learning plans.	Personal learning plans for other vulnerable pupils - such as Children Looked After.
Attendance data for the cohort.	Attitude to learning data.	Individual behaviour plans for pupils with behavioural support needs.

Some pupils have very specific needs within the classroom and will have plans, created by experienced and expert staff, which set out how you should adapt delivery for them. Part of your professional duty is to ensure that those plans are in place for the most vulnerable learners. However, these plans are usually evolving 'live' documents and the teams which generate them should welcome your feedback on what is, and is not, working. If you are struggling to implement some of the suggested adaptations for a pupil, or one is no longer working, ask to meet with someone in that team to plan adaptations together (see also Chapter 2). Where it is possible, there is great value in working with the pupil themselves, even their families if this is feasible, to implement these adaptations.

It is worth remembering that others in the school are likely to know these pupils better than you during your training and so you may make the decision to speak to other staff about their knowledge. This can be very beneficial and give you some 'ways in' with classes and/or individual pupils, but there is always a risk that you will also be given biased or unhelpful information. This can vary from "XXX is a little tinker, but if you try this approach, it generally works" (helpful), "Oh, they are never naughty for me!" (unhelpful), to "Oh my lord, you've got 8F3? I heard their last teacher is still in critical care!" (alarming).

A far more helpful approach is to observe the pupils in the classes of effective practitioners (identified for you by your mentor) who you can then work with to unpick their adaptations.

CASE STUDY

Reconnaissance / simplification / reflection

Scenario: Jane was working as an English ECT in September 2021. Her small Year 10 class of 16 had 11 pupils on the SEND register, several of whom had very pronounced needs, and many pupils with low attendance and low learner resilience. No matter how easy and accessible she made the delivery – often using a series of short, chunked activities – she always ended up working much harder than the pupils and as pupils could not retain or recall what she was teaching them, progress was not being made. Jane was diligently applying the guidance in the learning plans, but this was often conflicted (PowerPoints needed to have different background colours) and burdensome (three different styles of writing frame were suggested in passports). Rightfully frustrated, Jane raised this with her mentor.

Response: with the help of her mentor, Jane observed this class with other staff and in different subjects. While some was useful – for example, seeing them be more independent in maths and science, happier to work in groups in PE – it was the delivery in humanities that had the adaptations most likely to help in Jane's practice. Alongside her mentor, Jane observed the lessons with the humanities teacher and then deconstructed the adaptations being used. One immediate difference was that the experienced humanities teacher was not following the guidance of the learning passports, having grown frustrated with the conflicting strategies they suggest. Alongside the humanities teacher, Jane feedbacked to the Inclusion team that the SEND passports held guidance that made teaching the pupils together more burdensome. The Inclusion team reviewed the passports, taking into account that the pupils were almost always taught together, and made the suggested adaptations more aligned. Jane began to deploy a similar set of adaptations in English to those the pupils were used to using (successfully) in humanities. Jane also grouped the pupils differently, choosing to have them work in groups based on the way they engaged in learning rather than purely on 'ability'. This allowed her to provide groups of pupils with similar support within lessons, reducing the complexity of her delivery.

Impact: rapidly, Jane was able to see increased engagement and progress in lessons, both with individual pupils and with the group as a whole. Over time, the group was able to work more independently of Jane because she had provided them with effective adaptations. Consequently, she was able to provide more intense targeted support to individuals who needed it. Importantly, the curriculum-wide dialogue of what was, and was not, effective for these pupils allowed everyone who taught them to adapt more effectively.

- What are the ways you are adapting your prepared lessons?
- What other subjects can you draw upon for strategies?

HIGH CHALLENGE / LOW THREAT

One of the common pitfalls in relation to adaptive teaching is only thinking of lower attainers as in need of it. Learning should be challenging for all pupils, all the time. It might not be helpful for pupils to be given 'challenge' tasks as one-off events in lessons, even as 'extensions' when they have finished the main task. Ideally, all learning should require pupils to be in a zone of challenge, with adaptations used to lower the threat of that challenge or the complexity of the learning task.

If we remove the challenge from learning, for example by pitching the lesson to the middle/lower end of the ability range, we effectively place a glass ceiling on the potential progress of the class. This is not what teachers want to achieve and educators are not typically in the business of placing glass ceilings above the heads of their pupils. The danger with this approach is that when learning is pitched low, all pupils miss out on the opportunity to engage in and experience the higher-level content. Even if pupils cannot master this content, by being judiciously exposed to it, they will absorb some and it will enhance their own learning experience. If nothing else, it will reinforce messages about maximising your potential and taking opportunities to stretch oneself as a learner.

Wherever possible, learning should be pitched to the highest ability in the group with careful scaffolding to allow all pupils to engage effectively. In this regard, you are removing the glass ceiling and providing a cement floor. With your judicious support, responsive teaching and effective adaptation, no pupil will be left behind. Neither will they be limited.

It is also important to consider what adaptations are needed for the more able.

8 Adaptive teaching

> **REFLECTION POINT**
>
> How can you adapt the learning to become even more challenging for some in the group?

> **CASE STUDY**
>
> **Lowering the threat**
>
> Task: pupils are evaluating Elizabeth Tudor's various actions to mitigate the risk posed by her cousin Mary Stuart and Elizabeth's ultimate decision to resort to execution. From a one-word stimulus, pupils have to recall their knowledge of the threats Mary created, and then rank (and justify the ranking) in order of having the most influence on Elizabeth's eventual decision to execute her cousin.
>
> Adaptation: for all pupils, this is a challenging activity. You have lowered the threat for many by providing some additional information, and by ensuring you check their recall has been accurate thus prevent them building their evaluation on a misconception. For one pupil, you have provided the events and ranked the order of influence; they must focus on justifying your ranking. For pupils with stronger recall, you have not provided the one-word recall stimulus and simply told them there are six things to recall. For one pair of pupils, who you know are secure with this knowledge, you provide a subtly different ranking and ask them to evaluate why some historians may argue this view versus another.
>
> Impact: all pupils have engaged in the evaluation and justification task in a manner that challenges them. For some you have reduced the complexity of the tasks to maximise their thinking and processing on the most important bit of today's learning.
>
> - How can you adapt the learning to become even more challenging for some in the group without creating unnecessary complexity for others?

ADAPTIVE TEACHING POWERFULLY SUPPORTS PERSONAL DEVELOPMENT

Adaptive teaching is more than the way you sequence delivery within a lesson, or the resources you use – though these are crucial and an excellent place to start. It is also about the pace of learning in your classroom, about the language you use with pupils, about the space you create for them to strive independently and how you respond to them. Relationships are key in this.

There is much literature to suggest that pupils learn best in stable environments, where the cognitive complexity of the classroom has been reduced as far as possible, where routines are effective, predictable and consistent. Ultimately, pupils learn best when they know they are safe. For many years, I have considered my best classroom work to have been done with low-attaining pupils and those who have been historically disengaged (Sökmen, 2021). The first thing that has to happen for such learners is for me to make them feel safe *as learners* – I emphasise repeatedly that they will never be given anything they cannot do in my classroom; it will always be possible even if it is tough. Over time, this is proven in their continued ability to engage and succeed – all they need to do is *try*. This builds their learner confidence, their resilience and their self-esteem.

Adaptive teaching should take into account the personal development needs of pupils as much as their academic ones. All learning is a personal development opportunity, especially as we return and regenerate after the disruption of the pandemic. A responsive teacher knows their pupils well and makes adjustments to delivery based on this.

▪▪▪ — CASE STUDY

Managing interventions

Pupil A: entrenched poor attender for the last two academic years. Low self-esteem. Mid prior attainer. Apt to disengage from learning. Reluctant to ask for help.

Pupil B: consistently high attender. Mid prior attainer. Confident to ask for help and shows resilience to challenging learning and 'learning fails' (this is the term I use within the classroom for low-stakes errors, especially when they create an opportunity for metacognitive reflection. FAIL = First Attempt In Learning).

Task: use prior learning from last year, and recent lessons, to complete this series of mathematical problems.

Consideration: you may choose to intervene more quickly and offer help to Pupil A, who has low self-esteem and fragile prior learning, as there is more immediate benefit for their personal and mathematical development to see themselves as capable. The experience of striving could slip too quickly into struggling and result in their disengagement altogether. For Pupil B, (more comfortable to have to deploy resilience to challenge in lessons and more secure in their prior learning) being left to work through a problem themselves presents a positive learning opportunity for both their mathematical knowledge and their own personal development.

Response: prior to beginning the task, check in with Pupil A and reassure them they will get help on the next task. During the instructions, check Pupil B's understanding and encourage them to work with Pupil C, who you know will be able to work well with them. As the task begins, say to Pupil A, "If you like, I can get you going with this or you can start on your own and I'll check back in a minute or two when everyone else is settled." Give Pupil A the space to choose. If they choose independence, immediately and

(Continued)

> specifically praise this and check on the rest of your class. Come back to Pupil A at the time you said you would. Meanwhile, monitor Pupil B and 'nudge' if necessary. If Pupil A disengages, join them and work through the problem together. Be gently relentless in challenging closed mindset language. When taking feedback, praise resilience and independence.
>
> - What does XX need personally in order to be the best learner they can in this moment?

MEET THEM WHERE THEY ARE, BUT DON'T LEAVE THEM THERE

Adaptive teaching requires you to know your pupils' strengths and weaknesses well, which will allow you to maximise the opportunities for pupils to consolidate their strengths and provide scaffolding to support areas where pupils are less strong. However, it is important that our scaffolding and support do not lead to helpless and disempowered pupils. Think again about the earlier example of two pupils and how you may take an adaptive response to their personal development needs. Over time in that scenario, you should (safely) expose Pupil A to increased desirable difficulty in order to help enhance their resilience.

Careful reconnaissance will allow you to pitch the early lessons in a sequence or your first introduction to the class. Once you begin working with a group, the most useful data you can gather will be your early diagnostic and formative assessment with them (see Chapter 10 for more on assessment). Ultimately you are aiming to bring together this prior data alongside live data. This is a real challenge and to become more skilled at managing all of this information, work with your mentor to begin with (Hattie and Timperley, 2007). In partnership you can co-construct the likely adaptations that need to happen to the teaching sequence to benefit the whole class and the smaller scale ones that are needed for individuals.

TEACHING ASSISTANTS: WORK WITH THE OTHER ADULTS IN THE ROOM

In a number of lessons, you will find that you are not alone with the pupils but have teaching assistants (TAs) present – these may be generic to work with the class or, quite often, funded to work with a pupil or pupils with specific needs. The teaching assistants can be an invaluable asset and are there for you to work with. A report published by the EEF (Sharples et al., 2016) suggests seven strategies that are positioned as best practice for when working with teaching assistants. These are summarised opposite.

8 Adaptive teaching

Table 8.2 Effective use of teaching assistants (Sharples et al., 2016: 10–11)

Recommendation	Further information
TAs should not be used as an informal teaching resource for low-attaining pupils	This separates pupils from the rest of the class and there should be a review (and then emphasis) on how TAs can support learning throughout the school.
Use TAs to add value to what teachers do, not replace them	The role of the TA should be complementary to that of the classroom teaching to ensure that pupils who 'struggle' have as much time with the teacher as any other pupil.
Use TAs to help develop independent learning skills and manage their own time	High-quality talk between TAs and pupils can support development of skills associated with improved learning outcomes. Other strategies include offering minimum initial help, waiting time for responses to questions and intervention only when the pupil is unable to proceed.
Ensure TAs are fully prepared for their role in the classroom	Ideally TAs should be involved in the planning stages of lessons and have essential 'need to knows' such as conceptual knowledge, skills, the learning outcomes and expectations around feedback.
Use TAs to deliver high-quality one-to-one and small group support using structured interventions	For impact on attainment to be positive under one-to-one or small group interventions, there needs to be high-quality support and training available for the TAs – informal and unstructured approaches are found to negatively impact on attainment.
Adopt evidence-based interventions to support TAs in their small group and one-to-one instruction	Common elements of effective intervention include regular but brief interventions over a sustained period of time, structured supporting resources and lesson plans with objectives, support directed to the right pupil and connections being made with out-of-classroom contexts.
Ensure explicit connections are made between learning from everyday classroom teaching and structured interventions	Learning during interventions should be consistent with learning in the classroom and extend this work. Making the links between the two should be explicit – pupils will not necessarily make the links by themselves.

▰▰▰— REFLECTION POINT

Look at the table above.

- Consider how you as a classroom teacher can support better use of the TAs in your classroom.
- Think about what the specific challenges and needs are for your subject area in relation to these.

ASSESSMENT: THE FUEL OF ADAPTIVE TEACHING

Your knowledge of assessment is a critical foundation for the success of adaptations in your classroom (see also Chapter 10 on assessment). Teaching and learning are iterative processes. We plan, we teach, we review, we course-correct, we (re)teach, we review again, we amend plans for future use. We iteratively innovate our practice.

After you have 'done some assessment', you will have 'data'. Remember that 'data' might be a test score, but more usefully it would be whether specific learning/curriculum goals have been achieved, where misconceptions are common across a class, whether one component concept has been retained weakly and has made the composite concept unstable. The planned curriculum is a learning journey broken up into incremental stages. The goal is for students to reach composites of knowledge – complex, intricate, made up of a range of multi-facet concepts constructed by combinations of knowledge and skills. Each composite is made up of individual components, units of knowledge or know-how. The teaching of the components must be carefully sequenced so that students can build them up into secure composites. If individual components are weak – due to poor learning or poor retention – the resulting composite will be fragile also. Think about what you have gathered in flight about this class and their learning.

Once armed with that you should finish these statements:

- *Assessment of Pupil / Class XX has shown me that _____.*
- *Assessment indicates that _____ is successful.*
- *Assessment indicates that _____ is unsuccessful for _____.*
- *As a consequence I will _____.*

■■■ CASE STUDY

Using Assessment

You have completed the Year 7 midterm assessment on biodiversity. This includes questions about biodiversity in rainforests and also retests knowledge from a previous topic on habitat-based adaptations in camels, giraffes and hummingbirds. You have also kept hold of your teaching sequence (also known as scheme of learning, scheme of work, module, unit, medium-term plan ...), which you annotated as you went along with changes to your planned delivery – extra lessons, lessons lost, key student absences, etc.

Assessment of 7F4 has shown me that ... the majority (24/27) of the class have successfully explained how rainforests are biodiverse and retained this securely. Most pupils (17/27) are able to explain what the impact would be on biodiversity if there were changes to the habitat. Recall of habitat-based adaptations is less secure. The majority of pupils 22/27 were unable to accurately recall adaptations in all three example animals. All could recall the hump for camels but almost all had misconceptions about the

> benefit of this adaptation on survival. However, when compared to the summative data from the original end of term test on Habitat Adaptations, 22/27 were able to accurately recall the key adaptations of those three animals, including the camel's hump. Four pupils did not attempt the recall questions.
>
> **Assessment data indicates that the delivery of** ... biodiversity as a concept and (for the majority) engagement in recall quizzing ... **is successful.**
>
> **Assessment data indicates that** ... recall of prior topics **is unsuccessful** ... for specific data sets – such as animal adaptations. The ability to explain the impact on changes in habitat to biodiversity is less secure. For four pupils, confidence in recall quizzing is a real barrier to learning.
>
> **As a consequence I will** ... introduce quick recall tasks into lessons three times per week, focusing on key factual information and seeking 100 per cent accuracy. I will plan these with the other Year 7 teachers to reduce workload. This will include teaching pupils the look/cover/write/check memorisation strategy. I will link this forward to key revision needs in KS4 so pupils understand the value and impact of retention/revision. I will specifically reward pupils for secure/improved retention. I will adapt the delivery of biodiversity in the future to ensure that enough time is given to understanding how changes in habitat impact on biodiversity and give more opportunity for pupils to review cases – e.g. rainforests and coral reefs. For four pupils I will give advance notice of the next recall topic in end of unit tests to build confidence and I will check in on them during tests.

Please remember; assessment is wasted labour if you do nothing with the data/intelligence you have gathered and your FORMative assessment should FORM your strategy in the classroom. This goes for the big-ticket assessment at the end of a unit or in the check-in questioning you use following some explicit instruction in the classroom.

EVERYDAY ADAPTATIONS: A LITTLE GOES A LONG WAY

It is really important to understand that as teachers we all have pedagogical preferences. It is critical we also strive towards having a rich and well-established repertoire of strategies to use for the benefit of our pupils. As you gain in confidence and experience, do not be afraid of sticking to tried and tested strategies while they work, but don't continue to use them if they are unhelpful. Also look for opportunities to try new approaches with the support of your mentor.

These are a number of adaptions that can be adopted in order to adapt your teaching for your classes. Some work better in specific subjects, others for specific pupils. The one thing we do know about teaching is that there is no one size fits all magic solution. If a magic silver bullet existed to allow all students to learn as one, we would have found it by now!

SIMPLIFY

First and foremost, pupils who succeed with adaptation almost always benefit from simplicity too. Reduce the lesson content to its most critical knowledge, or at least signpost the most critical knowledge for these pupils. Identify the threshold concepts (the really important bits) and focus on those (Sweller et al., 2019).

In every way possible, reduce the cognitive burden of the learning environment, of your resources and your instructions. Allow the working memory to focus on the learning with minimal distraction.

Keep resources clear, streamlined and uncluttered.

Utilise simple and effective dual coding and carefully consider the graphological features of what you present to pupils. By this I mean how the page is arranged, the font used, the navigational features as all of this has an impact.

Remember, simplification does not mean dumbing down.

CURRICULUM (RE)SEQUENCING

You might need to make medium-term changes to the planned curriculum in order to make the best adaptations for key pupils or key groups. If your formative or summative assessment intel clearly shows that critical prior learning is not secure, you may need to adapt the teaching sequence.

Do this with care and with the support of your curriculum leader. Good teaching sequences take into account the need for some contingencies, and it may be you have some wiggle room planned into the curriculum plans you are following. If not, seek the guidance of your mentor and other colleagues in how to make larger-scale adaptations. Is there less critical content that can be left? Are there ways to create more time for a class or individual?

Use the exercise above linked with reflecting on assessment to identify where things may have gone wrong and how you can avoid the same happening again. All strong teachers do this. We all adapt as we go and know that in doing so we are meeting the needs of our pupils and securing their progress. This 'in-flight' approach is something that you develop with time and experience. Good leaders of curriculum will be maintaining a dialogue with you about how you are moving through the planned curriculum. Listen to the guidance of more experienced colleagues and be open and honest if you need to move at a different pace to the intended plan, especially if you have to circle back to secure critical content. If you feel you are falling behind, or have lost sight of the curriculum plan, raise this with your mentor or subject leader.

WRITING FRAMES / STRUCTURE STRIPS / SENTENCE STARTERS

These reduce the threat of extended writing, guide the writing process and support pupils in providing more detailed and extensive answers. This works as an effective

8 Adaptive teaching

adaptation for scaffolding writing, but the same strategy can be used for scaffolding thinking and speaking.

For Example A, this structure strip is designed to guide pupils in identifying the language devices used by a writer in order to then analyse how the audience is guided to respond in a particular way. I could reduce or increase the complexity by deleting some of the devices or requiring them to combine their analysis of two devices working in tandem.

In Example B, the structure strip includes the devices I would like my pupils to use in the opening paragraphs of a piece of narrative writing. I could increase or decrease the complexity by reducing the number of different devices to be used (literally crossing them out for some students) or giving them the options to choose 2/5 to be deployed.

Begin in media res with a paired adverb sentence.
Eyes Closed
Sensory paragraph – sounds, smells, feelings.
Build mystery, leave the audience waiting but not confused.
Skill AO5: simile or metaphor or personification + embedded onomatopoeia.
Skill AO6: semicolon sentence OR colon sentence OR triplet + colon starter.

Eyes open. Describe setting.
Pathetic Fallacy
Establish atmosphere.
Reveal more information but leave audience waiting.
Skill AO5: simile or metaphor or personification + embedded onomatopoeia.
Skill AO6: semicolon sentence OR colon sentence OR triplet + colon starter.

Figure 8.1 Example A

Her hand gripped the sapphire, its icy blue heart already corrupting her innocent soul.	Verbs
	Metaphor
	Adjectives
	Personification
Glowing brightly, the sapphires were like drops of luxurious Indian ink dotted prettily across the page.	Present Participle
	Simile
	Adjectives
	Verb + adverb
Staining the cloth like a pool of spilled blood, the rubies glowed evilly in the candle light.	Verbs
	Simile
	Noun
	Verb + adverb
Petals of passion. The scattered rubies shimmered in the warm candle light.	Metaphor + plosive alliteration
	Verbs
	Past participle
	Adjective

Figure 8.2 Example B

8 Adaptive teaching

NOTHING NEW

Another approach is to provide pupils with the knowledge required for the answer, so that the cognitive load is directed towards formulating the response rather than recalling the contents of the response.

This can be especially useful for pupils with patchy attendance or disrupted prior learning. This can be done by doing whole class Q&A to recall the knowledge and writing it on the board or providing a quick knowledge organiser to the pupils. Here is an example below from a religious studies unit.

VOCABULARY BANKS

Provide key terminology in simple and accessible formats. Pupils who need glossaries are likely to benefit from reduced 'word-load' and from being given a small number of very specific targeted terms to use. Simple definitions using the simplest words is a good approach. Consider providing accessible Tier 1 synonyms for more complex Tier 2 terms (especially if they are abstract in nature) so that pupils with lower working vocabulary don't feel overwhelmed.

An adaptation for pupils to be stretched further: consider banning simpler/less specific terms and targeting more challenging vocabulary choices.

MODEL ANSWERS

These should be the foundation of your daily practice so learners are consistently exposed to what a good one looks like (WAGOLL) and should use the sentence stems/writing frames as you will provide for them later. Once you have provided the model, deconstruct it with pupils so they understand how and why it is a successful expression knowledge and know-how. Consider also providing partial models that you complete together as a class as a group writing task.

When providing a model paragraph that will act as a springboard for pupils to then continue the written answer themselves, I think carefully about what to base the model on. For example, if pupils will be analysing the impact of four different factors on migration, I will intentionally choose the more challenging factor (or the one which most commonly produces misconceptions), leaving more accessible examples for the pupils to complete. Again, this reduces the threat of the task and guards against a common misconception becoming embedded.

LIVE/GROUP WRITING OR WALKING TALKING MODELLING

It is useful for pupils to experience the process of constructing a model answer, especially where the teacher is able to model the picking up of misconceptions as we write and self-editing. With this, consider the burden on pupils of listening and watching.

Some staff use silent modelling effectively, so that pupils only need to read along rather than read and listen.

Wherever possible, eliminate pupils spending time copying models. This is wasted learning time as most are unable to read, retain, write and listen at the same time. I prefer to provide the model, read and discuss it together, then silently model annotating as they make their own notes and annotations. This may take slightly longer, but it generates more secure learning and more opportunity for me to interrogate pupil understanding.

THINKING TIME – VERBAL REHEARSAL

As we question, or before pupils respond to a task, it is important to create appropriate thinking time. It is useful to form the habit, and regularly check you are sticking to it, of posing a question and pausing for a response. It is also useful to build in opportunities for pupils to check their answer with their desk-mates. Through verbal rehearsal, pupils practise their answer verbally with another pupil. Their partner can then correct/extend if needed. Again, this is a useful pedagogical strategy and is inclusive and accessible for all types of learners. It does need to be developed over time so that pupils don't use it as an opportunity to get a quick update on last night's *Love Island*.

Consider the difference here:

> Option 1: Rahul, what is the term for killing a king?
>
> Option 2: Everyone, what is the term for killing a king? [micropause while Rahul raises his hand] Yes, Rahul?
>
> Option 3: Okay, I want us to think carefully about the correct term for King Duncan's murder. What is the technical word for that crime? Think. [Pause for count of ten] Okay. Rahul, please share your answer.
>
> Option 4: Okay, everyone, Shakespeare is exploring the theme of treason here. Let's recall the term for killing a king. [ensure silence, pause for 10 seconds] Check the answer with your partner. [observe for 10–15 seconds, check in with targeted pupil] Okay, ready? The answer is … [choral response from class].

A choral response is useful but takes work to become a successful strategy. You must observe carefully who does and doesn't answer in a choral response and then follow up with a check-in later. Also, it is useful to remember that pupils sometimes get a bit of performance anxiety during observations and may suddenly get tight-lipped in front of an observer!

WORD / ACTION SCAFFOLDING

Practise the action of using your speech and gestures within the classroom. This could be as simple as deliberately pausing after a new key term and writing it on the board or offering accessible synonyms as you go. For key pupils, using gesture to pause and support their listening and thinking is a useful adaptation, especially if they can become distracted or struggle to listen to new information.

Consider:

> Within the Eucharist [pause, point to spelling of Eucharist on the board] there is a key difference between the beliefs and practices of Catholic Christians [pause, underline capital C in Catholic and Christians while looking meaningfully at Lily, who forgets this – she nods, understanding the hint] and Protestant denominations like the Church of England.
>
> In the Church of England, sometimes called CofE [underlines key letters on board], bread and wine are used to symbolise the body and blood of Christ.
>
> However, within the Catholic Church it is believed the bread and wine literally change state and become the divine body and blood of Christ. This is called transubstantiation [carefully spells out on the board and indicates key word sheet for some learners]. Say it with me [pauses for choral response, repeat as required, check for all learners' response].
>
> Good! This will help you to remember the term – *trans* [underline], linked with change or movement and *substan* [underline], like substance, linked to material. Change of material.
>
> Now. Turn in your pairs and practise explaining this key difference. I want to hear you using these key terms: Eucharist/Transubstantiation [circulates, pauses to listen, targets support].

When focusing on spelling or specific vocabulary, you could use this as an exciting opportunity to discuss the etymology of the term or break out your knowledge of grammatical terms or knowledge of Latin root words. However, your goal here is to simplify wherever possible until pupils are confident with the term. You'll know your class and your pupils best, and thus can make a professional judgement about whether this is the right time to do this.

WABOLL – WHAT A BAD ONE LOOKS LIKE

We have looked at some strategies for successfully adapting learning for pupils of different needs. It is also useful to consider what makes for unhelpful adaptations:

- inscrutable or complicated resources;
- burdensome resources to create/sustain;
- any strategy that creates future helplessness on the part of the pupil;
- any strategy that diminishes the dignity of a pupil;
- any strategy that significantly diverts from the intentions of the curriculum.

8 Adaptive teaching

▪️▫️▫️ CHAPTER SUMMARY

Adaptation, alongside its super partner formative assessment, is the most significant means by which you will promote the success and achievement of your pupils. Keep the following in mind:

- Teaching is a masterclass in iterative innovation and adaptation – we plan, we deliver, we adjust as we deliver, we assess, we review, we innovate, we solve, we re-plan, we re-teach, we move ever forward. This is the bedrock of teaching.

- Adaptive teaching is not about reducing or diminishing the challenge or quality of the curriculum; it is about lowering the threat and promoting the accessibility of learning.

- Adaptive teaching is always helped by considering how complexity can be reduced.

- Pupils learn at a different pace and with different approaches. Adaptiveness to their needs will demand your patience and flexibility.

- No two pupils are the same, and consequently all pupils require some degree of adaptation in their learning.

- Adaptive teaching need not be cumbersome or create drudgery for the teacher.

- Adaptive teaching is easier the more you invest in your technical pedagogy – questioning, instruction giving, explanation, modelling, formative assessment.

- Adaptive teaching can be accomplished effectively with low-workload strategies.

▪️▫️▫️ ASSIGNMENT LINKS

You may be asked to consider how you meet individual needs of learners in the classroom. This chapter will help you to apply the thinking behind your choices.

LEARNING AND CONSOLIDATION

KEY THINGS TO LOOK FOR WHEN OBSERVING LESSONS OR TEACHING

Ask for the teacher's planning folder, or access to shared planning in your school, where learning plans for key pupils are stored. Look at how those plans have been put into action by the staff delivering them. Ask yourself:

- Are they effective? Is the pupil able to make progress?

- How could I use the same strategy? Is it portable to my classroom?

- How could I enhance that strategy to be more effective?

After the lesson, ask the staff teaching to help unpick what was being used.

How many different strategies can you observe where teachers support the individual needs of pupils?

FURTHER READING

Fletcher-Wood, H. (2018) *Responsive Teaching: Cognitive Science and Formative Assessment in Practice.* Routledge.

REFERENCES

Alexander, R. (2018) *Towards Dialogic Teaching: Rethinking Classroom Talk.* Dialogos.

Dekker, S., Lee, N., Howard-Jones, P. and Jolles, J. (2012) Neuromyths in education: prevalence and predictors of misconceptions among teachers. *Frontiers in Psychology, 3.* Available at: www.frontiersin.org/articles/10.3389/fpsyg.2012.00429

Hattie, J. and Timperley, H. (2007) The power of feedback. *Review of Educational Research, 77*(1): 81–112.

Murdock-Perriera, L.A. and Sedlacek, Q.C. (2018) Questioning Pygmalion in the twenty-first century: the formation, transmission, and attributional influence of teacher expectancies. *Social Psychology of Education, 21*(3): 691–707. DOI: 10.1007/s11218-018-9439-9

Quigley, A., Muijs, D. and Stringer, E. (2018) Metacognition and self-regulated learning: guidance report. Education Endowment Foundation.

Sharples, J., Webster, R. and Blatchford, P. (2016) *Making Best Use of Teaching Assistants. EEF.* Available at: https://educationendowmentfoundation.org.uk/education-evidence/guidance-reports/teaching-assistants

Smart, J.B. and Marshall, J.C. (2013) Interactions between classroom discourse, teacher questioning, and student cognitive engagement in middle school science. *Journal of Science Teacher Education, 24*(2): 249–267. DOI: 10.1007/s10972-012-9297-9

Sökmen, Y. (2021) The role of self-efficacy in the relationship between the learning environment and student engagement. *Educational Studies, 47*(1): 19–37. DOI: 10.1080/03055698.2019.1665986

Sweller, J., van Merriënboer, J.J. and Paas, F. (2019) Cognitive architecture and instructional design: 20 years later. *Educational Psychology Review* (31):1–32.

9

TEACHING FOR INCLUSION

JANE ESSEX

▪▪▪— KEY WORDS

- Inclusion
- Disability
- Differentiation

CHAPTER OBJECTIVES

Through reading this chapter, you will learn how current ways of thinking about diverse learners have arisen and how they will impact on your work as a trainee and as an ECT. You will be encouraged to and directed how to identify the ways in which your school and wider organisations contribute to the achievement of inclusive education and the chapter will also support you in finding ways in which you can ensure that diverse learners are able to participate fully and succeed in your lessons.

The chapter also offers insights as to how the current understanding of inclusion evolved over the last few decades and the shifts that have been seen in policy and strategy as a result of this.

▪▪▪— LINKS TO THE CORE CONTENT FRAMEWORK

All of the Core Content Framework themes are referred to and applied in this chapter, but the following are the most relevant:

Standard 5 – Adapt teaching

(Continued)

1. Pupils are likely to learn at different rates and to require different levels and types of support from teachers to succeed.
2. Seeking to understand pupils' differences, including their different levels of prior knowledge and potential barriers to learning, is an essential part of teaching.
3. Adapting teaching in a responsive way, including by providing targeted support to pupils who are struggling, is likely to increase pupil success.
4. Adaptive teaching is less likely to be valuable if it causes the teacher to artificially create distinct tasks for different groups of pupils or to set lower expectations for particular pupils.
5. Flexibly grouping pupils within a class to provide more tailored support can be effective, but care should be taken to monitor its impact on engagement and motivation, particularly for low-attaining pupils.
6. There is a common misconception that pupils have distinct and identifiable learning styles. This is not supported by evidence and attempting to tailor lessons to learning styles is unlikely to be beneficial.
7. Pupils with special educational needs or disabilities are likely to require additional or adapted support; working closely with colleagues, families and pupils to understand barriers and identify effective strategies is essential.

WHAT IS INCLUSION?

The United Nations Educational Scientific and Cultural Organisation (UNESCO) website states that *inclusive education works to identify all barriers to education and remove them and covers everything from curricula to pedagogy and teaching.*

Inclusion is often seen as a tool for improving societal educational outcomes, to achieving educational, social and environmental justice. It is not, however, simply a case of being vigilant for the wellbeing of certain groups of pupils. Rather, it is understood as something that is achieved through ongoing change in the entire education system that requires shifts in thinking about diversity, inclusion in policy, revision of structures and systems and in day-to-day practices.

WHO NEEDS INCLUDING AND WHY?

By describing how we respond to diversity in learners as 'inclusion', we recognise that some learners have been excluded, completely or partially, from education. Some, by reason of disability, have been excluded from education of the kind that someone of their age would typically be receiving. In some cases, this was because they attended an alternative specialist school that catered to people with a similar disability, for example, in schools for the deaf or blind. However, one group of children, those with the greatest learning disabilities who had been judged 'ineducable', did not receive education of any kind. Until 1970 children who had what would now be termed 'profound and multiple learning difficulties' were simply considered not to have the capacity to learn, and so educational resources were not assigned to them. In the nineteenth century, such young people would be placed in 'asylums', places where they could be kept safe from the cruelty of society. Later, such young people were placed in junior training hospitals. Only when the Education (Handicapped Children) Act 1970 made education an entitlement for all children was universal education made available. Even then, children with learning disabilities were often segregated from their peers in special schools. The arguments for separate education varied from the positive, that specialist staff and resources could all be conveniently available in one place, to the rights of non-disabled children to have their education uninterrupted by children who were described as 'educationally subnormal' or 'retarded' (sic). Decisions about who was incapable of benefiting from education in a regular school, or indeed at all before 1970, were made by doctors alone until the 1970s and the legacy of this is found in the way that difference is commonly described in medical terms. Although the Warnock Report (1978) advocated that the aim of education should be to place all pupils in the same schools, the 'educational triage' of pupils that was established prior to 1970 has persisted in our ideas about separating some pupils from their peers.

We now recognise three major groups of ways of understanding difference, which are represented in three models of disability. (There are further models, but they all, broadly, align with one of these groups.) Equivalent approaches can be applied to any other group who is at risk of educational exclusion. The groups are:

1. <u>The medical model.</u> In this model, the focus is on what is different about the individual learner. It considers that most people fall within a normal range of values for any characteristic, such as academic attainment, walking speed or level of social interaction. Those who lie outside the normal range of values are considered abnormal and often biological causes are used to explain the difference. One result of using the medical model to understand difference is that cures of corrections are sought, such as the use of prosthetic limbs on children affected by thalidomide or using cumbersome hearing aids to 'correct' the hearing of deaf children. Notice that learning disabilities are not usually susceptible to this 'remedial' approach, and this may explain in part why such children remained excluded from education until relatively recently.

2. <u>The social (or socio-environmental) model.</u> This model grew up during the 1980s and was advanced by people with disabilities. It says that the adverse experience of people who are different ('have an impairment') are not simply due to the difference but are because society does not respond constructively to people who are different in some way. For example, if accommodations for differences were routinely available, such as having ramped access everywhere, wheelchair users would not experience any disadvantage. In schools, which are viewed primarily as institutions to further learning, it seems almost inevitable that people who do not learn as quickly or easily are disadvantaged. This, however, is based on the assumption that

all learning is of the same kind and overlooks the place that schools have in the socialisation of pupils and their role in developing skills and attitudes beyond those specified by the formal curriculum.

An important version of the social model is the so-called 'ecological model', which, like the social model, considers that difference is made a disadvantage by the environment that a child finds themselves in. It also recognises that the child is not a passive 'victim' of their environment but has agency and can change their environment (Brofenbrenner, 1977). Focusing on the environment enables teachers to think about the ways in which they and the pupils could change the environment to further learning.

3. <u>(Functional) diversity model.</u> This model actively challenges adverse responses to difference (Scotch and Schriner, 1997). The tenet of the diversity model is that everyone is different; difference is both normal and beneficial to a community. Ideas associated with this way of thinking about diversity include that a so-called disability (meaning a difficulty in doing things) can be a positive aspect of someone's identity; for example, people with dyslexia attribute their high levels of creativity to their condition. Similarly, many sign-language-using deaf people describe being part of a very supportive community with its own distinctive culture. The diversity model actively challenges the deficiency thinking of the medical model in arguing that unachievable expectations can prevent rather than enable progress, growth and development.

The diversity model suggests that institutions, such as schools, should not only respond to individual pupils' needs for adjustment but should proactively introduce anticipatory adjustments in order to facilitate the immediate inclusion of as many pupils as possible. This is the notion of universal design for inclusion. For example, if every school area was made accessible with ramps and lifts, pupils who use wheelchairs would not find anywhere in the school inaccessible. If all school resources were in a sans serif font and displayed on an off-white background, far more pupils would find them easy to read without further individualised adjustment.

■ ■ ■ — REFLECTION POINT

Look at your school's documentation relating to provision for pupils with special educational needs, such as school policies and descriptions of individual pupils. Carry out an analysis of the text to consider the way in which they represent pupil difference.

- How often is a medical diagnosis provided or a problem described? (medical model)
- How frequently is reference made to the learning environment that the pupil needs? (social model)

- How frequently do the documents refer to pupil strengths or things that they can do for themselves to enhance their learning? (diversity model)

Thinking about the focus and wording of the documents that you have looked at, which model or models of disability are most frequently represented? Which model is least commonly implied by the documents? Why do you think this is the case?

DIFFERENT CHARACTERISTICS, SAME NEED FOR INCLUSION

Other groups of pupils who are at high risk of under-attaining in school also need conscious consideration to improve their educational experience. It is very important that we distinguish between characteristics that are associated with more frequent underachievement and making assumptions that all pupils with such characteristics will inevitably achieve less than they should. These characteristics include:

- being Black and Asian Minority Ethnic (BAME), though not all ethnic groups are equally at risk of underachievement;
- those living in poverty;
- those who do not use English as their first language;
- those who are care experienced.

Pupils in any of these groups are liable to experience multiple barriers to full participation and success in school that beset children with disabilities. The way in which education prevents some pupils taking full part in the process of knowledge creation is called 'epistemic injustice' (Fricker, 2007). Some of these characteristics (gender identity, sexual orientation, skin colour and cultural markers, including language) are protected from disadvantageous treatment under the terms of the Equalities Act (2010). Others (living in poverty, as indicated by eligibility for free school meals, and being care experienced) qualify publicly schools for additional pupil premium funding, which is intended to mitigate their educational disadvantage. All of these groups of pupils have collectively experienced educational disadvantage, some individuals to a greater extent than others. They all merit active efforts to help them to achieve the wider aspirations of education. The fact that only disabled children have been actively excluded from education in the past means that they alone have required mechanisms to bring them into mainstream schools at all.

Their distinctive history has led some authors to suggest that, as our definition of those who should be considered as needing inclusion has extended, disabled pupils have suffered (MacKay, 2002). He suggests that considering multiple characteristics alongside disability may reduce the focus on those with disabilities and unintentionally lessen the support given to them. The generally held view now is that the point of inclusion is to benefit everyone (Schuelka, 2018) in line with the UNESCO definition given previously, rather than targeting support at identified groups. The ultimate aim is to build cohesive communities that foster opportunities for everyone, irrespective of their characteristics (Göransson and Nilholm, 2014).

Pupils with characteristics that are associated with exclusion or under-attainment commonly experience several common barriers in school. These include:

- stereotyping of groups of pupils, rather than getting to know them individually;
- low teacher expectations of certain pupils that depress attainment;
- assumptions about prior learning;
- a mismatch between the culture of school and the home culture of pupils;
- a failure to value what pupils bring to school in terms of knowledge, experience and skills;
- making value-laden judgements about pupils and what they do.

The ways in which teachers can avoid creating these obstacles are considered further in the section on 'Pedagogy for inclusion'.

REFLECTION POINT

- Think about your interactions with a class in which there are pupils with diversity characteristics.
- What practical steps do you take to ensure that they do not encounter the barriers listed above? How will these manifest in your planning?

HOW IS INCLUSION ORGANISED IN SCHOOLS?

In 2014, the Department for Education published a revised SEND (Special Educational Needs and Disabilities) Code of Practice, which was revised in 2015. This policy set out what all state-funded schools were expected to do for pupils with SEND. (It is not a legal document but has parts that are legally enforceable.) Schools are required to appoint a special educational needs co-ordinator, a qualified teacher who will oversee the implementation of the school's Special Educational Need and Disability (SEND) policy, liaise with parents/carers and other agencies (such as the local authority, Social Services or community health services). Their remit includes oversight of all four categories of SEND, which are:

- communication and interaction;
- cognition and learning;
- social, emotional and mental health difficulties;
- sensory and/or physical needs (Department for Education and Department of Health and Social Care, 2015).

The SEN co-ordinator is the person to whom staff or parents/carers should report concerns about any difficulties that are affecting learning. If a disability is suspected, the pupil is entitled to 'reasonable adjustment' under the terms of the Equalities (2010) Act, irrespective of whether they have been formally diagnosed. Although this is what we expect of a professional teacher, irrespective of legal requirements, knowing that adjustment is what the law stipulates should mean that they are made a very high priority. If the pupil experiences sustained difficulties that do not respond to reasonable adjustments made by teaching staff, the SEN co-ordinator can involve other SEN professionals, as the difficulties indicate. These might include the educational psychology service, speech and language therapist, occupational therapist or physiotherapist. Sometimes a pupil requires intervention from agencies beyond the school or requires more support in school that exceeds what the school can provide through its standard SEN budget, which comes as part of its overall funding. In this case, the SEN co-ordinator is likely to request a statutory assessment for an Education, Health and Care Plan (EHCP). This is a legally binding document that sets out exactly what the young person needs. It also comes with a budget to pay for the cost of meeting those needs.

The account above demonstrates the pivotal role of the SEN co-ordinator. Make sure that you know who they are in your school. If you have the opportunity, either through an organised training session or by an informal conversation, find out more about how they operate in the context of your school.

HOW WELL IS THE EDUCATION SYSTEM PROMOTING INCLUSION?

Despite the high ideals and political force behind many of the policies that have advanced educational inclusion in England, progress has been sporadic since the Warnock Report (1978). You may have anticipated that there would be problems in the early days executing a wholesale reform of the education system. However, it might equally be hoped that as discrimination was made illegal and equal treatment of diverse groups became widely accepted across society, schools would also become more inclusive. A spate of recent publications imply that this intention remains unfulfilled, partly confounded by the requirements of successive policies. Their failure may, in part, be attributable to rising expectations on the part of families, but a more frequent problem is a failure to involve stakeholders at an early enough stage, to maintain dialogue with them and to respond to their input. This was certainly a criticism that was levelled at the

Children and Families Act 2014, which was accompanied by the SEND Code of Practice 2014. The Act was passed very quickly and there was insufficient time to gather the views of those who would be affected by its terms, including pupils, parents/carers and teachers.

Two recent reports (Children's Commissioner, 2022; Ofsted, 2021) suggest that the major changes to the system of providing support introduced in 2014 has unintentionally created multiple points at which the system can fail. Ofsted (2021) spoke to young people, their families and carers, teachers, including SEN co-ordinators, and local authority staff. Based on the data, Ofsted reported several major difficulties that adversely affected their learning. One of these was that planning relies on the staff responsible knowing the young person well, which they did less often when the young person did not have an EHCP. Additional teaching assistant support, or withdrawal from the classroom for interventions, meant that the pupils were deprived of peer contact and were denied access to the curriculum that their peers were following. This meant that the support offered was simultaneously disadvantaging pupils, commonly without their input on which option they felt would be better for them.

The Children's Commissioner (2022) analysed the views of thousands of children and their parents/carers to provide four recommendations. Some of these relate to the organisational aspects of inclusion, such as the need to have early intervention and for it to be local. A key point was that diagnosis with a condition must be seen as only one route to having adjustments made, and that functional need should be considered as well. Pupils said that medical labels were felt to be stigmatising and led to low expectations, so support systems should not be structured around diagnoses.

Evidence from these reports highlights the ongoing difficulties in implementing the Children and Families Act (2014) and the SEND Code of Practice 2014. For that reason, a consultation was undertaken in 2022 (DfE, 2022), with the report due imminently at the time of writing. Such an exercise was felt to be needed because the 2014 provision, despite good intentions, has created a system that is too complicated, has not improved multi-agency working and stopped low academic achievement by pupils with SEN and which has been both costly and bureaucratic. As a trainee you may be given the opportunity to communicate with parents or carers at consultation evenings or in response to events in school (both positive and negative!). As an ECT it will be a key element of your role. It is important that you try to establish the formal (and informal) mechanisms in your school to counter the difficulties outlined.

CREATING MORE THAN JUST A SHARED SPACE

Creating an inclusive school is often understood as being about placing all pupils in a shared school environment. You can probably see why this is a focus now you know a little bit about the ways in which disabled children have been physically separated from their peers in the past. While sharing premises can assist with inclusion, there is considerably more to it than that. Schuelka (2018: 2) warns us against the use of crude metrics to monitor the implementation of inclusion, stating *Measuring the success of inclusive education should go beyond merely counting pupils to evaluate access but should include measures of educational quality.*

Göransson and Nilholm (2014) describe four different ways in which teachers understood inclusive education, of which only one refers specifically to the co-location of the pupils. These four categories are:

1. inclusion as the placement of pupils with disabilities in mainstream classrooms;
2. inclusion as meeting the social and academic needs of pupils with disabilities;
3. inclusion as meeting the social and academic needs of all pupils (called 'full inclusion' by some);
4. inclusion as the way of creating communities.

Slee (2019) takes a very critical view of the possibility of ever attaining full inclusion of the sort envisaged in 4. He says it is unattainable while education is obliged to focus primarily on assessment outcomes. He also argues that, so long as systems exist that can separate pupils on the basis of disability or other characteristic, they will be 'othered' rather than included. He describes the experience of being left out from the perspective of a parent or carer of a child with a disability,

> *Every day, a parent will arrive at a school and go to the 'inclusion room' where their child with a disability spends the day with the other children with disabilities in the school. Another parent will watch as other children receive invitations to a birthday party. Some might be checking their finances to see if they can provide money for the school to hire an aide for their child. Still another, will be told by a well-meaning principal, teacher, special needs coordinator or school psychologist that their child would be safer or cared for in another school* (Slee, 2019: 917).

REFLECTION POINT

- Based on your school experience to date, both as a pupil yourself, and as an ECT, which of Göransson and Nilholm's four types of inclusion have you seen put into practice?
- What do you see as the obstacles, practical and educational, to inclusion as described in their third and fourth categories? Does your list of obstacles include any of the points made by Slee?

By now, you should be aware that there are far more differences in opinions on what inclusion should look like than almost any other area of professional focus. You may also have encountered in school issues caused when different stakeholders hold very different views about the education of a single pupil. This makes practical implementation a great deal more difficult than many other policy requirements (Essex et al., 2021).

TEACHERS' CONCERNS ABOUT INCLUSION

The most immediate challenge that many ECTs report is uncertainty about how to meet the learning needs of a very diverse group of learners. Despite their commitment to the principles of inclusion, the majority report practical difficulties and a concern that there is a 'price to be paid' for inclusion. One of these is that the 'less able' pupils will impede the progress of the 'more able' (Essex at al., 2021). This is an especial pressure when ECTs are so conscious of the need to 'cover the curriculum'. They also reported that inclusion creates additional work at the point of planning their lesson. A major issue that emerged during one study was that ECTs harboured quite a 'medical' notion of diversity and thought that they needed to develop strategies for teaching pupils with each named diversity characteristic in order to know how to teach future pupils with the same characteristic. ECTs commonly identified a boundary of cognitive capacity below which they felt pupils should be removed from mainstream provision. This boundary appeared to be associated with the limits of their confidence in their own ability to teach very diverse learners, rather than the entitlement or otherwise of the very atypical pupils (Essex et al., 2021). For this reason, it is vital that trainees and ECTs identify common strategies that will benefit all learners, irrespective of their characteristics.

Beyond those immediate concerns, either your experience in schools or reading about EHCPs may have suggested that inclusion can have significant resourcing implications. Common 'costs' of inclusion are additional staff time, and possibly additional staff, and specialist equipment. Any additional financial costs beyond the routine provision for pupils with SEND, for which funding is provided, can be accessed through the EHCP. One criticism of the current system is the length of time that it can take to complete the EHCP process, meaning that the pupil has to wait for support, or the school may need to pay out of its own budget for support until the process is concluded. The administrative burden of co-ordinating support has shifted away from local authorities and into schools and created the need to appoint SEND co-ordinators who will undertake the administration. This leads to some staff questioning the justice of the way in which funding is allocated and that inclusion 'robs Peter to pay Paul'.

Teachers quite commonly (though wrongly) believe that teaching pupils with very varying levels of prior attainment reduces the learning of the most academically capable. This creates a great deal of pressure on them, knowing that they are judged, at least in part, by the academic success of their pupils. Inclusion can certainly make greater organisational demands of teachers but can also provide a powerful stimulus to pupils' development, including in non-assessed areas such as social awareness, empathy and respect. (It can also provide a stimulus to teachers to develop their classroom practice.) To mediate the curriculum for diverse learners requires a deep understanding of what is being taught, and this may require attention for inexperienced teachers. However, enhancing knowledge of one's teaching subject has to be of benefit to all pupils. Analysis of the attainment of 500,000 pupils led to the conclusion that there is no evidence that teaching diverse pupils together causes a reduction in individual academic attainment. Indeed, inclusion can enhance the attainment of those with SEN who might otherwise have been expected to do worst. Teachers and pupils also reported that inclusion could positively affect the wider achievements, such as social skills and empathy, of all pupils (Dyson et al., 2004). This is not to say that simply placing different pupils together will be successful but that with active management it is possible to create circumstances in which high academic attainment is compatible with full inclusion.

> ### REFLECTION POINT
>
> - What do you see as the most important outcomes for pupils, including both academic and other outcomes?
> - List four or five that you view as a priority. For each outcome, consider whether, in your opinion, inclusion enhances development in that area, detracts from development or has no net effect.
> - Based on this impressionistic analysis, do you think that inclusion can be argued to enhance the effectiveness of schools?

PEDAGOGY FOR INCLUSION

The very good news, at a point when teachers are having to assimilate so many new ideas and practical strategies, is that to teach inclusively is simply to teach very effectively. Despite comments, including in policy documents, about 'teaching for [name of disability]', teaching inclusively means that you are using effective teaching strategies in ways that enhance learning by those most likely to struggle (Davis et al., 2004). For instance you would be planning in any case but to be inclusive you need to plan for the very logical development of concepts with the links between different concepts articulated. Likewise, you might well be building in time for reflection and the rehearsal of new material anyway but now you are doing it in the understanding that some pupils need longer to process and understand fully than others. Some adjustments will be technical, but these are not specific to a diagnosis, rather they are specific to the functional support needs of a pupil. For example, if a pupil prefers to use, or can write more using, digital or assistive technology, you will need to plan for its effective use during your lesson. If you recognise that a pupil needs slightly longer to recall answers than their peers, you need to build in a longer pause than you might otherwise do between posing the question and asking for a response. But this type of responsive teaching is not 'specialist teaching for a disability'; it is specialist teaching for that specific pupil.

The first two recommendations consider the interpersonal dimension of teaching.

- Get to know the pupils as individuals so that you can tailor challenge and support to their capacities and needs, as well as their personal preferences and interests. Knowing the pupils will enable you to provide the flexible and responsive teaching that is at the heart of genuinely inclusive teaching (European Agency for Development in Special Needs Education, 2012).
- Set high expectations. Setting challenging but achievable learning goals signals high expectations, which raise achievement. However, it is important that support equal to the challenge is available. This includes frequent monitoring and feedback and offering reassurance to those who lack self-confidence in their ability (European Agency for Development in Special Needs Education, 2012).

What follows considers approaches to teaching and assessment that evidence suggests are effective, though some of these have a better evidence base upon which to base their recommendation, but all have shown signs of being promising (Education Endowment Foundation, 2018). However, only you, based on your growing experience, can judge whether, and how, to introduce them in your teaching context. Similarly, only you can judge their effectiveness with the pupils that you teach, and it is for this reason that the most important feature of effective inclusion is the 'disposition' of the teacher. This means that they hold and enact certain principles. A study conducted by the European Agency for Development in Special Needs Education (2012: 11) summarises the dispositions of an inclusive teacher as:

1. valuing learner diversity – learner difference is considered as a resource and an asset to education;
2. supporting all learners – teachers have high expectations for all learners' achievements;
3. working with others – collaboration and teamwork are essential approaches for all teachers;
4. continuing personal professional development – teaching is a learning activity and teachers take responsibility for their own lifelong learning.

From this you will see that while there are technical aspects of teaching in which you will need to develop, much of effective inclusion involves how you view and respond to diversity. Achieving an awareness of your own position on diversity requires reflection and is not something that you can be trained for. The practical steps set out opposite will be much more powerful if used in combination with ongoing reflection and revisions in your practice. The steps that you can take are considered in three groups: curriculum and assessment, (whole class) teaching strategies and differentiation.

CURRICULUM AND ASSESSMENT

Although a trainee or ECT is unlikely to be able to change the curriculum they are delivering, and can only modify internal assessments, you need to be aware of the degree to which both curriculum and assessment can be exclusionary. It is questionable whether a common curriculum, originally intended to provide a basic entitlement for all, is appropriate for a very diverse pupil body (McGinnis, 2013). In order to ensure that you are able to structure the learning well, you need to know the subject material well. In a report on how to enhance learning, Ofsted (2021) noted:

> *This again shows how important it is that teachers, TAs and SENCos have strong subject knowledge. With this, they can understand how best to develop and teach the curriculum to support pupils with SEND.*

A secure understanding of curriculum content, and the relationship between the different concepts and content, enables teachers to break down the curriculum strategically. A secure understanding lets them understand how the smaller 'chunks' are interrelated and to devise a carefully planned sequence. This is the basis of approaches such as 'mastery learning' for example, in which pupils have to show that they have mastered one chunk before moving on to new material. Secure subject knowledge also enables the teacher to choose what could best be left out, without loss of the core sense of the subject (Walshaw, 2012). Finally, a deep and analytical understanding of the demands of the subject material enables you to plan for a gradualised increase in conceptual demand, the learning equivalent of an uphill ramp.

Although diverse pupils can be very anxious about assessment, fearing further failure and the consequences, frequent feedback is an effective tool to enhance learning (Education Endowment Foundation, 2018) and especially so for diverse pupils. These two apparently contradictory statements can be reconciled by the use of formative assessment, sometimes called 'feedback that feeds forward', in other words assessment that constructively guides future learning and teaching. It does not need to be formal and can take the form of listening to a discussion or observing pupils undertaking a task. It can take the form of showing pupils what success in a task looks like, for instance by showing examples of good work or asking them to self-assess against shared criteria (McGinnis, 2013). Some of the attractions of formative assessment is that it gives pupils insight into how to improve, gives them agency in their own learning and facilitates metacognition (changing learning by actively thinking about learning). It is beneficial if assessment can recognise and reward different kinds of achievement. Many diverse learners have less prior learning and may be less able to recall what they have learnt before, so always praising pupils who remember well can be demoralising. By considering skills, subject specific and transferable, and personal qualities applied to the learning task, you create more opportunities for success by diverse learners.

9 Teaching for inclusion

In relation to your own development, try to identify what sources of support you would like to enhance your practice in your teaching subjects and where these might come from. Remember to consider colleagues' expertise, professional associations, subject associations, exam boards if relevant, independent reading and research, along with reflection on your own experiences as potential sources of help.

TEACHING STRATEGIES

There are many mechanisms by which teachers can enhance learning by all pupils. Some of these are likely to be disproportionately helpful to pupils with functional difficulties that impact on learning. Strategies that are especially helpful for pupils with learning difficulties (specific or global) are:

- Multi-modal (multi-sensory) learning, which is simply using more than one modality to represent key ideas, for instance displaying key terms and having an illustration representing what these terms mean. Hands-on ('haptic') learning is an especially powerful way to help understanding and assist with later recall.

- Metacognition (changing learning by actively thinking about learning) is considered a high-impact intervention and whose use is supported by an extensive body of knowledge (Education Endowment Foundation, 2018). By enhancing active and explicit thinking, for example by asking 'How do you know that?' or 'What made you choose that answer?' you encourage the active processing of information. This enhances understanding of material. This strategy benefits all learners, but the process of articulating their thinking is especially helpful for neuro-diverse pupils.

- Use grouping to enhance learning and by altering groups regularly so that pupils benefit from taking different roles and working in different groups and roles (Dyson et al., 2004). Collaborative learning enables wider sharing of ideas and skills, by SEND pupils as well as others, and is very high impact in terms of enhancing learning (Education Endowment Foundation, 2018). Do not assume that this is a back door means of getting additional help to those who are lower academic achievers, although it may facilitate the provision of peer support. For example, many of the 'low achievers' ask very perceptive questions that can usefully challenge the so-called 'high fliers'. (Be aware that pupils with social difficulties may need additional support with group work and it may be better to let them choose at least one member of their group, at least to begin with.)

Two strategies that will be helpful specifically for pupils with learning difficulties, but which will not disadvantage others, are:

- Allow ample time for reflection. This is the most frequent piece of advice that experienced teachers of SEN pupils say that they wish they had known at the start of their career. Allowing slightly longer for pupils to answer, possibly having given them advance notice of the question before you ask it, enables pupils with learning difficulties time to formulate their best response (McGinnis, 2013).

- Create opportunities for repetition of key ideas and terms. This is not to say that you should regularly teach the same material in the same way multiple times, though you should be willing to repeat teaching if there is evidence that there is a general difficulty in understanding. What I am suggesting should happen routinely is that you should link new learning back explicitly to previous learning.

The way in which we intentionally provide different pupils with different educational experiences is often seen as a way of accommodating diverse learning needs in one classroom – previously this would have been referred to as differentiation although it is part of the wider term of adaptive teaching you will see through your training and teaching. One study of ECTs found that they considered differentiation was a way of optimising knowledge transfer from the teacher to the pupils (Essex et al., 2021). Three broad categories of differentiation are recognised and this description groups strategies under the headings of differentiation by outcome, differentiation by task and differentiation by support. Combinations of these approaches can be used as well.

1. differentiation by outcome

This is probably the oldest form of differentiation, whereby a common task is set, such as a test, and pupils vary in their attainment. Formative assessment can also provide differentiation by outcome but, since the purpose is to guide future learning, can be less demoralising than a bad mark for a test. Pupils with learning difficulties are very easily deterred by failure and so it is helpful to ensure that everyone can achieve some level of success, even if the aim of the task is to identify varying bands of attainment.

2. by task

This may involve differentiating the amount of material that pupils are asked to engage with but should not mean that previously low-attaining pupils are given the least demanding and least interesting tasks. This can communicate low expectations, which depresses attainment. One way to differentiate by task in a non-judgemental way is to offer a choice of activities that offer equivalent learning outcomes.

3. by support

This can take the form of varying levels of prompts, as may be provided by writing frames or visual organisers. It can take the form of greater or lesser amounts of feedback. Quite commonly it is provided by assigning a support worker, who may be called a teaching assistant (TA) or Pupil Support Worker (PSW), to work with those pupils identified as needing support. The degree of support that is needed to successfully complete a task provides a mechanism for assessing learning; the less support needed, the more secure the learning.

The use of support workers, although widespread and certainly easing classroom management pressures upon teachers, is far from unproblematic. Evidence suggests that support has a moderate impact on learning for moderate costs (Education Endowment Foundation, 2018). One study showed that support workers actually depressed the attainment of pupils (Blatchford et al., 2009). This appears to be because the support workers, in order to prevent pupils getting into trouble with the teacher, 'mask' functional difficulties, such as by doing transcription for pupils who struggle to write the expected amount of text. Although this solves the acute practical needs of the pupil, it does not tackle the underlying issue and the pupil misses out on full engagement with the material that was being written down. Meanwhile the teacher does not realise the extent of the difficulties and so can be deprived of the stimulus to look at alternative means of generating a record of the material. For example, could they annotate a printed copy of the material instead of writing the text down? The best way to avoid this potential problem is to liaise with the support worker about the intended learning and how it will be delivered, by email if in-person meetings are difficult to arrange. This is ideally done before and after each lesson, but at least weekly, to identify difficulties as they arise and to confer on adjustments as the need arises.

CASE STUDY

Jonathan

Jonathan was on his first placement in school. He was given a number of classes that were grouped by ability and on his timetable had two Year 9 classes - a set 2 and set 5 - and was told that he should plan the same lesson for both in order to reduce planning time. Raksha was on placement in the same school and her mentor expected her to have two different lesson plans for different sets in the same year group. They discussed this on their journey to school and they could see there was probably some middle ground that would allow them to plan to meet the needs of each of the classes without full duplication.

- Of the practical strategies suggested, which ones have you used and found most successful so far?

- What support would you need to trial some of the other suggestions that you have not deployed so far?

ASSIGNMENT LINKS

University assignments often ask you to explore how you meet individual needs. This chapter will provide some rationale for that. Subject-specific literature should also be explored.

LEARNING AND CONSOLIDATION ACTIVITIES
IDEAS FOR GUIDED PRACTICE AND FEEDBACK

When observing lessons focus on how individual needs are being met – this is also worth exploring at the planning stage.

Ensure you meet with the SENCO within the school to better understand how they are providing support for pupils.

It is worth considering how you will make use of teaching assistants within the classroom (see also Chapter 8).

CHAPTER SUMMARY

Now you have read this chapter, you will have learnt:

- how current ways of thinking about diverse learners have arisen and how they will affect your work as an ECT
- to identify the ways in which your school and wider organisations contribute to the achievement of inclusive education
- ways in which you can ensure that diverse learners are able to participate fully and succeed in your lessons.

FURTHER READING

National Association for Special Educational Needs (NASEN) website: www.nasen.org.uk offers a wide range of resources relating to SEN, held in a searchable database.

Hodkinson, A. (2019) *Key Issues in Special Educational Needs, Disability and Inclusion* (3rd edn). SAGE. This book offers accessible and trainee-focused information around contextualising SEND.

Centre for Studies on Inclusive Education (2011) *Index for Inclusion*. Available at: www.csie.org.uk/resources/inclusion-index-explained.shtml. The *Index for Inclusion* is a set of materials to guide schools through a process of inclusive school development. It is about building supportive communities and fostering high achievement for all staff and pupils.

REFERENCES

Blatchford, P., Bassett, P., Brown, P., Martin, C., Russell, A. and Webster, R. (2009) Deployment and impact of support staff in schools: characteristics, working conditions and job satisfaction of support staff in schools. Available at: http://eprints.uwe.ac.uk/12342/

Bronfenbrenner, U. (1977) Toward an experimental ecology of human development. *American psychologist*, *32*(7): 513.

Children and Families Act (2014).

Children's Commissioner (2022) Beyond the labels: A SEND system which works for every child, every time. Available at: www.childrenscommissioner.gov.uk/report/a-send-system-which-works-for-every-child-every-time/

Davis, P., Florian, L., Ainscow, M., Dyson, A., Farrell, P., Hick, P. and Rouse, M. (2004) Teaching strategies and approaches for pupils with special educational needs: a scoping study. Available at: http://dera.ioe.ac.uk/6059/1/RR516.pdf

DfE (2022) *SEND Review: Right Support, Right Place, Right Time*. Available at: www.gov.uk/government/consultations/send-review-right-support-right-place-right-time

Department for Education and Department of Health and Social Care (2014) *SEND Code of Practice: 0 to 25 Years*. Available at: www.gov.uk/government/publications/send-code-of-practice-0-to-25

DfE and DfH (2015) *Special Educational Needs and Disability Code of Practice: 0 to 25 Years. Statutory guidance for organisations which work with and support children and young people who have special educational needs or disabilities.*

Dyson, A., Farrell, P., Polat, F., Hutcheson, G. and Gallannaugh, F. (2004) Inclusion and pupil Achievement. Department for Education and Skills. Available at: https://www.gov.uk/government/organisations/department-for-education/about/research

Education Endowment Foundation (2018) Sutton Trust-Education Endowment Foundation teaching and learning toolkit: Available at: https://educationendowmentfoundation.org.uk/evidence-summaries/teaching-learning-toolkit

Equalities Act (2010).

Essex, J., Alexiadou, N. and Zwozdiak-Myers, P. (2021) Understanding inclusion in teacher education – a view from student teachers in England. *International Journal of Inclusive Education*, *25*(12): 1425–1442. DOI: 10.1080/13603116.2019.1614232

European Agency for Development in Special Needs Education (2012) Teacher education for inclusion (TE41): profile of inclusive teachers. Available at: www.unicef.org//albania/reports/teacher-education-inclusion-te41

Fricker, M. (2007) *Epistemic Injustice: Power and the Ethics of Knowing*. Oxford University Press.

Göransson, K. and Nilholm, C. (2014) Conceptual diversities and empirical shortcomings – a critical analysis of research on inclusive education. *European Journal of Special Needs Education*, *29*(3): 265–280.

MacKay, G. (2002) The disappearance of disability? Thoughts on a changing culture. *British Journal of Special Education*, *29*(4) (December 2002): 159–163.

McGinnis J.R. (2013) Teaching science to learners with special needs. *Theory Into Practice*, *52*(1): 43–50. DOI: 10.1080/07351690.2013.743776

Ofsted (2021) *Supporting SEND: How Children and Young People's Special Educational Needs (SEN) Are Met in Mainstream Schools*. Available at: www.gov.uk/government/publications/supporting-send

Schuelka, M.J. (2018) Implementing inclusive education. *K4D Helpdesk Report*. Brighton, UK: Institute of Development Studies.

Scotch, R.K. and Schriner, K. (1997) Disability as human variation: implications for policy. *Annals of the American Academy of Political and Social Science*, *459*(1). DOI: 10.1177/0002716297549001011

Slee, R. (2019) Belonging in an age of exclusion. *International Journal of Inclusive Education*, *23*(9): 909–922. DOI: 10.1080/13603116.2019.1602366

Walshaw, M. (2012) Teacher knowledge as fundamental to effective teaching practice. *Journal of Mathematics Teacher Education*, *15*: 181–185. DOI: 10.1007/s10857-012-9217-0

Warnock Report (1978) *Special Educational Needs. Report of the Committee of Enquiry into the Education of Handicapped Children and Young People*. London: Her Majesty's Stationery Office.

10

DEVELOPING EFFECTIVE ASSESSMENT

ANDREW CHANDLER-GREVATT AND CHARLOTTE SAWYER

 KEY WORDS

- Assessment
- Formative
- Summative

CHAPTER OBJECTIVES

In this chapter we explore the challenges of using assessment effectively using examples, reflective questions and case studies to support your thinking. This chapter aims to start you on your journey of developing your assessment practice. In doing that we explore the purposes of summative and formative assessment. Then we encourage you to observe other teachers doing assessment in their lessons with suggestions of what to look for and a framework within which to analyse how assessment is used in the lesson. Effective assessment requires us to engage with recognising pupil progress from their work or tests, so they allow us to make valid and reliable inferences about this. We explore these concepts and consider the policy, practice and theory of pupil progress. Next, we support you in planning for assessment in your own lessons and using assessment strategies effectively while teaching, with a focus on developing good questioning skills. Then we consider how to give effective feedback and opportunities for pupils to respond to that feedback. Finally, we consider how to mark your pupils' work efficiently, balancing the impact with workload.

10 Developing effective assessment

> ### ■■■— LINKS TO THE CORE CONTENT FRAMEWORK
>
> All of the Core Content Framework themes are referred to and applied in this chapter, but the following are the most relevant:
>
> Standard 1 – Set high expectations
>
> 3. Teacher expectations can affect pupil outcomes; setting goals that challenge and stretch pupils is essential.
>
> Standard 2 – Promote good progress
>
> 2. Prior knowledge plays an important role in how pupils learn; committing some key facts to their long-term memory is likely to help pupils learn more complex ideas.
>
> Standard 6 – Make accurate and productive use of assessment
>
> 1. Effective assessment is critical to teaching because it provides teachers with information about pupils' understanding and needs.
> 2. Good assessment helps teachers avoid being over-influenced by potentially misleading factors, such as how busy pupils appear.
> 3. Before using any assessment, teachers should be clear about the decision it will be used to support and be able to justify its use.
> 4. To be of value, teachers use information from assessments to inform the decisions they make; in turn, pupils must be able to act on feedback for it to have an effect.
> 5. High-quality feedback can be written or verbal; it is likely to be accurate and clear, encourage further effort and provide specific guidance on how to improve.
> 6. Over time, feedback should support pupils to monitor and regulate their own learning.
> 7. Working with colleagues to identify efficient approaches to assessment is important; assessment can become onerous and have a disproportionate impact on workload.

WHY IS ASSESSMENT IMPORTANT?

When we use the word *assessment* at school, we often think of tests and examinations. However, these are only part of assessment processes in schools. Teachers use a set of practices as part of their everyday teaching toolkit to assess and make decisions about their pupils' learning and next steps in teaching. These practices include skilful questioning strategies, applying an understanding of progress within their subject, using feedback meaningfully and deciding on appropriate interventions to improve learning. In fact, this everyday assessment is far more important for improving pupil outcomes than the tests and examinations themselves.

The purpose of examinations in the secondary school context are to understand prior learning (in England pupils take national examinations, Standard Attainment Tests (SATs) in English and maths at Key Stage 2) and to assess their GCSE (in England) qualification (or A levels, T levels, etc.) and assign a grade (you can read more about accountability in Chapter 12). Assessment also has an important function in qualifications, where examinations are designed to assess knowledge, understanding and skills that informs employers and further education and higher education institutions on the pupil's educational attainment and whether they are suited to the next step in their education or career.

In general, assessment has a multitude of purposes and Newton (2007) identified at least 18 of them. It is worth thinking about how many you can identify as you work with more experienced teachers. When trainees start out the most relevant purposes of assessment are to:

- plan for teaching, based on prior assessment data;
- support and adapt learning, through diagnostic and formative strategies;
- understand attainment, through tests and examinations.

The purposes of classroom assessment include establishing prior knowledge, diagnosing misunderstanding, knowledge gaps and misconceptions, checking that blocks of knowledge or a concept has been learnt and understood before moving on through retrieval practice, and low-stakes tests to assess units of learning. Note, we avoid using the term *Teacher Assessment* in this context, because it has a specific meaning within the examination system (Newton, 2021).

In teaching it is rare that what you have taught will be perfectly understood by your pupils. Classroom assessment is the regular checking of to what extent what a teacher has taught is what the pupil now understands, challenging misconceptions and often adapting teaching to close any gap.

Although the purposes of assessment in your everyday teaching can be well defined, note that changes in the wider context can shift that focus. Changes in assessment policy have knock-on effects on what is taught, how often and when, within subjects, as well as which specific subjects are taught. This is known as the washback effect (Elshawa et al., 2016). The purpose of assessments, particularly examinations such as SATs, GCSEs and A levels, change. What is valued and therefore assessed is often based on political ideologies (e.g. Chandler-Grevatt, 2021; Torrance, 2018).

USES OF ASSESSMENT

There are two main uses of classroom assessment: summative and formative. Summative is usually in the form of a test or an examination that gives an outcome in the form of a score, percentage or grade. Formative assessment is focused instead on the process of learning, rather than the outcome. There are assessment strategies that are more suited to either summative or formative purposes, as we will see shortly.

SUMMATIVE ASSESSMENT

Summative assessment is what we traditionally associate with schooling. This is usually made up of school-based tests to check knowledge and understanding during school and external formal examinations to gain a qualification, such as a GCSE. It often occurs at an end point of a unit, course or key stage, giving an indication of attainment or achievement in a given topic or subject. In most cases pupils receive a raw score, percentage or grade. This can be used to infer how well a pupil has learnt and understood the material in a particular term, topic or qualification. External examinations such as GCSEs use a ranking method to assign grades, so that for a given cohort, a pupil with a grade 9 has done better than a pupil with a grade 4.

FORMATIVE ASSESSMENT

Formative assessment has been researched for many years (e.g. Sadler, 1989), but in the classroom it has been a focus for teachers and policy makers since the seminal research by Black and Wiliam (1998). They investigated how teachers used classroom assessment and argued that it was too focused on outcomes (summative purposes) and by focusing on improving processes of learning (formative purposes) would improve pupil outcomes. During learning, formative judgements are made, feedback given, and the pupil responds to that feedback with the aim of improving learning and eventually their attainment. Versions of Black and Wiliam's ideas were adopted by governments that recommended (or prescribed) strategies for use within schools. In England it was called Assessment for Learning (AfL), a term you may hear used as a reference to formative assessment. The key messages and strategies from *Working inside the Black Box* (Black et al., 2004) are worth reading as a foundation of any study on classroom assessment.

Some subjects, particularly maths, use a *mastery* approach to learning that employs the principles of formative assessment. The teaching has a particular approach of modelling, exemplifying and practice followed by a low-stakes test. The percentage scored (usually 80 per cent) is used to decide if the class has reached a threshold to continue with the next block of learning (Drury, 2018).

Good formative assessment relies on teachers developing not only a set of strategies to use but developing a *formative mindset*. This means that the teachers' (and their pupils') beliefs about assessment, attitudes towards assessment and the practices they use embrace the principles of formative assessment (Chandler-Grevatt, 2018). Embedding formative assessment into lessons takes time and is easier when a whole school approach is taken (Speckesser et al., 2018).

> ### ▪▫▫ REFLECTION POINT
>
> What kind of assessment takes place in your placement?
>
> - Does the school have an assessment policy?
> - Does your department have an assessment policy? How is it linked to the school policy?
> - How are pupils assessed in each year group?
> - How often are pupils assessed in each year group?
> - How is formative assessment used?
> - At what point do pupils start being prepared for their qualification examinations (GCSEs, A levels, etc.)?

WHAT DOES ASSESSMENT LOOK LIKE?

When experienced teachers use assessment in the classroom, it can be hard to see because the practices involved have been developed until they become tacit and somewhat invisible to an observer. Here are some practices to look for and some tips for understanding classroom assessment strategies so you can start developing the skills yourself.

STRATEGIES TO LOOK FOR

Asking questions. There are many techniques used, but they all involve the teacher posing a question and a pupil or pupils answering it. Teachers use verbal questioning to understand what pupils understand. Written questions are often displayed on the board, already in textbooks or on a worksheet for pupils to respond to, usually in writing.

Eliciting and challenging misconceptions. Misconceptions are ideas that pupils hold that are different to that expected by the subject. There are common misconceptions, e.g. the Sun orbits the Earth, which pupils bring with them from previous experiences. Teachers take opportunities to diagnose any common misconceptions, then challenge them. Teachers often monitor for misconceptions while they circulate during pupil-centred activities (see Chapter 6 on planning).

Low-stakes testing. Pupils are often given low-stakes tests like five retrieval questions at the start of the lesson. Not only does this assess what they have remembered, but the action of testing also helps retain knowledge in the long-term memory. Teachers often encourage pupils to make self-tests to help learn new material.

Self- and peer-assessment. This type of assessment engages pupils with the assessment of their own work (self-assessment) or that of other pupils in the class (peer-assessment). This type of activity requires structures and supports to start with, but once pupils get into a routine, they can use success criteria to make assessments about their achievements in a given activity.

Tests. Subject-based tests take place regularly. Sometimes this will be on an online digital platform, other times it will be a traditional paper style test. Some subjects have practical tests as well. Tests usually assess a topic as a whole and have a summative purpose.

HOW TO LOOK FOR ASSESSMENT IN ACTION

With formative assessment strategies there are three main stages of the assessment process, sometimes seen as a cycle. It is summarised as:

- Where am I now? What pupils know now.
- Where do I need to get to? A shared learning goal (where they are going).
- How do I get there? Next steps in learning (interventions to meet that goal).

When observing or planning an assessment activity, you can ask yourself these key questions:

- *What?* What body of knowledge or application of skills is going to be assessed at this particular time?
- *How?* Select your assessment strategy so that you can draw valid inferences from the outcome. Think carefully about your assessment tasks; can they provide valuable feedback about student learning specific to your subject? What does progress look like in your subject? What domain-specific knowledge, skills or language will they need to show? It can be useful to write your own mark scheme or success criteria, to keep you on track as you are planning the assessment.
- *Why?* Is it to inform next steps, checking for understanding, to plan the next lesson, feeding into the next scheme of learning? Or is it a summative assessment to capture end of term or end of year grades? What are you going to be doing with the results of this particular assessment and is it likely to link back to how you are going to assess?

Use the questions below as a guide to the types of assessment activities you may observe in lessons. For each one apply the What? How? Why? questions when you see it used in context. Think about how you can integrate this thinking into the planning stage of your lessons.

10 Developing effective assessment

▬■■■▬ REFLECTION POINT

Observing teachers using assessment in the classroom. Can you identify the What/How/Why in their assessment? After the lesson, deconstruct and discuss the questions with the teacher.

Think about each of the questions from three perspectives:

- assessment of the whole class
- assessment of groups of pupils
- assessment of individual pupils.

How does the teacher:

- share any learning objectives?
- communicate expectations of learning or success criteria?
- establish prior knowledge?
- elicit and address misconceptions?

Questioning – verbal

- What types of questions does the teacher use? (open, closed, hinge, multiple choice, see section below)
- What are the expectations for answering? (immediate, think-pair-share, thinking time)
- What is the approach to getting answers? (hands up, no hands up, mini whiteboards)
- How does the teacher respond to incorrect or incomplete answers?
- How does the teacher encourage pupils to elaborate their answer?

Questioning – written

- Does the teacher provide written questions to answer?
- How are these questions presented?
- What are the expectations for answering them?
- How does the teacher monitor pupil responses during the lesson?
- How does the teacher use the questions for assessing pupils' knowledge, understanding or skills?

(Continued)

Feedback strategies

- How does the teacher feedback?
- What strategies are used to provide verbal or written feedback?
- What does the teacher feedback upon? (learning behaviours, task completion, misconceptions, use of literacy, use of maths, approach to tackling learning)

CHALLENGES OF ASSESSING LEARNING

Teachers do try to really grasp what their pupils know, understand and can do; however, this relies on a proxy because we cannot see directly into the minds of the pupils. These proxies are usually observing what a pupil can say, write or do, but they can be problematic because what often seems to be an indicator for learning are often poor proxies.

■ ■ ■ — POOR PROXIES FOR LEARNING

- Engagement or doing tasks
- Neat writing, lots of writing
- Completing tasks quickly
- Confidence (over competence) when getting involved
- Repeating answers without context (rote learning)
- Enthusiasm (over competence) in practical activities e.g. sport, drama, science, art
- Working silently or lots of talk

(adapted from Coe, 2013)

Exactly what good proxies for learning are varies depending on the subject you teach. However, they may include:

- Retrieval of knowledge (at different intervals of time: within lesson, next lesson, next week). This is better within a context, where knowledge in a topic is built up, making connections to previous knowledge.
- Answering questions (recalling, retrieval) without cues or prompts.
- Comparing new knowledge to prior knowledge (e.g. comparing the meaning of a new key word to a previously learnt key word). In science diffusion compared to osmosis, in history significance compared to causation.

- Applying concepts to new examples or situations.

Based on a review of academic literature, Coe (2013) suggests that there is a high chance of learning taking place if pupils are made to think when teachers plan to:

- explain what the pupils should do;
- demonstrate it;
- get pupils to do it (with gradually reducing support);
- provide feedback;
- get them to practise until it is secure;
- assess their skill/understanding.

Some of these can be observed within a lesson, though how much we can infer that pupils have learnt within a lesson is contested. Classroom assessment is focused on checking, correcting and intervening as required as new knowledge is taught. In the longer term, the content of the lessons taught can be assessed more synoptically. This is when pupils have the opportunity to bring knowledge and concepts together and demonstrate how they are connected or how they be applied. This can often be done with a task that allows pupils to bring these concepts together, but more often it is assessed by way of questions in a test or examination.

It is impossible to assess everything a pupil knows or how well they know it. Even in formal written examinations we only can check, by proxy, a sample of what a pupil knows of an exam specification.

INFERENCE, VALIDITY AND RELIABILITY

As a teacher, we are making *inferences* (conclusions that we draw based upon evidence and reasoning) from pupils' responses to our assessment strategies, be it spoken questions, written questions or responses to other tasks using a set of knowledge, understanding and skills. The inferences we make are subject to the concepts of *validity* and *reliability* (Wiliam, 2017).

Kime (2017a) describes validity in two ways:

- the ability of the assessment to test what it intends to measure;
- the ability of the assessment to provide information that is both valuable and appropriate for the intended purpose.

In short, does the assessment measure what we think and need it to measure?

Kime (2017b) also states that *There are lots of factors which contribute to the reliability of an assessment*, but two of the most critical for teachers to acknowledge are:

- the precision of the questions and tasks used in prompting students' responses;
- the accuracy and consistency of the interpretations derived from assessment responses.

These terms support us in determining how confident we are with an assessment we have made about a pupils' knowledge, understanding or skills (Black, 2002). If we think about an examination such as a GCSE, it has been carefully constructed to test a number of areas across the specification and should have high validity and reliability. Let's consider this in the context of school examinations.

Exams are seen as being objective, statistically sound and therefore reliable in the scores that are provided. Writing exam questions and constructing exam papers is a highly skilled job and it is often not until pupils sit the exam that grading boundaries can be applied based on statistical judgements (Harlen, 2007). Despite the best efforts, there will be variability within (e.g. marking errors) and between examinations (e.g. variation in pupils on the day of the exam) that can reduce reliability. However, we infer that pupils who gain GCSE grade 5 in particular subjects have enough knowledge to take on the next level of study, such as A levels. This is seen as a valid use of the grades. Though it would not be valid to infer that every pupil starting that A level subject would have the same prior knowledge of the entire GCSE specification because they were only tested on a sample of areas.

In topic tests or assessments used in school, this can be even more problematic, particularly if the test is constructed by teachers with little knowledge of designing tests. It is better to use existing, authenticated tests; however, even then it is not valid to infer that pupils know everything they have been taught based on a high grade. Christodoulou (2017), who discusses these issues in detail, concludes that there is little that can be reliably inferred from a topic test and suggests alternative ways of assessing. To consider a practical example, read the below case study.

CASE STUDY

Assessing Make or Bake Tasks

Even though some assessment activities seem engaging, they are not suited to all subjects. Charlotte explains how using a make or bake task for history can be difficult to assess.

In the past I have been asked to get students to complete a 'make or bake' task based on their learning of the Battle of Hastings. The task set as homework is to make (a model or diorama) or bake (usually a decorated cake) a scene that the pupils had learnt from their lesson.

10 Developing effective assessment

I had some wonderful cakes produced showing Harold Godwinson with an arrow in his eye, alongside some rather questionable cardboard boxes with roughly cut crenulations. Applying the What? How? Why? assessment questions, it is clear that this task does not tell me about what my students have understood about this period of English history.

What am I actually assessing? The make or bake is not allowing the pupils to show what they understand about the Battle of Hastings. So the *How?* is an inappropriate task, I cannot make valid inferences about learning of history from the outcome or give meaningful feedback. So the question *Why?*; well, because someone thought it would be fun.

However, applying the same questions to a task for design and technology, the making could be assessed meaningfully or a food technology teacher could apply appropriate learning objectives to be assessed by the baking task.

- What are the advantages of using the 'make or bake' homework as an assessment activity?
- What are the limitations?
- Would it work in your subject? How would you assess it?
- What inferences about learning objectives could you make from this activity?

PERSPECTIVES ON PROGRESS

Progress is a term used in policy and practice in England relating to the attainment of pupils. What it actually means in policy, practice and theory can be problematic. In this section we explore *progress* from these three perspectives.

PROGRESS IN POLICY

When you read the Teachers' Standards (DfE, 2021), progress is mentioned some 14 times; it's clear teachers have a responsibility for ensuring progress of their pupils. When looking at current policy, progress is often framed with other terms, 'attainment' and 'curriculum'. For example, Ofsted (2019) state that:

> *If pupils attain within a well-sequenced, well-constructed curriculum, they are making progress.*

This is within the context of a lesson or a series of lessons and is often inferred through qualitative evidence, such as how well pupils can answer questions using the expected vocabulary, or the work they produce against a particular outcome, how well they can articulate their thinking. Progress is also quantified in accountability measures – with quantitative evidence being focused more on test scores and assessment marks and what we might think of as hard data. Schools are judged based on the *Progress 8* and *Attainment 8* calculations and compared to other schools in league tables (DfE, 2014, 2019). In this context, these are the definitions:

> *Attainment: the academic standard that pupils reach in, for example, assessments and exams. It's usually recorded as grades, scores or levels, and it indicates a pupil's result at the end of a key stage (KS).*
>
> *Progress: pupils' achievements over a period of time, for example from KS2 to KS4. It's the difference between pupils' previous attainment and current attainment. When measuring a pupil's progress, the DfE also takes into account the progress of pupils with similar starting points.*

Therefore, in policy terms, progress can be talked about in the context of classroom assessment, which is often a qualitative judgement, and also using quantitative measures to make judgements about schools. In both cases, it is in the context of attainment within the curriculum.

PROGRESS IN PRACTICE

Consider teaching a class being taught a lesson mid-way through a topic. At the end of the lesson, your mentor asks you what progress the class has made. What could you say meaningfully about progress? What inferences can you make? With your mentor or peers, discuss the good proxies for learning. Look at these suggestions below and think about which of these are indicators of progress.

- The class really enjoyed the lesson, they were really engaged, keen to answer my questions and chatting about the work.

- The starter activity of retrieval practice showed me that most pupils remembered the key concepts from the previous lessons. Emily and Raj had misconceptions, which I challenged through questioning.

- I planned the lesson so that I could explain the concept, modelling it using questions, gave pupils a chance to practise it and apply it to a new example. By checking their understanding through questions, I could correct Iesha's misunderstanding of the model. Rik's table had trouble getting started on the practise questions but got going once prompted.

- Stuart and Brunilda finished the practise tasks quickly and moved onto the independent task ahead of the others.

- In the mini whiteboard activity I used to check progress, only about half the group gave the correct answers to the three key questions. At the end of the lesson, most of the class could answer those three questions.

It is hard to make any claims about progress within the lesson, though retrieval from previous lessons and using evidence-informed approaches to teaching can support pupil progress. You could claim that due to the activities you have planned that facilitate thinking and memorisation, the pupils are making progress through the curriculum. You will only have more certainty about the extent to which they have learnt it and can apply it when tested at an interval after that lesson, e.g. end of topic test or retrieval practice at a week, term and year. These statements are, however, reflections that we often hear after a lesson or see through the development records student teachers are asked to keep. They are a starting point for thinking about progress but, like with many aspects of teaching, identifying and measuring progress is not quite that simple.

PROGRESS IN THEORY

Current education policy emphasises cognitive theories to explain learning and therefore progress in a given subject. Cognitive theory focuses upon teachers maximising the opportunities for their pupils to commit knowledge to their long-term memory (Sweller, 2011). In order to do so, they need to develop understanding through making connections to prior knowledge as well as practise becoming more fluent at retrieving knowledge in their long-term memory (Willingham, 2021).

There is criticism that favouring one set of theories over others limits our understanding of learning and how pupils make progress, the limited view of progress as attainment through a curriculum, and values a restricted perspective on educational development (e.g. Biesta, 2020; Chandler-Grevatt, 2019). There are also critiques of the progress measures used (Prior et al., 2021).

USING ASSESSMENT FOR PLANNING

Assessment should always form part of lesson planning. Previous summative assessments can inform you of prior attainment, so you can pitch your lesson accordingly. For each learning activity you should plan how that could be assessed formatively. Knowing what you are going to assess allows you to plan to feedback effectively. After a sequence of lessons, you are likely to be working towards an assessment that covers specific learning objectives. There is more detail on this in Chapter 6.

PLANNING LESSON STRUCTURES THAT ALLOW ASSESSMENT AND FEEDBACK

Each learning activity should have some assessment purpose: establishing what they know already, diagnosing misconceptions, actively learning new material and checking they have learnt the new material. This can be done by regular reviews within the lesson, at the end of the lesson and checked again at points within the topic. Table 10.1 shows some examples.

10 Developing effective assessment

Table 10.1 Examples of activities and their assessment opportunities

Activity	Assessment opportunity
Diagnostic tasks	Checking prior knowledge (Where am I now?)
Retrieval practice	Checking prior knowledge has been retained (Where am I now?) and active retrieval supports learning (How do I get there?)
Lesson objectives	Establish the purpose of learning (Where are we going?)
Learning outcomes/success criteria	Establishing the aim and a shared understanding of what success looks like (Where are we going?)
Verbal questioning	Quick checks of knowledge before moving on (Where am I now?)
Circulating when the class do a task	Spotting mistakes and misconceptions, answering questions (How do I get there?)
Feedback on task	Once a task is completed, it can be assessed using teacher, self- or peer-assessment (Where am I now? and Where are we going next?)

USING ASSESSMENT IN THE CLASSROOM

There are many ways in which assessment is used in the classroom and you will need to try, reflect upon and improve how you use them in your early years of teaching. Different subjects and different schools have different approaches. Here are the main strategies used.

ESTABLISHING LEARNING INTENTIONS AND SUCCESS CRITERIA

Learning aims, learning objectives, learning outcomes, success criteria and many other iterations are used in different schools. Some teachers do not like using learning outcomes, others weave them into their lesson narrative. Whatever they are called, there are two aspects to this: what it is we are going to learn and what success looks like.

The purpose of *what we are going to learn* statements is to have something to aim for. It is the *where am I going?* part of formative assessment. They can be presented in a variety of ways and different subjects and schools have different approaches.

Typical approaches to sharing objectives include:

- a specific question;
- a big question;
- a content statement;
- by the end of the lesson, I will be able to …

Next, both teachers and pupils need a shared idea of what success looks like. This can be done on a task-by-task level as well as for a whole lesson. The purpose is to explain what success looks like to the pupils. These are often called learning outcomes or success criteria. This can be seen as the threshold to reach before moving on, which is part of the mastery model. Some schools use descriptors such as *developing, secure and extending*. These should not be used to label or limit pupils, but as a way to communicate that a pupil needs further support, has reached the threshold, or has exceeded it.

EFFECTIVE QUESTIONING (VERBAL AND WRITTEN)

As a trainee, paying attention to developing effective questioning strategies will set you up to be able to:

- establish prior knowledge;
- diagnose misconceptions;
- check current understanding;
- encourage pupils' deeper thinking;
- assess whole class, small group and individual pupils' understanding.

When questioning, teachers often use the IRF (Initiate-Response-Feedback) approach. That is, the teacher initiates a question, a pupil responds, the teacher responds by giving feedback ("That's right, well done"). When done poorly, questioning can limit pupils giving a full, well-considered response (see Tom's case study below). To increase the number of pupils participating and quality of answers, teachers often use strategies to increase the wait time between the question being asked and the answer given.

There are a variety of effective questioning practices. For example:

No hands rule. This is established to ensure that all pupils are ready to participate in questioning. To ensure all pupils feel comfortable participating, care needs to be taken to create a safe environment to do this. There are techniques such as pose, pause, pounce, bounce that support good-quality questioning.

Think-pair-share. This is a strategy that increases 'wait time' and allows pupils to think before they answer, which improves the quality of their responses. The teacher will often pose an open question and ask pupils to write down their first thoughts over a minute, then in the next minute or two share with the person next to them. This part allows pupils to refine their response. Finally, the pairs share their responses with the class under the direction of the teacher.

Hinge questions. There are questions that identify a key concept that a pupil needs to understand. They usually are posed as a multiple-choice question, designed to tease out any misconceptions. They can be difficult to write, but there are plenty for most subjects available on the internet.

10 Developing effective assessment

 **CASE STUDY**

Improving your questioning

Examples of how trainees Tom and Ben improved their questioning.

When Tom started teaching, his questioning was often vague; he would ask questions that equated to *guess what's in my head*. For example, "Can anyone tell me that writing technique beginning with m?" Confused-looking Year 7 pupils looked as Tom started to give them clues. He stumbled over his words a little as he said, "It then has an e ..." Perplexed pupils start to shout out random words beginning with 'm' until Tom finally starts sounding out, "M-e-t-a ..." A pupil picks up on this and shouts, "Metaphor!" Tom breathes a sign of relief and with a big smile says "Yes, excellent" and then moves on.

This is quite a common occurrence for Early Career Teachers. With support from his mentor, Tom's questioning improved rapidly. Now when Tom plans his lessons, he identifies and plans questions that he is going to ask throughout the lesson. This focus on planning questions has helped him to ensure that he asks good questions that either give him diagnostic data (check for understanding) or that develop student learning. To do this, Tom looks at his lesson objectives and thinks about when and why he is going to ask questions. They form part of his lesson planning process, they are well thought out and relevant to each particular stage of the lesson development.

Ben's questioning had been identified as a strength in his lessons, but there was a little tweaking to be done still. For Ben, it isn't what he asks or how he asks it, but how quickly he ends up answering it himself. For example, the average wait time between posing the question and either selecting someone to answer or answering himself was less than two seconds. This doesn't give pupils an opportunity to even process the question let alone think about it, formulate an answer and raise their hand to offer what they have to say. The advice to Ben was to pose his question and then tell himself in his head that pupils need enough time to think clearly before they offer an answer; at this point he could then look for pupil responses. This removed the awkwardness Ben felt about the wait time and gave pupils the valuable time needed to process the question and formulate an answer. Ben found that by doing this more pupils were willing to volunteer answers and they were of a better quality than before as they had time to think. It is worth considering with wait time that some questions will require less wait time than others; lower-level recall for example will take around one to three seconds, with more complex questions needing around ten seconds or more.

- What questions have been asked in lessons you have observed or taught?
- What different purposes did these questions have?
- How do questions change at different points in the lesson?
- How has the teacher responded to student answers?

MAKING FEEDBACK MEANINGFUL

Feedback is a key element in the process of classroom assessment. Black and Wiliam (1998) recognised that formative assessment involves perceiving a gap between the pupil and the learning goal and providing feedback to decrease that gap. Since then a lot of research has gone into what constitutes effective feedback.

Through combining studies on feedback in the classroom (a meta analysis), Hattie and Timperley (2007) demonstrated that effective feedback is one of the most powerful ways to improve pupil outcomes. Hattie and Yates (2013) later conceptualised feedback into three types: feed up (where am I going?), feedback (how am I going?) and feed forward (where to next?). You may see the similarities with the mantra: where am I now? Where am I going? How do I get there?

They then identified the four levels at which teachers give feedback:

- the task level (how well the task is understood and performed by the pupil);
- the process level (how the pupil is approaching the task, e.g. information being drawn upon, methods to approach learning a list of information);
- the self-regulation level (how the pupil employs strategies such as plan, monitor, review to check their own progress);
- the self-level (personal evaluations of the pupil such as ability to reflect, emotional engagement with tasks).

You will see that most feedback in lessons takes place at the task level, with some at the process level in most classrooms, unless you are observing a teacher who is expert in giving feedback. You might find some feedback forms that encourage all four levels of feedback.

Feedback is only effective if pupils receive it positively and act upon it. Pekrun et al. (2014) demonstrated that when pupils anticipate feedback, that is, the teacher tells them that they will receive feedback on a task, the pupils are more likely to be motivated and show improvement in outcomes. There are also cultural implications of how pupils receive feedback from their teachers. This can be tackled by making the expectations clear of any feedback activity.

Feedback is most effective when it is valued by both teacher and pupil, teacher and pupils have a mutual understanding of what is expected, the feedback is specific, related to the task, given immediately or soon after the task is completed, and time is given to the pupil to improve the task.

APPROACHES TO FEEDBACK

In your placement schools there are often policies for feedback. This may be a formalised 'feedback sheet' or a set of expectations of what feedback should include. However, if

10 Developing effective assessment

you develop your questioning skills, your instant feedback to individuals, groups or classes will be effective. Finding opportunities for verbal feedback when planning is a quick and effective way to improve learning.

Within a sequence of lessons, often mid-point or towards the end of a topic, teachers often plan a *feedback lesson*. This is an opportunity to demonstrate that responding to feedback is valued and an important part of learning. It means that the teacher can direct specific individuals and groups, supporting their learning through careful selection of tasks that help to bridge gaps. It can be that pupils are given a task the previous lesson or for homework that they complete. The teacher can mark that task in detail, identify the types of mistakes and misconceptions that occur and plan a lesson to address those. Different pupils do different tasks to improve their learning. This has a variety of names, including 'DIRT' (as you can see from the case study below).

Instead of going through the paper with the whole class question by question when tests are marked (you may have had that inflicted on you at school), the teacher identifies the common issues and sets tasks that remedy those, which pupils select based on their marked paper. This is a much more effective approach as it is meaningful, targeted and specific to individual pupils.

Whatever form it takes, feedback should be meaningful, understood and the pupil should be given time to respond to or address the feedback.

CASE STUDY

Feedback through DIRT

DIRT (Directed Improvement and Reflection Time) tasks or activities are used differently in different subjects. For example, in literacy-based subjects such as English or history, DIRT often takes the form of redrafting a written answer. For this to be effective, quality feedback needs to communicate to pupils what is expected of them. After all, if they knew how to write this better, they would have done so first time around. Here are some examples:

- In English after marking the essays, Laura identifies areas of whole class feedback: areas where the class have done well and where they need to improve. She will give some general feedback verbally to the whole class. Then she provides specific DIRT tasks that are identified on the individual pupils' work. For example, Abdul's might be to 'Rewrite your opening paragraph, making sure you have included key details about the main character's personality.'

- In history, a pupil may be asked to rewrite a paragraph, making sure they have used domain-specific language, the language of change and continuity, for example, slowly, rapidly, catastrophic change – language that would have been explicitly taught and modelled previously.

- Design technology take a different approach by using an ongoing system of continuous improvement, whereby pupils are encouraged to compare their project to modelled examples and identify similarities and differences, then discuss their next steps with their peers and teacher before actioning those changes.
- Maths operates on a system of DIRT templates, where peers are given a modelled step-by-step example of how to complete a particular equation, and then a series of questions that allow them to practise that in different situations getting progressively more difficult.
- Discuss with your mentor:
- How does your school or subject offer time for pupils to respond to feedback?
- When does this take place and how often?
- How does the teacher go about planning this type of lesson?

MANAGING ASSESSMENT AND MARKING

You may have experienced the traditional approach to marking of *tick and flick* where the teacher goes through each page of your book to tick the work you have done, in a way of acknowledging that they have read it. You have also experienced teachers that laboured for hours highlighting every error and writing comments to help you improve, much of which you were unlikely to read or act upon (Education Endowment Foundation, 2016).

We have a good understanding of the features of effective feedback, and we are more mindful of the workload on teachers (Gibson et al., 2015; DfE, 2018). Whenever you make a decision to mark work, you need to balance the time you put in to the impact on learning that results from that marking. This is also about you managing your workload (see Chapter 4). The term *marking* seems to be replaced with the term *feedback*, to emphasise that it is an activity that should involve a response from the pupils.

THE PURPOSE OF MARKING OR FEEDBACK

When marking, you will want to be able to feedback to the pupil (or pupils) what they have achieved and what they can improve on.

At the start of any piece of work, emphasise how the work will be assessed, usually based on learning objectives and outcomes, so that you and the pupils know what they are trying to achieve. This clearly establishes the purpose of the task and the focus of marking.

Focus the marking on improving learning rather than managerial aspects such as presentation (title, date, underlining, etc.). Ask yourself, how will this marking improve the pupil's knowledge, understanding or skills in my subject?

EFFICIENT AND EFFECTIVE FEEDBACK STRATEGIES

To be effective, as we have seen before, feedback needs to be positive, specific, timely and ideally expected. To be efficient, teachers have developed a range of strategies, including:

- Having standard expectations for presentation and literacy of all work. Pupils who need to improve this are directed back to these expectations.
- Using abbreviations to feedback on presentation or literacy.
- Completing feedback forms for a specific piece of work to which pupils have to respond.
- Giving verbal feedback as pupils work in lesson to which pupils respond.
- Whole class marking strategies, where a teacher spends some time going through a sample of books and identifies concepts that the class seem to have understood, the key misconceptions and common errors. The teacher feeds this back to the whole group, provides interventions, and the pupils attend to the issues relevant to them personally.

Ask your mentor and peers for other strategies used to improve efficiency of marking.

USING A MARK BOOK

Mark books, either paper or digital, can be used to build a picture of each pupil's progress over time. It is worth setting up your own mark book before you teach your first lessons. Ask to look at your mentor's mark book to get an idea of what they include.

- Find out about the assessment system of the whole school and your department/year group. What data needs reporting? Where does it come from?
- Observe (and take part in) report writing and parents evening. What do teachers draw on to feedback to parents?
- Once teaching, use your mark book to track progress and decide effective feedback and interventions, but keep efficiency in mind.

An important consideration is how you will keep the data in your mark book safe and within General Data Protection Regulation (GDPR) guidelines. Your school will have policies on this.

CLOSING THOUGHTS

Assessment can seem like a dark art because it is something that is done tacitly by experienced teachers and relies on a wealth of professional knowledge and skills. As a trainee, this chapter offers you some of the secrets of what to look for when observing assessment in action and provides structures and cautions upon which to develop your practice. It takes time, but practise and good mentoring will allow you to develop the skills you need to support your pupils' learning and success.

▰▱▱ ASSIGNMENT LINKS

If you have an assignment on assessment, make sure you are clear about the type of assessment you are researching and writing about. Summative or formative. If formative, which part: teacher questioning, peer-assessment, self-assessment, etc.

The theory (educational research), policy (expectations from the DfE, Ofsted and Ofqual) and practice (what schools and teachers do in the classroom) do not always align. There are tensions between teacher performance and authentic formative assessment (e.g. the case study on make or bake tasks).

Inferences from pupils' work have to be valid. What steps can teachers take to establish valid inferences? How can teachers improve the reliability of their inferences?

LEARNING AND CONSOLIDATION ACTIVITIES

KEY THINGS TO LOOK FOR WHEN OBSERVING LESSONS OR TEACHING

Use the 'what, how, why' method of observing teachers using assessment and when planning your own lessons.

Apply the 'formative assessment cycle' – where am I now? Where do I want to get to? How do I get there? – to the whole lesson and individual learning episodes when observing or planning your lessons.

When focusing on feedback, use Hattie's types and levels of feedback as a way to focus how, when and why feedback is given in lessons.

DISCUSSION POINTS FOR TUTORIALS AND SEMINARS

What are good proxies for learning in your subject? What are poor proxies? How can you ensure that you focus on good proxies when making assessment judgements?

Assessment is a key part of every lesson. Why is it important to plan how you are going to assess activities before teaching them? How do you think this changes as you become more experienced?

What would you consider good practices to use when using questions in class? What are the pitfalls?

Giving pupils grades is a common practice in schools despite the research showing that grades can demotivate and impede engagement with feedback. Why are grades often given throughout secondary education?

IDEAS FOR GUIDED PRACTICE AND FEEDBACK

Ask your mentor to focus an observation on your use of questions during your lesson and feedback on the good practice and areas for development.

How can you plan lessons so that pupils have opportunities to respond to your feedback? What can you do, as a teacher, to ensure that pupils value time to respond to feedback?

Find out the school's marking policy and shadow your mentor when they are marking pupils' work or books. Take on responsibility for marking the work of the classes you teach.

CHAPTER SUMMARY

Now you have read this chapter, you will:

- be able to explain the importance and uses of summative and formative assessment
- observe assessment being used in a variety of ways in other teachers' lessons
- evaluate assessment strategies using the concepts: inference, reliability and validity
- plan and teach lessons with assessment opportunities embedded and used
- mark efficiently, give effective feedback and opportunities to respond.

REFLECTION POINT

- To what extent is assessment done *to* pupils or *with* them in your context?
- When observing activities in lessons, what inferences can be made from pupil responses?
- How do the teachers that you observe use questioning? Which part(s) of the formative assessment cycle do these inform?
- What are the advantages of planning assessment strategies when lesson planning? How much detail is needed?

FURTHER READING

This Education Endowment Foundation report on Effective Feedback uses an evidence base from educational research to distil five recommendations for teachers and schools to use in practice.

EEF (2021) Teacher Feedback to Improve Pupil Learning. Six recommendations for using teacher feedback to improve pupil learning. EEF, London. Available at: https://educationendowmentfoundation.org.uk/education-evidence/guidance-reports/feedback

Professor Dylan Wiliam, one of the leading researchers on formative assessment, applies his research to practical examples in the classroom.

Wiliam, D. (2017) Assessment, marking and feedback, in C. Hendrick and R. McPherson (eds) *What Does This Look Like in the Classroom? Bridging the Gap Between Research and Practice*. Woodbridge: John Catt.

The following book not only charts the research base for Assessment for Learning across the UK and US; it also shows how principles of formative assessment can support self-regulation and metacognition.

Harrison, C.A. and Heritage, M. (2019) *The Power of Assessment for Learning: 20 Years of Research and Practice in UK and US Schools*. London: Corwin.

REFERENCES

Biesta, G. (2020) What constitutes the good of education? Reflections on the possibility of educational critique. *Educational Philosophy and Theory*, 52(10): 1023–1027.

Black, P. (2002) *Testing: Friend or Foe? Theory and Practice of Assessment and Testing*. London: Routledge.

Black, P. and Wiliam, D. (1998) Assessment and classroom learning. *Assessment in Education: principles, policy & practice*, 5(1): 7–74.

Black, P., Harrison, C., Lee, C., Marshall, B. and Wiliam, D. (2004) Working inside the black box: assessment for learning in the classroom. *Phi Delta Kappan*, 86(1): 8–21. Available at: https://eric.ed.gov/?id=EJ705962

Chandler-Grevatt, A. (2018) *How to Assess Your Students: Making Assessment Work For You*. Oxford: Oxford University Press.

Chandler-Grevatt, A. (2019) *How To Teach For Progress: Classroom Approaches For Improving Practice*. Oxford University Press.

Chandler-Grevatt, A. (2021) The wilderness years: an analysis of Gove's education reforms on teacher assessment literacy. *The Buckingham Journal of Education*, 2(1): 101–117.

Christodoulou, D. (2017) *Making Good Progress: The Future of Assessment for Learning*. Oxford: Oxford University Press.

Coe, R. (2013) *Improving Education: A Triumph of Hope Over Experience*. Centre for Evaluation and Monitoring. Available at: www.cem.org/attachments/publications/ImprovingEducation2013.pdf

DfE (2014) *Secondary Accountability Measures (Including Progress 8 and Attainment 8)*. Available at: www.gov.uk/government/publications/progress-8-school-performance-measure

DfE (2018) *Guidance: School Workload Reduction Toolkit*. Available at: www.gov.uk/guidance/school-workload-reduction-toolkit

DfE (2019) *Guidance: English Baccalaureate (EBacc)*. Available at: www.gov.uk/government/publications/english-baccalaureate-ebacc/english-baccalaureate-ebacc

DfE (2021) *Teachers' Standards*. Available at: www.gov.uk/government/publications/teachers-standards

Drury, H. (2018) *How to Teach Mathematics for Mastery*. Oxford: Oxford University Press.

Education Endowment Foundation (2016) *A Marked Improvement? A Review of the Evidence on Written Marking*. Available at: https://educationendowmentfoundation.org.uk/education-evidence/evidence-reviews/written-marking

Elshawa, N., Heng, C.S., Abdullah, A.N. and Rashid, S. (2016) Teachers' assessment literacy and washback effect of assessment. *International Journal of Applied Linguistics and English Literature*, 5(4).

Gibson, S., Oliver, L. and Dennison, M. (2015) Workload challenge: analysis of teacher consultation responses. Department for Education. Available at: https://assets.publishing.service.gov.uk/government/uploads/system/uploads/attachment_data/file/485075/DFE-RR456A_-_Workload_Challenge_Analysis_of_teacher_consultation_responses_sixth_form_colleges.pdf

Harlen, W. (2007) *Assessment of Learning*. London: Sage.

Harrison, C.A. and Heritage, M. (2019) *The Power of Assessment for Learning: 20 Years of Research and Practice in UK and US Schools*. London: Corwin.

Hattie, J. and Timperley, H. (2007) The power of feedback. *Review of Educational Research*, 77(1): 81–112. DOI: 10.3102/003465430298487

Hattie, J. and Yates, G.C.R. (2013) *Visible Learning and the Science of How We Learn*. London: Routledge.

Kime, S. (2017a) Four Pillars of Assessment: Validity, EEF.

Kime, S. (2017b) Four Pillars of Reliability: Validity, EEF.

Newton, P.E. (2007) Clarifying the purposes of educational assessment. *Assessment in education*, 14(2): 149–170.

Newton, P.E. (2021) *The Ofqual Blog: Bias in Teacher Assessment Results*. Available at: https://ofqual.blog.gov.uk/2021/05/17/bias-in-teacher-assessment-results/

Ofsted (2019) *School Inspection Update January 2019*. Special edition. Available at: https://assets.publishing.service.gov.uk/government/uploads/system/uploads/attachment_data/file/772056/School_inspection_update_-_January_2019_Special_Edition_180119.pdf

Pekrun, R., Cusack, A., Murayama, K., Elliot, A.J. and Thomas, K. (2014) The power of anticipated feedback: effects on students' achievement goals and achievement emotions. *Learning and Instruction*, 29: 115–124.

Prior, L., Jerrim, J., Thomson, D. and Leckie, G. (2021) A review and evaluation of secondary school accountability in England: statistical strengths, weaknesses and challenges for 'Progress 8' raised by COVID-19. *Review of Education*, 9(3): e3299.

Sadler, D. (1989) Formative assessment and the design of instructional systems. *Instructional Science*, 18(2): 119–144.

Speckesser, S., Runge, J., Foliano, F., Bursnall, M., Hudson-Sharp, N., Rolfe, H. and Anders, J. (2018) Embedding formative assessment: evaluation report. [Online] Available at: https://educationendowmentfoundation.org.uk/public/files/EFA_evaluation_report.pdf

Sweller, J. (2011) Cognitive load theory. *Psychology of learning and motivation*, 55: 37–76.

Torrance, H. (2018) The return to final paper examining in English national curriculum assessment and school examinations: issues of validity, accountability and politics. *British Journal of Educational Studies*, 66(1): 3–27.

Wiliam, D. (2010) What counts as evidence of educational achievement? The role of constructs in the pursuit of equity in assessment. *Review of Research in Education*, 34: 254–284.

Wiliam, D. (2017) Assessment, marking and feedback, in C. Hendrick and R. McPherson (eds) *What Does This Look Like in the Classroom? Bridging the Gap Between Research and Practice*. Woodbridge: John Catt.

Willingham, D.T. (2021) *Why Don't Students Like School? A Cognitive Scientist Answers Questions About How the Mind Works and What It Means for the Classroom*. John Wiley & Sons.

11

'WHAT IF ...' SCHOOLS AND SOCIETY

AMANDA NUTTALL AND TOM SHAW

▪▪▪ KEY WORDS

- Social justice
- Equity
- Education policy

CHAPTER OBJECTIVES

In this chapter we will develop your understanding of education policy and practices and how these relate to wider societal and cultural issues. You will be encouraged to think critically about *what* you know about schools, pupils and teachers and *how* you know these things. You will consider and critique some of the social and cultural messages that shape our understanding of the lives and work of teachers. This chapter is deliberately more provocative than those you have read so far.

Following a brief history of policy making in England, we will look at how some pupils, families and communities in education are privileged, and how others are disadvantaged. Through case studies and educational research, you will have opportunity to examine your own views about individuals or groups of pupils, considering stereotypes and learning how to challenge behaviours and discourses that replicate existing inequalities. The learning around policy, social justice and inequalities in relation to education that forms this chapter will help you in your professional development as a critical, inclusive practitioner.

▪▪▪ LINKS TO THE CORE CONTENT FRAMEWORK

All of the Core Content Framework themes are referred to and applied in this chapter, but the following are the most relevant:

(Continued)

> Standard 5 – Adapt teaching
>
> 1. Pupils are likely to learn at different rates and to require different levels and types of support from teachers to succeed.
>
> Standard 8 – Fulfil wider professional responsibilities
>
> 1. Effective professional development is likely to be sustained over time, involve expert support or coaching and opportunities for collaboration.
> 2. Reflective practice, supported by feedback from and observation of experienced colleagues, professional debate and learning from educational research, is also likely to support improvement.
> 3. Teachers can make valuable contributions to the wider life of the school in a broad range of ways, including by supporting and developing effective professional relationships with colleagues.
> 4. Building effective relationships with parents, carers and families can improve pupils' motivation, behaviour and academic success.
> 5. SENCOs, pastoral leaders, careers advisers and other specialist colleagues also have valuable expertise and can ensure that appropriate support is in place for pupils.
> 6. Engaging in high-quality professional development can help teachers improve.

INTRODUCTION

The title of this chapter is inspired by the late Sir Ken Robinson, an internationally recognised leader of creativity, innovation and uncovering new potential in education. In his book *Imagine If...*, published posthumously (Robinson and Robinson, 2022), we are challenged to imagine what the future could be like if we were to revolutionise typical western notions of education and schooling. The book begins simply but provocatively, *How should we educate our children? For generations we have been getting this badly wrong* (*ibid*: xix). In this chapter, you will be encouraged to reflect critically on these two points. We will begin by exploring how education policies and practices and societal messages shape our understanding of the role of teachers and pupils in schools in the UK context.

We will then consider issues of equity and social justice in relation to education and schooling, and reflect on some relationships between schools, communities and society as a whole. This will bring us to consider the role of the teacher in relation to pupils' education and development – or, as Robinson puts it, how we work with children's 'boundless capacities' (*ibid*: xix). You will be challenged to reflect critically on your own previous experiences, preconceptions and identities that shape how you think and act as a teacher. Finally, we conclude with some comments on how we, as individual teachers, *can* make a difference to the children and disadvantaged or marginalised groups we work with.

'THE PROMISE OF EDUCATION'

You may not have wondered too much about what education is actually for – or maybe you have thought about this a lot, and this has compelled you to join the teaching profession. Either way, when you start to consider your response, you will find that you have many ideas about the purposes and promises of education, as will your colleagues, the pupils and families that you work with, your family and friends, your community; they may not always be the same and may, in fact, be contradictory. Our understanding about the purpose of education is informed by social and cultural messages that surround us, which means that without realising it, your conceptualisation of what education *is* and what it is *for* is constantly constructed, deconstructed and reconstructed. In academic terms, we would describe this as socio-constructivist and socio-cultural influences that shape how we understand particular actions and actors related to education (Holland et al., 1998; Rutten and Soetaert, 2013). For example, you will have a very particular conception for terms such as 'teaching', 'learning', attainment', 'pupil', 'school', 'teacher' and so on. These conceptions are created by you as an individual in interaction with others around you, meaning that you will have many shared ideas and ideals but that your conceptions are also unique to you.

Take a moment to think about the way in which schools, teachers and pupils are represented in screen media; how attainment results of pupils and university trainees are presented in the media each summer; how debates around behaviour play out on social media. Later in this chapter we will come to reflect in more depth on how these kinds of social and cultural messages can lead to us (unintentionally and unconsciously) holding stereotypical views and replicating existing inequalities in our schools. It could be uncomfortable to reflect on some of these ideas as it may lead to you uncovering some of the assumptions that you hold, but this kind of critical reflection is a crucial part of your professional development and, as you will see in this chapter, essential for us as teachers to challenge some of the harmful assumptions and biases we may come across in our personal and professional lives.

THE INFLUENCE OF EDUCATION POLICY(IES)

A particular influence on the way in which we conceptualise and locate ourselves in education is through national education policies that are translated regionally and actioned locally in individual schools or groups of schools. At the start of your teaching career, it is important to recognise and understand some of the context and ideologies that underpin education policy making in the English context. These policies and practices have shaped, and will continue to shape your understanding of what it means to be a teacher and how you understand your role in relation to others: pupils, colleagues, families and communities. In England we have a very particular system of policy and inspection in education that is critiqued by some educationalists as being highly centralised and controlled to the extent that England is considered to be an outlier compared to European systems (Ball, 2016; Lupton and Hayes, 2021; Sahlberg, 2015).

11 'What if ...' schools and society

Some would argue that current policy directions and trajectories for school policy making seemingly continue to follow industrial drivers of the nineteenth century, promoting a highly regulated and regimented schooling system (Crook and McCulloch, 2013; Nuttall and Podesta, 2020; Robinson and Robinson, 2022). Since the late 1970s, teacher voice, progressive education and 'the common good' at primary and secondary level in England have faced consistent attack from successive governments, regardless of their political leaning. Governments have made significant criticisms of past progressive practices for being left-leaning, overly child-centred and lacking in aspirations for pupils. This is typified by the current Conservative government in England who promote the work of educationalists such as E.D. Hirsch and Doug Lemov, who believe that a centralised, knowledge-rich curriculum and stringent behaviour controls in schools are the key to success (particularly economic success) for all pupils, regardless of their context and backgrounds. Philosophies of democratic ideals in education, such as those put forward by John Dewey and Michael Apple, and teaching of critical social theories have come under increasing fire, in what some have termed 'culture wars' related to education ideals. This has taken place alongside an evolution of education as a marketised system, marked by parental choice, league tables and competition and accountability as methods to 'drive up standards' (Gunter et al., 2015; Ozga, 2011). The interplay of both of these moves has meant that the aim of a common educational experience for all groups and individuals and concerns about the impact of multiple cumulative disadvantages on pupils have gradually been diluted or downplayed.

Perhaps most significant has been the growing emphasis on principles of accountability, driven by the ideology that public expenditure on education should be justified by the extent that it contributes to economic growth. Hand in hand with this has been a fear that disadvantaged pupils are falling behind their peers internationally, and in turn holding back economic development of the country. Ball (2003) sums this up as the way in which:

> *social and economic purposes of education have therefore been collapsed into a single, overriding emphasis on policy making for economic competitiveness and an increasing neglect or side-lining (other than in rhetoric) of the social purposes of education (pages 11–12).*

■ ■ ■ — **REFLECTION POINT**

Thinking differently

The Universal Declaration of Human Rights emphasises that *education shall be directed to the full development of the human personality and to the strengthening of respect for human rights and fundamental freedoms.* Robinson and Robinson (2022) argue that policy makers and educators have lost sight of this basic principle. In your experience of the classroom, do you observe practice shaped by Hirsch/Lemov

11 'What if ...' schools and society

> or Dewey/Apple – for instance a focus on developing rote-memory or a focus on the application of knowledge? How does each influence shape the pupils' experience of education in relation to their development personally, culturally, socially and economically? Do these experiences align with your values in education? If not, how might you do things differently?

A BRIEF HISTORY OF POLICY IN ENGLAND

The Conservative government's policy (1979–1997) was one of 'endogenous competition', which means bringing features of market mechanisms and behaviours into the publicly funded and owned school system (Ball, 2016). This was achieved through local management of school budgets, the establishment of a National Curriculum, and standardised testing to allow for measures of performance and increased accountability. The creation of Ofsted allowed government to enforce the uptake of these policies as the inspectorate were set the task to monitor and report on the implementation of centrally directed policies and practices. This not only enforced standardisation across schools but at the same time effectively muffled dissent from school inspectors who had previously publicly reported on the impact of government policy without fear or favour (Lupton and Hayes, 2021).

From 1997, New Labour and the subsequent Cameron-Clegg Coalition governments brought 'exogenous competition' to bear on the school system, enabling and encouraging external providers to enter the 'market' in school education (Ball, 2016). Under New Labour (1997–2010) these changes were focused on 'under-performing' schools. The Academies Programme, for instance, sought to match failing schools to philanthropic business and charity sponsors, in order to bring business ethos, practices and investment to challenged schools. New Labour's policies to tackle school improvement and issues of educational inequalities were typified by sequences of compensatory measures that focused on how to make 'them' and 'their' schools (the disadvantaged, vulnerable and non-white) more like 'us' and 'our' schools and businesses. This tended towards unhelpful deficit models of disadvantaged pupils and their schools, alongside increased marketisation, which reinforced inequalities and hierarchies of social class despite the intention for policies to be a contrast to those of the previous government (Burn and Childs, 2016; Mutton et al., 2021).

Under the Cameron-Clegg Coalition government (2010–2015) and the subsequent Conservative majority government (2015 onwards), radical acceleration of the exogenous competitive policies of New Labour saw the state education sector transformed while developing a rhetoric of social equality, interpreted as individual social mobility. Its first Education Secretary, Conservative Michael Gove, claimed the attainment gap between rich and poor to be 'a scandal' (DfE, 2010) and denigrated New Labour's approach of modular examinations, skills-based curricula and credential inflation. One response was to challenge school improvement through curricular reforms, which referenced 'core knowledge' movements from the United States (especially Hirsch) and the work of British sociologist Michael Young in emphasising the role of traditional knowledge and 'the best that has been thought and said'. These changes, under the label of 'powerful knowledge' and 'knowledge capital' borrowed sociological terms while ignoring wider sociological concerns about the ability of disadvantaged pupils to access and use such privileged knowledge (Burn and Childs, 2018; Lupton and Hayes, 2021).

Both the Coalition government and the subsequent Conservative government stated a commitment to improving educational outcomes of disadvantaged pupils through a policy of 'pupil premium' additional funding. This may appear to represent a more focused initiative on reducing inequality, but in reality, the ways in which this funding is tied to rigid accountability measures and rapid results in improving attainment in standardised tests has been critiqued by some as steering schools and teachers towards the most superficial of interventions (Burn and Childs, 2016; Wrigley, 2016). Many schools implemented practices that identified and (unintentionally) stigmatised disadvantaged pupils, such as colour-coded seating plans and lunch wristbands, targeted intervention groups in core subjects, provision of resources and openly published lists of names of those accessing free school meals (Mazzoli Smith and Todd, 2019). The policy solutions put forward have thereby continued to drive particular conceptualisations, expectations and 'norms' about education, centred around traditional curricula, norm-referenced attainment, standards, accountability and competition, arguably most disadvantageous for vulnerable pupils, their families and local communities.

SOCIAL JUSTICE

When we talk about the ways in which individuals and/or particular groups access and experience education, we are often drawn to notions of 'social justice'. Social justice is an ambiguous and contested term and one that is often not defined or articulated clearly, particularly in relation to education (Cochran-Smith and Lytle, 2009). For the purposes of this chapter, we consider social justice as related to inclusion, diversity and marginalisation, recognising cultural, social and economic contexts that impact an individuals' ability to engage with and be successful in education.

At the start of your teaching career, it's important that you develop an understanding of issues related to social justice and your role as a teacher. This is not just because you will need to consider pupils' progress and attainment and how individual needs affect these, but you will also need to critically reflect on the progress and attainment of particular groups of pupils that you work with and the impact you can (and sometimes cannot) have on these groups. England has multiple, wide social, gender and race divisions in educational attainment. Despite many policies designed to tackle inequality, the gap between the most and least well off is great and the relationship between school achievement and family background continues to be strong (Adjogatse and Miedema, 2021; Littler, 2018; Wrigley, 2014). It could be said that pupils from disadvantaged and marginalised communities face 'savage inequalities' (Kozol, 1991), and that these inequalities are exacerbated and replicated by social policies (Bibby et al., 2017; Dorling, 2015; Littler, 2018). Children's early learning experiences up to the age of three are crucial, but for families who experience multiple cumulative disadvantages such as stress, insecure housing, marginalisation from mainstream education and limited access to physical and cultural resources, it is harder to provide stimulating and social experiences for young children (Doherty and Nuttall, 2023). Pupils are then at a distinct disadvantage compared to their better-off peers as they begin school without the positive cultural and social resources that give them an understanding of and secure access to schooling systems and expectations (Smyth and Wrigley, 2013). These inequalities continue throughout school life, as disadvantaged pupils are more likely to have interrupted schooling, experience the debilitating effects of tiredness or malnutrition, be stigmatised by their peers, and have less access to cultural and social artefacts (Mazzoli Smith and Todd, 2019; Smyth and Wrigley, 2013).

One very striking feature of England's education policy environment is the insistence that gaps in educational attainment can be narrowed, and indeed removed entirely, within the schooling system – despite the persistence of inequities and years of austerity measures leading to rising levels of wage inequality, child poverty and increased marginalisation of vulnerable and non-white groups (Bibby et al., 2017). Indeed, politicians and policy makers are keen to blame individuals for their educational failings. For example, Ofsted Chief Inspector Amanda Spielman's criticism of families' lack of engagement and schools prioritising feeding poor pupils rather than educating them during the Covid-19 pandemic response (Weale, 2021) and former Education Secretary Damian Hinds blaming 'strife at home and parents being disengaged' for the continued gap in attainment between disadvantaged pupils and their better-off peers (Hinds, 2019). Wrigley (2014) and Beckett and Nuttall (2019) critique school improvement programmes that purport to help disadvantaged groups do better academically, access higher education or increase employability through superficial and short-term interventions. For example, schools may have career 'aspiration' programmes to introduce disadvantaged pupils to potential high-earning professional careers. This is based on the assumption that these pupils do not already have high aspirations and that their lack of attainment in education is due to their unwillingness to engage with academic study. This could be termed as a 'deficit discourse', where poor educational outcomes for particular groups of pupils are inappropriately located in the individual rather than their circumstances.

REFLECTION POINT

Uncovering deficit discourses

Teachers regularly make what appear to be instinctive decisions and responses, especially when in a high-pressure environment. This means that teachers may tend towards making decisions that are informed by deeply ingrained class, gendered and

(Continued)

racialised expectations of pupils (Lampert et al., 2017). Considering what we discussed around social justice, what kinds of deficit discourses are you aware of? Think about messages you see in social media, documentaries on TV, reports of 'stop and search' of young Black boys by police, conversations with colleagues and your family. You might hear words and phrases like 'disruptive youth', 'deserving poor' and 'benefit scroungers'. What other words are associated with those who experience poverty, poor mental health, insecure employment, homelessness or addictions? What kinds of messages do you hear that locate 'problems' within young people and their families? And how might these deficit discourses affect decision making or responses to these pupils in the classroom?

CHALLENGING DEFICIT DISCOURSES

Burn and Childs (2016) criticise externally driven and policy-focused improvement strategies in which disadvantaged pupils are viewed as deficient in some way compared to white middle-class ideals. They call this an 'othering' agenda, which means that professionals – including teachers – misinterpret the outcomes of structural inequity. Rather than blaming existing inequities for pupils' low attainment or disenfranchisement from education, teachers are pressed to implement compensatory interventions intended to 'fix' the deficiencies of disadvantaged pupils by improving their academic performance and attainment (Nuttall and Beckett, 2020; Wrigley, 2014). A different approach would be to start with a more contextualised understanding of what is at issue. Beckett and Wrigley (2014) identify how 'contextual intelligence' underpins authentic interventions that are more likely to meet the needs of particular groups and that are designed to build connections with pupils' interests and lived experiences (Burnett, 2011; Nuttall, 2016).

At the most basic level, it is clear that different schools with different communities, demographics and histories need differing ways of tackling attainment gaps. This involves careful reflection on the purposes of schooling (including giving thought to the moral purpose of education), which then leads to intelligent and sustainable reform at all levels and for all learners (Nuttall and Podesta, 2020). Anyon (2014) provokes teachers to question, how can school interventions truly benefit disadvantaged pupils when their educational outcomes cannot lead to a funded college place or secure employment that provides a living wage or secure housing? She argues that genuine socially just policies and practices in education are intrinsically linked to national (and international) social and economic reforms. Providing economic and social opportunity for the vulnerable and marginalised groups in society creates conditions in which schools and teachers can make a meaningful difference for all pupils.

CASE STUDY

Extra-curricular activities

Often adults in schools are encouraged to offer opportunities for extra-curricular activities. These are activities that sit outside the assessed curriculum. They create experiences for the full development of the human personality.

Some schools market themselves on the added value that their extra-curricular programme contributes to child development. All teachers are expected to contribute from their own experience and expertise. They are expected to provide a programme that gives every child a range of opportunities and supports them to make a connection with a pursuit that brings them joy. Experiences in sport, music, drama, etc. are to complement formation through the curricula experience and ensure the whole child is developed.

Ofsted's 2019 inspection framework expects schools to provide for pupils' personal development. This includes the range, quality and take-up of extra-curricular activities. It states that *the curriculum extends beyond the academic, technical or vocational. It provides for learners' broader development, enabling them to develop and discover their interests and talents*. However, creating these opportunities requires using staff-directed time or relies on staff giving their time to create a programme of activity. Many adults working in schools may have had a limited experience of extra-curricular programmes and may not have expertise in areas that are valued by their employing school or may have expertise in an area that the school does not value. For example, cricket, rowing, rugby and clay-pigeon shooting are perceived by many to be activities of a particular class and therefore are not open to all. But when staff are reflective of the community in which they work, their passions and pursuits will connect with the wants of the community and the children in the school. As a result there will be opportunities for children to develop their 'soft skills' and character and connect with a pursuit that brings them joy.

The provision of extra-curricular activities can be problematic in all settings. Consider:

- Do you think adults in schools should be expected to provide extra-curricular activities?
- If staff in school are not representative of the children in the school, how will this affect the impact of the extra-curricular programme?
- What passion or interest beyond your subject would you want to share with children? Should you be expected to share this in addition to your teaching? How might this give agency to staff to challenge a performance-driven curriculum?
- To what extent does the Ofsted expectation that schools provide extra-curricular activities perpetuate a deficit discourse?
- How could an extra-curricular programme challenge deficit discourse? How could it move toward social justice?

THE ROLE OF THE TEACHER

So far in this chapter, we have considered in depth the broader social and cultural influences that form our identity as a teacher, shape our understanding of our place in the profession and the way in which we view and respond to pupils who experience multiple cumulative disadvantages. Now let's consider your position as an individual. Why did you choose to be a teacher? Historically there has been a pervasive perception of teaching and education as serving 'the common good' (Hansot and Tyack, 1982). Teaching is often cited as a values-oriented enterprise: it may feel as if, as a teacher, your role is to focus on educational attainment, but teachers' work goes beyond the academic to encompass pupils' emotional and social development, their understandings of their place in the world and their interactions with society around them (Flores and Day, 2006; Grudnoff et al., 2016) (see Chapter 2 for a more detailed account of teacher identity). Janzen and Phelan (2019) describe teachers as having an obligation to respond to the child who is *constantly tugging at our sleeves* (Caputo, 1993: 6). This *visceral sense of obligation* (Janzen and Phelan, 2019: 17) underpins a moral enterprise of teaching that locates teachers' work far beyond the performance of 'teaching', 'learning' and 'attainment'.

One aspect of teachers' moral enterprise relates to how their work is framed within the context of social justice as explored above, and how this relates to teachers' individual moral beliefs and value systems. Grudnoff et al. (2016) describe issues of social justice for teachers as related to concepts of equality and fairness. For teachers, social justice embodies aspects of distributive justice, such as access to resources, as well as recognising and challenging society's systemic inequalities. Putting social justice and equity at the centre of a teacher's role means enabling them to understand and address the ways in which groups of pupils have been historically disadvantaged by systemic inequalities, but perhaps more importantly, to actively challenge the systems that reproduce inequality (Burn and Childs, 2018; Mazzoli Smith and Todd, 2019).

CASE STUDY

Understanding low attainment of a particular group of pupils

Nuttall and Doherty (2014) report a case study where concerns about the attainment and engagement of a small group of disadvantaged white British boys in an inner-city primary school came under scrutiny. In this work, the class teacher moved away from focusing on attainment data alone and investigated different questions about this group of young boys that centred on their broader social and emotional dimensions, asking how they responded to different learning experiences, how they managed various social aspects of their school day, and constructing a rich description of their home lives that brought together information from multiple agencies. Central to this work was the prioritising of the boys' voices, a significant step change to previous interventions that were applied to 'raise standards' and improve attainment in English and maths in the short term.

Following this investigatory work, a very different set of interventions was designed by the school leadership team to attempt to address some of the complex interplay between the realities of pupils' lived experiences, including insecurities in housing, poor health and wellbeing linked to poverty, drug and alcohol addictions, criminal activity, domestic violence, and their engagement and attainment at school. While it was essential not to make a 'deficit reading' (Thompson et al., 2016) of these kinds of issues, it became clear that attention needed to be paid beyond the bounds of daily classroom practice and this led to action within the local community. For example, this school, along with others in its local partnership, engaged with a national campaign against domestic violence to encourage children and their families to become involved in this movement; built active relationships with local children's centres to offer wider support for families, including access to play therapies; and developed relationships with community policing and fire service to tackle juvenile anti-social behaviours and to build more positive relationships with local services.

- What links does your school make with external partners?
- How does the school ensure that the content from external partners meets the needs of their pupils and is not 'off the shelf'?

The kind of work presented by Nuttall and Doherty (2014) exemplifies how attainment gaps are only part of a broader picture of social, cultural and economic inequalities related to many factors within and outside the context of an individual classroom or school. If we consider that to teach to one's best necessitates an investment of the personal and professional self (Day, 2017), then asking critical questions and reflecting on our own individual responses and assumptions to the experiences we have in the classroom are an essential part of our role.

But herein lies a conundrum: much literature in the field of teacher education suggests that teachers' pre-existing experiences shape their teacher training and their early career and that these views are often resistant to change (Lupton and Thrupp, 2013; Thompson et al., 2016). As we highlighted above, many teachers *do* hold stereotypical views of some pupils, families and communities, particularly those who are perceived as 'different' or 'other' to the individual teacher (Burn and Mutton, 2015; Mazzoli Smith and Todd, 2019).

Consequently, issues of disadvantage and marginalisation are located by teachers in individuals rather than in the institutional policies and practices that give rise to disadvantage. Some teachers also report feeling powerless to challenge stereotypical views of others, or may lack agency to challenge or change the impact of a knowledge-rich and performance-driven curriculum (Thompson, 2017). As a result, teachers are left in a contradictory space where education is framed as a means of improving social mobility and enriching life chances, yet which, as a system, also maintains existing social inequalities and formations of class (Bibby et al., 2017; McCulloch, 2011).

So, how do we, as individual teachers, challenge these systemic issues? You have already made a good start by engaging with this chapter! The British Educational Research Association (BERA) research commission report on Poverty and Policy Advocacy (2016) highlights how many teachers and school leaders have little or no access to sociological, cultural or historical understanding of social class, race and educational disadvantage, which can leave them ill-informed and ill-equipped to understand complex issues of underachievement, alienation and disaffection (Gorski, 2016; Reay, 2006). In response, the report recommends that practitioners engage in forms of research-informed practice or enquiry in their local contexts in order to build rich understandings of the disadvantaged and marginalised communities they serve and then design and implement 'authentic' and contextualised responses to improve pupils' outcomes.

CASE STUDY

Curriculum review

The 2019 Ofsted framework inspects 'quality of education' by exploring three aspects: intent, implementation and impact of the school curriculum. Schools are expected to offer a broad and balanced curriculum and address questions like:

Intent – what do children need to know and be able to do?

Implementation – what are the best ways to teach these things?

Impact – how do we know when they have been taught them?

This prompted many schools to conduct a curriculum review. Primary schools looked at the extent to which they focused too narrowly on maths and English to the detriment of the wider curriculum and the time spent on SATS prep. Secondary schools looked at the extent to which they had shortened KS3, leading to children lacking the depth and breadth of experience prior to narrowing the curriculum for KS4. Also, the breadth of subjects experienced in KS3 and on offer at KS4. Between 2011 and 2019, following the introduction of the EBacc, subjects in the arts, religious studies and alternative qualifications experienced a significant decline in numbers. (https://ffteducationdatalab.org.uk/2019/06/if-the-ebacc-were-scrapped-would-anything-change/). They were prompted to ask questions like: why is the curriculum shaped the way it is? What values have guided our decisions about the curriculum that is in place? How does our curriculum reflect our school's context? How does it include different pupil groups, such as pupils with special educational needs (SEN) or disadvantaged pupils? Has a focus on exam results led to children being excluded from parts of the curriculum or pushed toward less rigorous qualifications?

As we make curriculum choices about intent, implementation and impact, we should consider ...

Who wins? Who loses? Who decides?

CONCLUSION – BE THE CHANGE

Teachers make a difference: when pupil backgrounds are held constant, it is the practices of individual teachers that contribute more to variation in pupil outcomes than any other school effect (Mayer and Mills, 2021). But, at the same time, teachers and schools cannot make *all* the difference (Thrupp, 1999). As we have seen, there are significant social and cultural influences that play out in the policies and practices of education in England and beyond. It would be naïve of us, as teachers, to think that we can compensate for deep-rooted inequities in society through improving pupils' educational attainment and future prospects.

But, at the same time, we acknowledge that teaching is inevitably a moral endeavour and that *the contributions that teachers make to the moral life of classrooms, to the moral lives that our … pupils lead, and to the character of our society, are critical* (Sanger and Osguthorpe, 2011: 570). The aim of this chapter has been to help you, as a beginning teacher, to understand some of the complexities and nuances involved in this moral endeavour of teaching. In response to some of the challenges that we have highlighted, we could consider that what is needed in our current education system in England is a pedagogy of compassion (Zembylas, 2013), which signifies empathy and an orientation of kindness, respect and fostering a sense of belonging rather than judgement and 'othering'. To meet this ideal it is essential that you, personally and professionally, reflect on your own ideas about individual and groups of pupils that you work with, challenging unhelpful stereotypes and biases that you and others may hold. Positive change for your pupils, your school and the communities you serve starts with you. After all, *Educational change depends on what teachers do and think. It's as simple and complex as that* (Fullan, 1991: 17).

ASSIGNMENT LINKS

1. Knowledge of some of the history of education policy making in England will help you understand how policy and practice decisions are made in the current political and social climate in England.

2. Being able to identify stereotypes and deficit discourses around pupils who experience disadvantages will help you to critique the way in which these pupils are presented in policy and practice.

3. Understanding of social and cultural influences will support your critiques of the teaching profession as a whole.

4. Being able to reflect critically - to be reflexive - is an essential part of professional development. It is important in your assignments that you acknowledge your own experiences and beliefs and that you understand how these will shape your understanding of and response to particular policies and practices.

LEARNING AND CONSOLIDATION ACTIVITIES

KEY THINGS TO LOOK FOR WHEN OBSERVING LESSONS OR TEACHING

- How do teachers identify gaps and misconceptions in pupils' knowledge and experiences?
- How does poverty or disadvantage manifest physically, mentally and/or emotionally for pupils?
- What differences – or gaps – in language are present for pupils who experience poverty and disadvantage?
- How are pupil premium pupils identified?

DISCUSSION POINTS FOR TUTORIALS AND SEMINARS

- What is the cultural nature of the community your school serves? What might you need to know about families in the local area?
- How does your school provide for pupil premium pupils? What key outcomes do senior leaders look for?
- What additional or extra-curricular experiences are provided? How do these support pupils' social and cultural development?

IDEAS FOR GUIDED PRACTICE AND FEEDBACK

- Consider how you will identify and plan for any gaps in pupils' knowledge and understanding for the sequences of lessons you will teach.
- What outcomes (beyond curriculum learning objectives) will your lessons provide for pupils?
- How can you make connections between the curriculum content of your lessons and pupils' real-life experiences?

CHAPTER SUMMARY

Now you have read this chapter, you will:

- understand how social and cultural messages influence your perception of yourself as a teacher and of the pupils you work with
- understand some of the political influences on current educational policy making in England

- know about some of the disadvantages that particular groups of pupils will experience in relation to their lived experiences and schooling
- be able to identify deficit discourses and damaging stereotypes about particular groups of pupils and consider how to challenge these.

> **REFLECTION POINT**
>
> 1. Sir Ken Robinson asks, 'How should we educate our children?' After reading this chapter, what policies and practices might you change to create a more equitable and inclusive schooling experience for all?
> 2. Is the current curriculum that you teach fit for purpose for the twenty-first century? What about the way in which the curriculum is assessed? Why/why not?
> 3. How can we provide interventions for pupil premium pupils that does not stigmatise or 'other' them?
> 4. How could participating in extra-curricular activities remove barriers between schools and those perceived as 'different' or 'other'?

FURTHER READING

Potts, R. (2021) *The Caring Teacher: How to Make a Positive Difference in the Classroom.* John Catt Educational Ltd.

A warm, encouraging and realistic overview of teaching with practical tips and anecdotes that will help you to develop your own pedagogy of compassion. This is a very enjoyable read that will guide you in addressing some of the bigger questions about how to sustain a caring professional identity in the classroom.

Robinson, K. and Robinson, K. (2022) *Imagine If… Creating a Future for Us All.* Penguin.

A short read that places education in the context of wider society. Each chapter asks the reader to consider how we can make changes for a more sustainable future that is based on key principles of creativity, collaboration and compassion.

Biesta, G.J.J. (2014) *The Beautiful Risk of Education.* Routledge.

A slightly more challenging read that is organised around seven areas of provocation in education: creativity, communication, teaching, learning, emancipation, democracy and virtuosity. The reader is challenged to engage in critical reflection on pedagogy and the broader aims of education through a lens of risk-taking.

REFERENCES

Adjogatse, K. and Miedema, E. (2021) What to do with 'white working-class' underachievement? Framing 'white working-class' underachievement in post-Brexit Referendum England. *Whiteness and Education*, *7*(2): 1–20. DOI: 10.1080/23793406.2021.1939119

Anyon, J. (2014) *Radical Possibilities: Public Policy, Urban Education, and A New Social Movement* (Second). Routledge.

Ball, S.J. (2003) The teacher's soul and the terrors of performativity. *Journal of Education Policy*, *18*(2): 215–228.

Ball, S.J. (2016) Neoliberal education? Confronting the slouching beast. *Policy Futures in Education*, *14*(8): 1046–1059.

Beckett, L. and Nuttall, A. (2019) Education and activism, in *Oxford Research Encyclopedia of Education*. Oxford University Press. DOI: 10.1093/acrefore/9780190264093.013.375

Beckett, L. and Wrigley, T. (2014) Overcoming stereotypes, discovering hidden capitals. *Improving Schools*, *17*(3): 217–230.

BERA (2016) *BERA Research Commission 2015/2017 – Poverty and Policy Advocacy*. Available at: BERA Research Commission 2015/2017- Poverty and Policy Advocacy | BERA

Bibby, T., Lupton, R. and Raffo, C. (2017) *Responding to Poverty and Disadvantage in Schools: A Reader for Teachers*. Palgrave Macmillan.

Burn, K. and Childs, A. (2016) Responding to poverty through education and teacher education initiatives: a critical evaluation of key trends in government policy in England 1997–2015. *Journal of Education for Teaching*, *42*(4): 387–403.

Burn, K. and Childs, A. (2018) Responding to poverty through education and teacher education initiatives: a critical evaluation of key trends in government policy in England 1997–2015, in O. McNamara and J. McNicholl (eds) *Poverty Discourses in Teacher Education*, pages 14–30. Routledge.

Burn, K. and Mutton, T. (2015) A review of 'research-informed clinical practice' in Initial Teacher Education. *Oxford Review of Education*, *41*(2): 217–233. DOI: 10.1080/03054985.2015.1020104

Burnett, B. (2011) Teacher education and the targeting of disadvantage. *Creative Education*, *2*(5): 446–451. DOI: 10.4236/ce.2011.25064

Caputo, J.D. (1993) *Against Ethics: Contributions to a Poetics of Obligation with Constant Reference to Deconstruction*. Indiana University Press.

Cochran-Smith, M. and Lytle, S.L. (2009) *Inquiry as Stance. Practitioner Research in the Next Generation*. Teachers College Press.

Crook, D. and McCulloch, G. (2013) History, policy and the professional lives of teacher educators in England, in M. Ben-Pertez, S. Kleeman, R. Reichenberg and S. Shimoni (eds)

Embracing the Social and the Creative. New Scenarios for Teacher Education, pages 21–34. Rowman and Littlefield.

Day, C. (2017) *Teachers' Worlds and Work : Understanding Complexity, Building Quality*. Routledge.

DfE (2010) *The Importance of Teaching. The Schools White Paper 2010*. Her Majesty's Stationery Office. Available at: https://assets.publishing.service.gov.uk/government/uploads/system/uploads/attachment_data/file/175429/CM-7980.pdf

Doherty, J. and Nuttall, A. (2023) The effects of disadvantage on children's life chances and educational outcomes, in L. Hayes (ed.) *The Early Years Handbook for Students and Practitioners: an Essential Guide for Levels 4 and 5* (Second). Routledge.

Dorling, D. (2015) *Injustice: Why Social Inequality Still Exists*. Policy Press.

Flores, M.A. and Day, C. (2006) Contexts which shape and reshape new teachers' identities: a multi-perspective study. *Teaching and Teacher Education*, *22*(2): 219–232.

Fullan, M.G. (1991) *The New Meaning of Educational Change* (2nd edn). London: Casell Educational Limited.

Gorski, P.C. (2016) Poverty and the ideological imperative: a call to unhook from deficit and grit ideology and to strive for structural ideology in teacher education. *Journal of Education for Teaching*, *42*(4): 378–386.

Grudnoff, L., Haigh, M., Hill, M., Cochran-Smith, M., Ell, F. and Ludlow, L. (2016) Rethinking initial teacher education: preparing teachers for schools in low socio-economic communities in New Zealand. *Journal of Education for Teaching*, *42*(4): 451–467.

Gunter, H.M., Hall, D. and Mills, C. (2015) Consultants, consultancy and consultocracy in education policymaking in England. *Journal of Education Policy*, *30*(4): 518–539. DOI: 10.1080/02680939.2014.963163

Hansot, E. and Tyack, D. (1982) A usable past: using history in education policy, in A. Lieberman and M.W. McLaughlin (eds) *Policy Making in Education*, pages 1–21. National Society for Study of Education.

Hinds, D. (June 2019) *Education Secretary Challenges Misconceptions of Disadvantage*. Available at: www.gov.uk/government/speeches/education-secretary-challenges-misconceptions-of-disadvantage

Holland, D.C., Lachiotte, W., Skinner, D. and Cain, C. (1998) *Identity and Agency in Cultural Worlds*. Harvard University Press.

Janzen, M.D. and Phelan, A.M. (2019) 'Tugging at our sleeves': understanding experiences of obligation in teaching. *Teaching Education*, *6210*: 1–15.

Kozol, J. (1991) *Savage Inequalities: Children in America's schools*. New York: Crown Publishing.

Lampert, J, Burnett, B., Comber, B, Ferguson, A. and Barnes, N. (2017) 'It's not about punitive': exploring how early-career teachers in high-poverty schools respond to critical incidents. *Critical Studies in Education*, *61*(2) 149–165. DOI: 10.1080/17508487.2017.1385500

Littler, J. (2018) *Against Meritocracy: Culture, Power and Myths of Mobility*. Routledge.

Lupton, R. and Hayes, D. (2021) *Great Mistakes in Education Policy and How to Avoid Them in the Future*. Policy Press.

Lupton, R. and Thrupp, M. (2013) Headteachers' readings of and responses to disadvantaged contexts: evidence from English primary schools. *British Educational Research Journal*, *39*(4): 769–788.

Mayer, D. and Mills, M. (2021) Professionalism and teacher education in Australia and England. *European Journal of Teacher Education*, *44*(1): 45–61. DOI: 10.1080/02619768.2020.1832987

Mazzoli Smith, L. and Todd, L. (2019) Conceptualising poverty as a barrier to learning through 'poverty proofing the school day': the genesis and impacts of stigmatisation. *British Educational Research Journal*, *45*(2): 356–371. DOI: 10.1002/berj.3506

McCulloch, G. (2011) *The Struggle for the History of Education*. London: Routledge.

Mutton, T., Burn, K., Thompson, I. and Childs, A. (2021) Teacher education policy and research, in *Teacher Education Policy and Research*. Springer Singapore. DOI: 10.1007/978-981-16-3775-9

Nuttall, A. (2016) The 'curriculum challenge': moving towards the 'storyline' approach in a case study urban primary school. *Improving Schools*, *19*(2): 154–166. DOI: 10.1177/1365480216651522

Nuttall, A. and Beckett, L. (2020) Teachers' professional knowledge work on poverty and disadvantage, in L. Beckett (ed.) *Research-Informed Teacher Learning: Critical Perspectives on Theory, Research and Practice*. Routledge.

Nuttall, A. and Doherty, J. (2014) Disaffected boys and the achievement gap: 'the wallpaper effect' and what is hidden by a focus on school results. *Urban Review*, *46*(5): 800–815.

Nuttall, A. and Podesta, E. (2020) School reform in England, in *Oxford Research Encyclopedia of Education*. Oxford University Press. DOI: 10.1093/acrefore/9780190264093.013.848

Ozga, J. (2011) *Fabricating Quality in Education [electronic resource : Data and Governance in Europe]* (1st edn). Routledge.

Reay, D. (2006) The zombie stalking english schools: social class and educational inequality. *British Journal of Educational Studies*, *54*(3): 288–307.

Robinson, K. and Robinson, K. (2022) *Imagine If… Creating a Future for Us All*. Penguin.

Rutten, K. and Soetaert, R. (2013) Narrative and rhetorical approaches to problems of education. Jerome Bruner and Kenneth Burke revisited. *Studies in Philosophy and Education*, *32*(4): 327–343. DOI: 10.1007/s11217-012-9324-5

Sahlberg, P. (2015) *Finnish Lessons 2.0: What Can the World Learn from Educational Change in Finland?* (Second). Teachers College, Columbia University.

Sanger, M.N. and Osguthorpe, R.D. (2011) Teacher education, preservice teacher beliefs, and the moral work of teaching. *Teaching and Teacher Education*, *27*(3): 569–578. DOI: 10.1016/j.tate.2010.10.011

Smyth, J. and Wrigley, T. (2013) *Living on the Edge: Rethinking Poverty, Class and Schooling.* Peter Lang.

Thompson, I. (2017) *Tackling Social Disadvantage Through Teacher Education.* Critical Publishing.

Thompson, I., McNicholl, J. and Menter, I. (2016) Student teachers' perceptions of poverty and educational achievement. *Oxford Review of Education*, *42*(2): 1–16.

Thrupp, M. (1999) *Schools Making a Difference: Let's be Realistic! School Mix, School Effectiveness and the Social Limits of Reform.* Open University Press.

Weale, S. (September 2021) Ofsted head: schools' focus on food parcels may have hit learning. *The Guardian.* Available at: www.theguardian.com/education/2021/sep/14/ofsted-head-schools-focus-food-parcels-may-have-hit-learning

Wrigley, T. (2014) Poverty and underachievement: false trails and new directions. *Improving Schools*, *17*(3): 197–202. DOI: 10.1177/1365480214557935

Wrigley, T. (2016) Not so simple: the problem with "evidence-based practice" and the EEF toolkit. *FORUM*, *58*(2): 237–252.

Zembylas, M. (2013) Critical pedagogy and emotion: working through "troubled knowledge" in posttraumatic contexts. *Critical Studies in Education*, *54*(2): 176–189. DOI: 10.1080/17508487.2012.743468

12

ACCOUNTABILITY AND GOVERNANCE

JULIAN BURKINSHAW AND RACHEL RUDMAN

 **KEY WORDS**

- Accountability
- Governance
- Ofsted

CHAPTER OBJECTIVES

This chapter will define accountability in education and explore ways in which teachers and schools are held accountable for the provision of high-quality education. Arising from this are issues around how we define and measure educational success, whether through examination performance or other data that is gathered by various stakeholders. The chapter will then explain how national accountability measures are likely to affect you and impact on your practice within the classroom.

The content will encourage you to identify what accountability means for you as a teacher and know the nature of national and local accountability measures. Each school will have some form of governing body and this chapter will examine what a governing body might look like, the function of school governance and how this might impact on your everyday practice as a teacher. By the end of the chapter, you should have a greater appreciation of the role and function of a school's governing body.

Finally, the chapter will explore the Ofsted framework for inspection of schools and consider how the principles that underpin the Ofsted framework will affect you as you begin your teaching career. These principles are Intent, Implementation and Impact. The chapter will then conclude with insight into how the Ofsted framework impacts a secondary subject teacher, with recent individual experiences drawn upon from a subject-specific perspective. This should allow you to develop an insight into the Ofsted regulatory body and analyse how it might affect you as a new teacher.

12 Accountability and governance

> ■ ■ ■ — **LINKS TO THE CORE CONTENT FRAMEWORK**
>
> All of the Core Content Framework themes are referred to and applied in this chapter, but the following are the most relevant:
>
> Standard 1 - Set high expectations, with a focus on:
>
> 1. Teacher expectations can affect pupil outcomes; setting goals that challenge and stretch pupils is essential.
> 2. High-quality teaching has a long-term positive effect on pupils' life chances, particularly for children from disadvantaged backgrounds.
>
> Standard 3 - Demonstrate good subject and curriculum knowledge
>
> 1. A school's curriculum enables it to set out its vision for the knowledge, skills and values that its pupils will learn, encompassing the National Curriculum within a coherent wider vision for successful learning.

WHAT IS MEANT BY ACCOUNTABILITY IN AN EDUCATIONAL CONTEXT?

From the moment you embark on a career in teaching, you begin to take responsibility for the provision of a high-quality education for the pupils you teach. Indeed, in order to gain Qualified Teacher Status (QTS), new teachers have to demonstrate that they have met the teacher standard to *promote good progress and outcomes by pupils* by being *accountable for pupils' attainment, progress, and outcomes* (DfE, 2011). In real terms, this means that you will focus on ensuring your planning and teaching of lessons are effective so that pupils can make progress both in the short term and more finally in the results they attain in externally marked examinations at the end of Key Stages 4 or 5. Individual teacher accountability feeds into a much bigger picture, since departments and schools as a whole consider how pupils have attained in those external examinations in order to measure success and this then feeds into accountability from a national perspective. Judgements about the effectiveness of a school will focus to a large extent on external examination results in relation to national benchmarks. As an Early Career Teacher (ECT), you will be aware of the need to ensure that pupils attain as well as they are able across all year groups taught, whether measured through internal or external results.

Accountability is usually seen as a 'top down' or vertical concept, by which the government holds educational professionals to account to ensure that public money is being used effectively to provide high-quality education. While there is a middle layer of oversight through local authorities or multi-academy trusts, accountability is primarily focused onto leadership teams within individual school contexts. This responsibility is then passed on to teachers to ensure the ultimate aim of high-quality education for all pupils. The key ways in which schools are held to account are through scrutiny of examination results and outcomes of Ofsted inspections. Brill et al. (2018) asserted that horizontal accountability might provide more positive and sustainable opportunities for school improvement, through peer-to-peer or school-to-school partnerships. This is an emerging focus for schools that are beginning to work in networks or clusters to share improvement strategies, develop trust and share visions for effective education. This is supported by the government-focused 'self-improving school-led system' (DfE, 2019), which acknowledges the high value of this form of accountability.

In monitoring the degree to which pupils are receiving a high-quality education, it is important to analyse what is actually meant by high-quality education. While examination results can provide 'hard data' on how pupils within schools are performing, it is also critical to realise that education is about much more than examination results. Biesta (2010) defined the function of education in three ways: qualification, socialisation and subjectification. The first of these focuses on the knowledge, skills and understanding that we *can* measure through those external examination grades. Socialisation is far more difficult to measure but identifies the development of pupils' capacity to integrate within a community and interact in a way that will support their transition to adult life. The final of these, subjectification, recognises the importance of pupils becoming autonomous and independent: again, arguably essential life skills but also difficult to measure. Coe (2013) suggested that we have to be clear about what learning we value. While hard attainment data can provide evidence for some of what we are responsible for as teachers, it does not account for those less measurable elements like socialisation and subjectification that are nevertheless essential.

REFLECTION POINT

- When you are in a school, how might you measure the quality of education in terms of socialisation and subjectification as mentioned above?
- Beyond data tables, what other accountability measures might be in place to gauge the impact of the education that pupils are receiving?

Using externally marked examination results as an ultimate measure of pupil progress has become increasingly problematic across both primary and secondary provision. Pupils in Year 6 will sit Standard Attainment Tests (SATs) in English and mathematics and secondary schools have the annual pressure of General Certificate of Secondary Education (GCSE) examinations for pupils in Year 11 and Advanced levels for pupils in Year 13. These are all efficient ways of measuring how successfully schools are promoting good progress for their pupils and can also allow for comparative analysis across other schools in the area and across schools with similar demographics. From a national perspective, this data can provide policy makers with numerical data that provides oversight of performance across different subjects, different schools and different areas of the country.

The impact of these data-driven accountability measures has been significant. Secondary schools have often had a 'three-year GCSE' course, which meant that pupils started Key Stage 4 curriculum content in Year 9 to develop deeper knowledge of the required specifications on which they will be assessed at the end of Year 11. This means that curriculum content might be more restricted to allow for more exam preparation time. Another accusation levelled at schools is that if external examination results are a key accountability measure, then the focus of an educational institution might shift accordingly, through either narrowing the curriculum or prioritising those areas where pupils are getting measured on their performance to the detriment of other areas of school life (Hutchings, 2015 and Brill et al., 2018). This has led to explicit referencing in the most recent Ofsted framework to the need for schools to keep the curriculum as broad and balanced for as long as possible to counter this culture of narrowing the curriculum to prioritise the measurable areas, *teaching a full range of subjects for as long as possible, 'specialising' only when necessary* (Ofsted, 2022a).

NATIONAL ACCOUNTABILITY MEASURES AND YOU AS A SECONDARY TEACHER

Accountability became a major focus in education following the Education Reform Act of 1988, as discussed in Chapter 11. This led to significant changes to how schools operated, not least the introduction of local management of schools, which meant that head teachers and governing bodies became responsible for school budgets. This change meant that schools became far more like businesses and this sense of marketisation was enhanced further by the introduction of objectives for pupils to achieve at each key stage, thus making progress and attainment more prominent.

In 1992, as a direct result of this act, Ofsted and school performance tables were introduced to provide both annual data about school performance and regular periodic inspections of schools. Alongside these measures, another change at this time was that parents could specify preferred schools, thus strengthening the need for accountability and adding to the perception of parentocracy (a term coined by David in 1993 to suggest the power of parents as 'users' of the education system to influencing the 'service' provided for their children). For the first time, parents as key stakeholders were able to hold schools to account, judge how well the school was performing and compare performance across different local schools.

Since those league tables were first introduced, the way in which data is collected has evolved. While early league tables identified raw data on performance, it did not place that data into any wider context. The Value-Added National Project report (Taylor-Fitzgibbon,

1997) acknowledged that different starting points for pupils would affect the outcomes at GCSE. To that end, the 'Unique Pupil Number' (UPN) was introduced in 1999, which meant that any child enrolled at a government-funded school would have a UPN that then enabled data to be gathered about performance against starting points and relative to the social context in which the pupils were situated.

Currently in secondary education, attainment is considered in relation to the following accountability measures (DfE, 2022a):

- number of pupils attaining a good pass (grade 5 or above) in English and mathematics;
- proportion of pupils achieving the English Baccalaureate (which measures the number of pupils achieving a good pass in English, mathematics, science, history or geography and a language);
- progress eight scores, which are calculated by benchmarking KS4 results against prior attainment at KS2 and expected attainment based on that. This value-added data determines how pupils are performing at any given school relative to other pupils with similar prior attainment. Attainment is measured across a pupil's highest performing eight subjects in relation to performance of all pupils with the same prior attainment.

Table 12.1 Shows how scores are calculated for progress eight, with maths and English holding a double weighting.

Maths	Double weighted
English	Language or literature – double weighted
Three EBacc qualifications	Sciences (and computer science)
	Geography/history
	Modern foreign language
Three other qualifications	Any remaining EBacc qualifications or the second English GCSE if taken
	Other full GCSEs
	Approved high-value qualifications (e.g. BTECs)

While many of these measures look at the performance of a whole school, it is inevitable that the focus on pupil achievement will filter down to the individual class teachers, particularly when teaching at GCSE and A level. As pupils enter secondary school, there will be a clear profile for each pupil who has taken Key Stage 2 SATs about expected performance at Key stage 4. Often a 'flight path' is identified, with clear expectations about performance at GCSE based on prior attainment (and Cognitive Ability Tests or CATs, which are often taken in the first few weeks of Year 7). Through close monitoring of where pupils are in relation to these predictions, additional support and interventions might be introduced for pupils to encourage an enhanced rate of progress. Given the pressure that schools – and teachers – are under to ensure pupils perform to meet those attainment expectations, it has been suggested that a disadvantage of this system is that teachers become more 'controlling' and less likely to allow pupils autonomy as learners, since they are aware of the high-stakes measures that will be applied (Pelletier et al., 2002).

REFLECTION POINT

- What effect might it have on you as a teacher and on your pupils if those predicted grades are shared with them? Try to think about positive and negative effects.

- How might the focus on these external accountability measures impact on your practice as a teacher? Again, try to think about both positive and negative effects.

WHAT IS MEANT BY GOVERNANCE IN AN EDUCATIONAL CONTEXT?

Until 1988, schools were administered by local bodies that took responsibility for oversight of educational administration, known as local education authorities (LEAs). Greater freedom around governance and control emerged after the Education Reform Act of 1988, which allowed schools to decide (contingent on parent votes) to move away from this LEA control and to be funded directly from government as a grant-maintained school. While these no longer exist, the Academies Act of 2010 enabled all schools to have the opportunity to leave LEA control and establish themselves as multi-academy trusts. You may be aware of MATs operating in your local area and as of August 2019, there were 1,180 MATs in the country (cited by Matthews and Ehren, 2022). There has been much political speculation about whether all schools will eventually be attached to a MAT, which the government set out as its intention in 2022 to have happened by 2030 (DfE, 2022b).

Whether a school is part of a MAT or still attached to local authority funding, there will be school governance in place. Usually, a multi-academy trust will have an overall board of governors and then a 'local' governing body attached to the individual school. Other schools will have a governing body that has oversight from the local authority (or sometimes the diocese if it is a church school).

Governors will usually work alongside senior leadership within a school, which means that teachers may not have much direct contact with governors attached to their schools. Governors are important members of the school community though, as they perform an important role in relation to the strategic vision for a school and can be key drivers for school improvement as they can view the institution through a more objective lens, thereby acting as 'critical friends' (Costa and Kallick, 1993).

Governors have varied responsibilities and should support, question and challenge as needed in order to promote the best possible outcomes for the school. The governing body should encourage self-evaluation that can lead to an authentic 'desire to improve' (Wrigley, 2003: 46), which tends to be more developmental than external scrutiny and might lead teachers to feeling they are under surveillance and not trusted as professionals (Hextall and Mahoney, 2000). If you are aware of the decisions being made by a governing body and the vision that it has for your school, this can further develop your appreciation of some of the decisions being made about how the school operates on a day-to-day basis.

THE SHAPE AND ROLE OF THE GOVERNING BODY

A secondary school governing body will usually have around 15–20 members (dependent on the size of the school) who will meet between three and six times per year for full governing meetings with a co-opted chair and vice-chair. The governing body will be made up of school staff members, members of the wider community, local authority representatives, parents – and church schools will have foundation governors who are diocesan representatives. Each governor will usually have responsibility for an area appropriate to their knowledge and expertise (for example, health and safety, Special Educational Needs and Disabilities, safeguarding, head teacher performance management, resources) and there will be a range of sub-committees which meet regularly to focus on specific areas that can then feedback to the main governing board meetings. Sub-committees will cover areas such as teaching and learning, resources and head-teacher performance management.

The governing body has responsibility for strategic oversight of what happens within the school and is seen as similarly important to leadership as those school leaders with more formal, paid positions in a school. All governors undertake the role in a voluntary capacity but, to be done well, being a governor can take time and effort. The Ofsted framework provides a judgement about effectiveness of leadership and management and expects that:

- *Those responsible for governance understand their role and carry this out effectively. They ensure that the provider has a clear vision and strategy and that resources are managed well. They hold leaders to account for the quality of education or training; and*

- *those with responsibility for governance ensure that the provider fulfils its statutory duties, for example under the Equality Act 2010, and other duties, for example in relation to the 'Prevent' strategy and safeguarding, and promoting the welfare of learners.*

(Ofsted, 2022a)

These two bullet points encompass a range of responsibilities and show that governors are held accountable for the overall direction in which the school is travelling. Brill et al.

(2018) suggested that this strategic accountability might be seen in four ways: financial, pupil wellbeing, behaviour and safety, and pupil attainment and progress.

The National Governance Association (2022) suggested that school governance should be ethical, effective and accountable. Accountability can be seen through the prominence given to governance within the Ofsted framework. Ethical governance speaks of working with integrity and following codes of conduct for governors to work for the best interests of the school by fulfilling roles and responsibilities, working confidentially, declaring any interests and demonstrating commitment to the role. These codes of conduct are usually shaped in their content by Nolan's seven principles of public life (Committee on Standards in Public Life, 1995), which identify how those in roles of responsibility should behave with selflessness, integrity, objectivity, accountability, openness, honesty and leadership.

The National Governance Association (2022) also suggest the key characteristics of a governing body as a whole that can enable the board to operate effectively:

1. good chairing;
2. professional clerking;
3. the right people around the table;
4. understanding roles and responsibilities;
5. courageous conversations;
6. knowing the school/trust;
7. asking challenging questions;
8. good relationships based on trust.

Ultimately, through forming positive relationships with members of the school community, and from knowing what goes on within the school, governors should be able to ask questions and challenge the leaders of the school to get a clear sense that the school is moving in the right direction.

▬▬▬ CASE STUDY

How might governance impact on you in your early career?

Many governors are given subject-specific responsibility to make contact with subject leaders to act as 'critical friend' and discuss the long-term plans and intent with them to understand the strategic direction of the school from a curricular perspective (and to support changes to the Ofsted framework of 2019). This kind of responsibility might also involve discussions with other members of the subject department.

Luke has been asked to oversee history and has contacted Beth, the history leader, in order to meet and discuss the curriculum. When he met Beth, he was also introduced to Rob, an Early Career Teacher (ECT) who has just joined the school after a successful PGCE year. While chatting with Rob about how he is settling into the school and department, it becomes clear that he does not seem to be getting the expected support for him as an ECT and new member of staff and Luke is concerned that Rob has not been given access to departmental strategic plans so cannot really explain the rationale for the approaches to teaching history across Key Stages 3 and 4. It is also clear that he is struggling with the workload and some challenging issues around support for some pupils in his classes. When Luke raises this with Beth, she agrees that she has not had enough time to work alongside Rob and support his induction to the school.

In this situation, it becomes challenging for both the subject teachers and the governor. While responsible for asking questions where needed, Luke does not have the level of subject expertise to fully appreciate the kind of support that Rob needs and he is mindful of not adding to Beth's workload further.

Think like a governor

- What do you think Luke might do in this situation to be an effective governor?
- Are there any areas of potential conflict or difficulty if Luke takes his concerns back to the main governing body?
- What problems could emerge if Luke does not take issues back to the governing body?

HOW DOES SCHOOL GOVERNANCE AFFECT YOU AS A TEACHER?

School governance will have an important impact upon your teaching practice every day. The results of this impact, however, may not be felt quite as directly when compared to other responsibilities such as curriculum development, marking or lesson delivery. One of the main interactions you will have with the governing body, or a particular governor, will be during governor visits to school. The most significant of these visits to you as a teacher will be a focus on the quality of education across school. To prepare for an Ofsted inspection, the link governor for quality of education will need to familiarise themselves with the work being conducted in school and the best way to do that is to observe, discuss, challenge and celebrate the quality of education on offer within departments. These visits will provide you with the chance to explain the curriculum and learning intentions, to reinforce the rationale about why you are teaching what you are, how it links to past and future learning, and how learning is tailored to pupil needs.

Outside of these direct governor interactions, and as the governing body is accountable for the overall direction of the school, school-wide policies and budgets will be discussed, challenged and ratified. While not as visible an interaction as link governor visits, this work will have significant, direct implications for your teaching practice. For example, governing bodies are responsible for agreeing the budget for future academic years, policies such as behaviour and uniform, safeguarding and pupil wellbeing, staff wellbeing and workload, among many other considerations. Teachers are stakeholders in these processes, with a staff governor sitting on the governing board. The staff governor will be able to relay important information regards daily school life back to the governing body and identify needs, issues or areas of celebration. It is important to interact with the governing body where practicable through requests, questions and queries, particularly any staff voice surveys. If senior leadership and governors are not aware of issues within the school from a teacher perspective, then they do not know what to prioritise to improve wellbeing, reduce workload and update policies to reflect feedback.

BRINGING ACCOUNTABILITY AND GOVERNANCE TOGETHER

In the UK, Ofsted are the regulatory body responsible for inspecting services providing education and skills for learners of all ages (Ofsted, 2022b). As a result, it is likely in your teaching career that your education provider, typically a maintained school or academy, will be inspected by Ofsted. Inspections typically last two full days, with inspectors spending most of their time observing lessons and speaking with pupils and staff to inform judgements about the school. Under the new Ofsted Education Inspection Framework (Ofsted, 2022a), judgements will be made about schools in terms of overall effectiveness, quality of education, behaviour and attitudes, personal development and leadership and management.

A judgement of the provider will then be made, either outstanding, good, requires improvement or inadequate, and shared with the local authority, governing body, academy trust (if applicable) and parents of pupils at the school (Ofsted, 2022a). Ofsted considers its role to be more than just inspection and regulation, recently releasing research and insight series around subjects that aim to identify trends, highlight issues and share good practice (Ofsted, 2022b). The geography research review series is an excellent example of how Ofsted are seeking to identify the nature of high-quality teaching in subjects through reviews of pedagogy, assessment and whole school policies (Ofsted, 2021).

WHAT IS OFSTED LOOKING FOR DURING INSPECTIONS?

The Education Inspection Framework (EIF) was published for use from September 2019, with the most notable change from previous frameworks being the judgement for quality of education. The change in this judgement has placed curriculum back to the centre of focus within education. Providers will now be judged based on the intent, implementation and impact of the curriculum within their setting, rather than being weighted towards data and outcomes. The three sub-sections to the quality of education framework are important to distinguish, as they will impact upon you as a teacher in differing ways.

- Intent – what does the school want pupils to learn?

This focuses upon the construction of a curriculum that is ambitious and challenging, meeting the needs of all learners. Ofsted will want to see a curriculum that is coherently planned and sequenced towards cumulative knowledge and skills that will help in future learning and employment. The curriculum is accessed by all learners, only specialising where necessary (for example, at GCSE or A level).

- Implementation – what are teachers going to teach pupils?

This aspect focuses upon the delivery of subject content by teachers with good knowledge of their subject. Understanding is checked regularly with clear and direct feedback given. Teaching is responsive and adaptive to needs in the classroom. Teaching helps pupils remember more over the long term, using assessment to help pupils embed and use knowledge in different contexts. Curate environments that focus upon learning and reading, with resources that reflect the intent of the curriculum.

- Impact – what evidence will the school show that this curriculum has worked?

This considers the detailed knowledge and skills that are developed across the curriculum, reflected in achievements from national tests and examinations. Knowledge developed prepares pupils for further study, employment or training to meet their interests, aspirations or course of study.

ACCOUNTABILITY, GOVERNANCE AND INSPECTION – WHAT HAPPENS IN AN INSPECTION

Inspections under the previous guise of Ofsted had a reputation of being intensely focused upon performance data and outcomes as a barometer for success. This accountability model was detrimental to other subjects outside the core of English, maths and science, and was considered unable to capture the wider development of pupils, particularly the experiences and cultural capital gained during their school careers. The current Education Inspection Framework has moved away from this previous data-driven mantra towards a more holistic approach to evaluation of learning across the curriculum.

Included within this more holistic approach are new 'deep dives', which include observations, interviews, work scrutiny and document reviews. Secondary schools will likely have around five subjects involved in the deep dive process, with evidence collected from a large sample of pupils across the year groups under consideration. The deep dives include an evaluation of senior leader intent for the subjects chosen, together with their overall understanding of the implementation and impact of the school curriculum. Middle leaders will be assessed through long- and medium-term planning and why they have sequenced, planned and chosen the content taught within their subjects.

Senior leaders are the first point of contact for an Ofsted inspection, as inspectors will have a telephone conversation with the headteacher to assess the effectiveness of the school's vision, strategy and culture. The curriculum will be a significant consideration – what is on offer, who it is on offer to, and when it is offered. Understanding of the curriculum across school and why specific choices have been made will also be explored.

The responsibility of a governor is to drive up standards, therefore inspectors will be seeking evidence that governors are holding the headteacher to account. The simplest place to demonstrate this is during governing body minutes, when probing questions and clarifications are recorded that challenge leadership of the school. Governors are also expected to hold a working knowledge of school progress across behaviour, attendance and achievement. Therefore, governors will also need to understand the school's ethos and curriculum narrative, in addition to the plans in place to improve behaviour and attendance.

THE IMPORTANCE OF MIDDLE LEADERS DURING OFSTED INSPECTIONS

Middle leaders with responsibility for the curriculum within subject areas will be scrutinised on how well they have curated, implemented and reviewed the impact of curriculum plans. Middle leaders are therefore assessed on their choices for what content has gone into the curriculum and how it is organised to meet the needs of all learners to make progress. This section will introduce some of the key considerations middle leaders might take when developing a curriculum in line with the new EIF.

Curriculum development is often referred to as the 'progression model', and by this it means that knowledge progresses in difficulty through a clearly defined sequence, with a clear rationale, to alter the long-term memory of pupils. It is therefore this alteration of long-term memory that is at the core of pupils 'remembering more'. As such, judgement of pupil progress will be based upon how much of the curriculum a pupil has learned. This can be a challenging task. Curriculum must therefore be developed clearly with enough specificity regarding what pupils need to know, need to remember, and how they apply knowledge. These considerations will of course differ across a pupil's learning journey, as knowledge of subjects will become more specific, complex and abstract as they move from EYFS to KS4 and beyond.

Sequences of learning across the curriculum should therefore allow pupils to build confidence in learning and how to apply this knowledge across different contexts, before introducing more challenging and abstract subject content. In doing so, pupils will have robust foundations upon which to build and therefore feel more comfortable with the increase in challenge that they may not have experienced before. It is understood that any curriculum should be inclusive and meet the demands/needs of all pupils.

Curricula also need to be agile and reflective, so they can be reshaped through assessment, to ensure that pupils are given the best opportunities to remember more of what they are being taught.

Underpinning all of this is an acknowledgement that a pupil's memory can only hold so much information at once. It is important to build pupil knowledge up, with routine opportunities for reflection and repetition of learning to improve retainment. Doing so will encourage pupils to make connections with learning across subjects and disciplines – to piece together the jigsaw that is their memory. Providing these links within lessons can help remove barriers to remembering, as pupils have opportunities to repeat and apply knowledge in different contexts.

The Ofsted Education Inspection Framework can therefore be helpfully captured by the phrase 'knowing more, remembering more'. While this phrase may seem oversimplistic, it is a useful starting point to consider how a curriculum can be sequenced and linked to ensure pupils can recall knowledge accurately over longer periods of time – altering the long-term memory of pupils. Within this it is helpful to distinguish between knowledge and know-how. Pupils need to be taught knowledge and then how to use it. For example, pupils need to be taught how to read a map. Pupils then also need opportunities to practise this 'know-how' in different contexts using different maps, to alter long-term memory and retain the knowledge of map reading for the future.

WHAT WILL TEACHERS DO AND BE ASKED ABOUT DURING AN INSPECTION?

While trainees and ECTs are unlikely to be expected to defend the practice of the school during an inspection, it is useful to understand what teachers will do and be asked about. Secondary subject teachers will need to be able to explain what they are teaching and why they are doing it that way. They will need to be reflective in their practice, asking *'where does this learning link together with previous and future learning?'*, *'why am I wanting the pupils to know this information?'* and *'how and why are pupils going to apply the knowledge I am teaching them?'*

To answer these questions, secondary subject teachers will need to engage with curriculum development within their department. Doing so will help explain the rationale of what they are doing daily and why this is the best approach for the pupils in front of them. Teachers will then receive a fuller picture of what topics/texts/knowledge are important to the community the school serves, and how lessons are tailored specifically to the pupils served by the curriculum that has been developed. These explorations into department curriculum will assist in triangulating what teachers are doing, what the department is doing and what the school is seeking to do with the curriculum offer. Secondary subject teachers will therefore likely need to explain how, with examples, the whole school ethos and vision for curriculum is reflected in the department and own teaching.

In summary, the importance of different accountability measures has changed significantly since 2019. Instead of heavily weighted data-driven inspections, Ofsted are offering a counterpoint to this in expecting to see the quality of education more holistically. Inspections seek to explore the texture and context of the curriculum and teaching through middle leaders and teachers, rather than SLT, to ensure a good-quality education for all learners is being offered consistently. To prepare for these discussions, teachers need to engage with curriculum development with departments and how this links to the whole school ethos and vision of curriculum. A result of this will then be a more in-depth, confident rationale of teaching practice, lesson planning and adaptations to classes being taught.

REFLECTION POINT

Ofsted and intention

- Where in lesson planning do you engage with curricular intent?
- What short- and medium-term plans have you used in your placement? How do they communicate the longer-term intention of the school?
- When you are reflecting on lessons you have taught, how much weight do you give to thinking about curriculum intent and what pupils are learning?

ASSIGNMENT LINKS

1. You might use information in this chapter if you are asked to think about progress and accountability measures in school.
2. You might get asked to think about how we assess learning and the success of schools.
3. You could get asked to reflect on the importance of Ofsted as a regulatory body, evaluating the ways in which it enhances education and risks of this system too.

LEARNING AND CONSOLIDATION ACTIVITIES
IDEAS FOR GUIDED PRACTICE AND FEEDBACK

Find out about your school's data; how does the school perform against the national accountability measures? Can you talk with your mentor about what this data means for the school?

When you begin your school-based placement, investigate the school website to find out a little bit about the governing body – who is on the board, what are the sub-committees and what do the meeting minutes tell you about the focus of their meetings?

Ask your mentor about what governor involvement there is through either subject-specific visits or engagement with wider school life.

CHAPTER SUMMARY

This chapter has introduced you to the notion of accountability within the secondary school system and what measures are in place to judge the success of a school in relation to pupils' progress. You were also encouraged to consider how the external accountability measures will impact on you as a new teacher. The chapter has also discussed school governance and explained how this is connected to your role as a teacher. The function of Ofsted within the education system was explored with a particular emphasis on how this will impact on you in the first few years of your teaching career.

FURTHER READING

Brill, F., Grayson, H., Kuhn, L. and O'Donnell, S. (2018) What impact does accountability have on curriculum, standards, and engagement in education? A literature review. Slough. NFER.

Ofsted (2022) *Education Inspection Framework*. UK Government. Available at: www.gov.uk/government/publications/education-inspection-framework/education-inspection-framework

REFERENCES

Biesta, G. (2010) *Good Education in an Age of Measurement: Ethics, Politics, Democracy.* London: Routledge.

Brill, F., Grayson, H., Kuhn, L. and O'Donnell, S. (2018) *What Impact Does Accountability Have on Curriculum, Standards and Engagement in Education? A Literature Review*. Slough: National Foundation for Educational Research (NFER).

Coe, R. (2013) 'Improving education: a triumph of hope over experience'. Inaugural lecture, presented at Durham University. (Microsoft Word – Improving Education Coe Inaugural June 2013.docx (eachandeverydog.net).

Committee on Standards in Public Life (1995) 'The seven principles of public life'. UK Government. The Seven Principles of Public Life – GOV.UK (www.gov.uk).

Costa, A.L. and Kallick, B. (1993) Through the Lens of a Critical Friend. Educational Leadership, 49–51. Available at: www.ascd.org/publications/educational-leadership/oct93/vol51/num02/Through-the-Lens-of-a-Critical-Friend.aspx

David, M. (1993) *Parents, Gender and Education Reform*. Cambridge: Blackwell.

DfE (2011) *The Teacher Standards Guidance*. (Teachers' Standards guidance (publishing.service.gov.uk)).

DfE (2019) *What Works in Delivering School Improvement Through School-to-School Support*. (What works in delivering school improvement through school-to-school support (publishing.service.gov.uk)).

DfE (2022a) *Secondary Accountability Measures – Update for the 2021 to 2022 Academic Year*. (Secondary accountability measures – update for the 2021 to 2022 academic year (publishing.service.gov.uk)).

DfE (2022b) *Next Steps Towards a Strong School System with All Schools in Strong Trusts*. (Next steps towards a stronger school system with all schools in strong trusts – GOV.UK (www.gov.uk)).

Hextall, I. and Mahoney, P. (2000) *Reconstructing Teaching: Standards, Performance and Accountability*. London: Routledge.

Hutchings, M. (2015) 'Exam factories? The impact of accountability measures on children and young people'. National Union of Teachers. ((PDF) Exam Factories? The impact of accountability measures on children and young people (researchgate.net)).

Matthews, P. and Ehren, M. (2022) Accountability and improvement in self-improving school systems, in T. Greany and P. Earley (eds) *School Leadership and Education System Reform*. Great Britain: Bloomsbury.

National Governance Association (2022) 'Eight elements of effective governance' (Eight elements of effective governance – National Governance Association (nga.org.uk)).

Ofsted (2021) *Research Review Series: Geography*. UK Government. Available at: www.gov.uk/government/publications/research-review-series-geography/research-review-series-geography

Ofsted (2022a) *Education Inspection Framework*. UK Government. Available at: www.gov.uk/government/publications/education-inspection-framework/education-inspection-framework

Ofsted (2022b) *Ofsted Strategy 2022–27*. UK Government. Available at: https://assets.publishing.service.gov.uk/government/uploads/system/uploads/attachment_data/file/1070946/Ofsted_Strategy_2022_2027.pdf

Pelletier, L.G., Séguin-Lévesque, C. and Legault, L. (2002) Pressure from above and pressure from below as determinants of teachers' motivation and teaching behaviors. *Journal of Educational Psychology 94, no. 1 (2002)*: 186–96.

Taylor-Fitzgibbon, C. (1997) 'The value-added national project final report'. The University of Durham. (Microsoft Word – durham report.doc (hubspotusercontent30.net)).

Wrigley, T. (2003) *Schools of Hope: A New Agenda for School Improvement*. Stoke-on-Trent: Trentham.

13

YOUR PROFESSIONAL FUTURE: GETTING A JOB AND DEVELOPING YOUR EXPERTISE

AMANDA MEIER, MARK DEACON AND LEIGH HOATH

 KEY WORDS

- Network
- Collaboration
- Job application

CHAPTER OVERVIEW

In this chapter you will learn about how you apply for and secure your first teaching position. We will also help you build, engage with and extend a professional support network as an ECT. The overall purpose of this chapter is to further highlight that your ITT year is just the first year of your development journey as a teacher, and that you can draw on a wealth of experience, community and support as you establish your teacher-self.

INTRODUCTION

One of the themes that has emerged through this book, appearing in many of the chapters, is the need to work with others in order to progress, be successful and develop fully as a teacher. Even though you are relying on yourself in the classroom, or in the job interviews you take part in, your development and practice is best developed with the advice, views and experience of others. This chapter therefore starts with advice about searching, applying and interviewing for your first job. Your development obviously doesn't end when you achieve an exciting first teaching post; arguably the community aspect of your work and development becomes of greater value at this point. So, the second part of this chapter will cover your activities and development post-qualification in the Early Career Teacher and later years of your profession.

13 Your professional future: getting a job and developing your expertise

---

▀▀▀ — LINKS TO THE CORE CONTENT FRAMEWORK

All of the Core Content Framework themes are referred to and applied in this chapter, but the following are the most relevant:

Standard 8

1. Effective professional development is likely to be sustained over time, involve expert support or coaching and opportunities for collaboration.
2. Reflective practice, supported by feedback from and observation of experienced colleagues, professional debate and learning from educational research, is also likely to support improvement.
3. Teachers can make valuable contributions to the wider life of the school in a broad range of ways, including by supporting and developing effective professional relationships with colleagues.
7. Engaging in high-quality professional development can help teachers improve.

GETTING YOUR FIRST TEACHING JOB

▀▀▀ — CASE STUDY

Should Jasmeet Apply?

Jasmeet is coming to the end of her PGCE. She has done well and is an enthusiastic and effective new teacher. Jasmeet is engaged to Zain, who is settled in his first engineering job in Lanchester. They intend on marrying and living in Lanchester. Neet Street Academy, Lanchester, has advertised for a teacher. The location is perfect for Jasmeet, but she is concerned that Neet Street has a less than excellent reputation. The school has been through Special Measures but was then taken on by a successful MAT. Since then, there have been big changes to the school. New teachers have joined and the curriculum and even the uniform have been completely changed. Jasmeet is aware that some parents in the community are not happy with all of these innovations. Neet Street was classified as Requires Improvement in an Ofsted inspection in 2020.

- Should Jasmeet apply?
- What are the pros and cons for Jasmeet in this job opportunity?
- What steps could Jasmeet take to find out more information and help her make a decision about applying?

It is important that you do not let labels commonly applied to schools put you off a job application. A poor Ofsted report can mean this is a school working really hard to improve. An unpopular school can be intimate and supportive; a poor local reputation can come from people who remember it as a bad place 30 years ago. If you talk to teachers in schools that seem to have a tough reputation, you will often find that their work brings a great deal of satisfaction and reward. Indeed, one of the authors had the time of his life working to turn around a school that rejoiced in the label 'The worst school in Britain'.

WHAT DO YOU WANT?

Teaching is a satisfying yet demanding job. It is the kind of job that will be a significant part of your life. This means that it is important to find a role that is a good fit for your values as much as for the practical aspects of getting to work on time and in sound mind. So, before you dive into job listings, it is probably a good idea to draw up a list of priorities and preferences that you can use to help you decide where to apply.

REFLECTION POINT

What do you want in your first teaching job?

- Are there restrictions on where you can live?
- Where is your current friendship group and family?
- Where do you want to live?
- What sort of school can you see yourself working in: leafy suburbs, inner city, multi-academy trust, free school, local authority federation?
- What kind of curricular approaches interest you most?
- What would put you off applying to a school? Are these well-grounded objections?
- What about career development – do you already have an idea about what kind of school can give you the kinds of experience you want?
- Are you keen to develop extra-curricular experience, such as running clubs, leading Duke of Edinburgh schemes?
- Perhaps you want to learn about pastoral and wider care and the related curriculum?

These sorts of reflection can be done alone or with your mentors or with friends on your programme. Getting others' ideas and perspectives can often help you clarify your own.

WHERE TO APPLY FOR A JOB

If you are anchored to a relatively small area, you will get fewer options in your choice of school. We will discuss how to approach this situation when we consider your application. England is a country with wide economic disparities between regions. It might be a perfectly reasonable decision to move to an area with lower living costs. Your teaching salary will be largely the same wherever you go, apart from in London (see below). It can also be easier to find work in these areas – coastal towns, for instance, can offer many different jobs each year and often cheaper house prices, though they can also bring significant (and rewarding) educational challenges.

THE LONDON ALLOWANCE

Some of the additional costs of London are recognised in terms of the London Allowance. This is a supplement to your pay depending on where you are working. There are three bands:

Fringe allowance – £1,000

Outer London – up to £3,800

Inner London – up to £8,000

These allowances are linked to your pay and in which London borough you work. These allowances do contribute to your teacher's pension. Your pension scheme is based on your career average earnings. This may not be a significant factor now but one day you might be glad of the early uplift.

THE EDUCATION JOB MARKET

The market for teachers is dynamic – it can change every year. The number of jobs for teachers will fluctuate in line with government policy, the economic climate, teacher pay and conditions and society's perceptions of teachers. Of these, the economy and government policy probably have the most impact. For instance, when science GCSE was taught as a combination of three subjects by the National Curriculum, demand for physics and chemistry teachers rocketed. Up to that point chemistry and especially physics were minority subjects – and demand for physics teachers has been very high ever since.

Some of us may choose to look with envy at our colleagues training to teach 'shortage subjects' as they will have more choice when it comes to applying for jobs. But at the time of writing this chapter, there is a general shortage of teachers that does not show any signs of being changed in the near future. Some trainees, perhaps those looking for work in teaching PE or history, will have to be more flexible around type of school, location, role and nature of contract but most can expect to get a job that suits them, and that is supportive (Spencer et al., 2018).

WHAT DO SCHOOLS WANT?

Even when they're looking to fill shortage subject positions, head teachers will be looking for someone who can bring good teaching to their school. Later in this section we will talk about completing an application that shows you have the skills and experiences of a successful ITT trainee, and you will need to think about which of your experiences and values best shows that to prepare for writing that application. Schools are also looking for rounded candidates who can offer other skills and experience.

So, it would be a good idea to consider what else you can offer. Perhaps you have a second subject you can teach. Think about your A levels – you might be able to offer some teaching in a subject that the school might really appreciate. Science teachers, especially physics graduates, can often find that schools need them to teach some maths too. One of the author's recent biology trainees is now happily teaching sports science.

Perhaps you have a passion that can add to the curriculum? Head teachers will be looking at the whole of life in the school – will you be up for running a STEM club, or helping with the school choir?

DIFFERENT TYPES OF SCHOOL

Local authority schools – a school funded, supported by and accountable to the local authority.

Academies – in many respects these schools are just local schools, but they enjoy freedoms in organisation, curriculum and staffing not available to local authority schools. They are funded by and accountable to the Department for Education. Most academies have banded together into groups called multi-academy trusts. You will probably train in a school that belongs to a MAT.

Free schools – free schools are a type of academy. They are set up in response to local demand, often by groups of parents who have a view on the local provision and want to do something different.

Faith schools – these are academies, free schools or local authority schools that are supported and run by faith groups. Do not rule yourself out of applying for a job in a faith school just because you do not share that faith. Most faith schools only require that you are in sympathy with its teachings. Most faith school heads would rather have an excellent teacher who is an atheist than a poor teacher who fully embraces a faith.

Special schools – children in special schools often have particular physical, medical, psychological or other learning needs that mean that their teacher has to overcome significant barriers to learning. To work in a special school setting requires patience, resilience and a profound understanding of learning because they represent an intellectual and pastoral challenge. Special school heads look for experienced teachers who have demonstrated a high level of skill in a mainstream setting. However, Early Career Teachers can apply and, of course, some have experience of working in these settings through work experience, training route or perhaps having a family member with additional needs.

Private schools – are paid for by parents directly, though some of the pupils will be receiving bursaries and scholarships. Like state schools, they tend to emphasise broad pastoral, extra-curricular as well as academic achievements, but in a context where school funds can provide excellent learning environments and facilities. Sports, arts and personal development are often a focus of considerable activity, alongside teaching the curriculum.

Private schools do have longer holidays. While this is great, during term time a lot will be required of teachers, and you can expect to do very long days. There will also be an expectation that you take a full role in the wider curriculum, so you can expect to run sports teams, weekend activities and trips. There are often excellent fringe benefits to working in the private sector. In boarding schools there will be opportunities to take on house duties. These usually come with free accommodation and free food – this can be great if you are saving for a house deposit for instance.

PAY, ECT YEARS AND FIXED-TERM CONTRACTS

Despite this diversity of provision, national agreements on pay, conditions, union recognition and pension arrangements are still in effect. In most schools, including some private schools, you can expect to be paid on the Standard National Pay Scales, with National Conditions of Service. If you are applying to a private, academy or free school, check out their pay and conditions policies before signing a contract to see if this is the case.

Wherever you decide to apply for your first post, do check that they can support an Early Career Teacher. That support is going to involve mentor support, time off for training, a training provider and registration with an appropriate body to sign off the ECT programme.

Most head teachers are risk averse. They will want to be confident that you are a good choice. You may find that you are offered a fixed-term contract, which means that the school can use this as a kind of probation period. While this is becoming more normal, if you are in a shortage subject, you might be able to push back on that in negotiations. You might also be able to shop around and find schools where this isn't what is on offer.

WHEN AND HOW TO LOOK FOR YOUR FIRST JOB

When you have got a clearer idea of your preferences, you can start to use these as criteria to help you decide where to apply. The job market for Early Career Teachers will open in late January and early February, but you can start your search at any time. In shortage subjects you may find that you are approached by your placement school or even see some adverts appearing in November or December. In most cases you'll find your job online.

Table 13.1 Finding a job to apply for

www.tes.com/jobs/	The TeS Jobs website is where many new teachers find their first job. It offers an alert service. This is very useful if you are limited to working in a particular area.
https://jobs.theguardian.com/jobs/schools/	The *Education Guardian* offers posts in schools – this includes teaching jobs alongside admin and other support or specialist posts. If you are looking for education sector work that isn't teaching, then this can be a good place to start.
https://teaching-vacancies.service.gov.uk/	In an effort to help schools with the cost of advertising jobs, the government has set up this site. You can use it to search for teaching, school leadership and education support jobs in England. It will also allow you to apply for jobs and set up job alerts.
School, faith and diocesan websites	Faith schools, private schools and others often also advertise on their websites, or through parent organisations such as the local diocese, faith council or multi-academy trust.
Unsolicited applications	You can apply directly to schools that you are interested in, even if they have not advertised. Follow the advice in the rest of this section, but don't be disappointed if you do not receive a reply.

PREPARING YOUR APPLICATION

Successful applications are usually built on good research about the school you are applying for. Knowing about the school and its curriculum can help you tune your application so that it shows the head what a good candidate you are, and how you fit well with what they need and want. Doing this research can also help you decide whether the school seems like a good fit for you. You can do this by looking at different sources of information, but you shouldn't rely on any one of these alone. Get an overall picture (Allen and Sims, 2018) – don't let one piece of off-putting information dissuade you.

- The school website: this is the world's window into the school, but it is completely in the head's control. Read it carefully and be aware that the site will be designed to show the school in the best positive light.

- Ofsted reports: these can be useful (but they might also have been done quite a while ago). As we have already seen, however, an Ofsted grade can't tell you the whole story about a school.

- Performance tables: the government service at www.gov.uk/school-performance-tables allows you to find a range of performance information about the school and compare it to other similar schools. Be aware of the impact of the Covid-19 pandemic on school data when using this website.

- Teachers who work there: this can be a really informative source. Teachers will tell you about the day-to-day experiences of working in the school.

- Trainees who have been placed there: your peers might also be useful – especially if they work in the department where you are applying. Do consider whether you and your informant are similar people, or whether you might have different views or experiences to them.

- Visiting the school: it is a good idea to try and negotiate a visit to the school before you send in your application. If you do visit, then dress and be prompt. In other words, act as if this were an interview, as a first impression is important.

▰▰▰— REFLECTION POINT

Use one of the websites we have outlined above; pick a job, and then do some research about the school using some of these methods. What kinds of key ideas and themes emerge that you might put in an application?

APPLYING FOR A JOB

The application procedure for most jobs follows a typical pattern. After contacting the school you will get a pack, usually consisting of information about the school, a job description, a person specification and an application form. Follow these steps to get your application ready:

The golden rule is that schools will specify the format of your application and will want you to follow the instructions given, e.g. no. of pages, font size, word count, etc. If they use an application form, fill that in. If they want a covering letter that sets out a personal statement, and a CV, do that.

Table 13.2 Steps for job application

Closing date	Note the closing date – it is easy to miss when you are busy
Job description	Read the job description. Is this the job you were expecting to be doing? Are there any unexpected duties listed? Highlight or make a note of the features that you want to make clear links with.
Person specification	This usually sets out the qualifications and characteristics of the ideal candidate, sometimes as 'essential' and 'desirable' criteria. Read through it, and as with the job description, note down how you can address these requirements in your application.
Application form	Complete this, with accurate information, and make sure that you have: 1. sought permission from referees 2. given a complete employment and education record – or you explain any gaps 3. checked your grammar, spelling and use of standard English.
Statement/covering letter	Some application forms have space for a personal statement on the application form. In other cases you will be asked to do this in a covering letter. We have set out some more advice on your statement below.
Your placement school	Let your placement school know you're applying so that they have warning if you're asked for an interview.

YOUR PERSONAL STATEMENT

If we assume that many people applying for the role will be ECTs, and will have similar qualifications, it is often your personal statement that secures you an interview. You need to make the statement interesting and give a good account about your teaching, values and personality. There's quite a bit of advice online (Beckett, 2020; Drury, 2013), but in particular you should write about:

- Your life before teaching: perhaps you have had another career, or worked your way through university; what skills did you develop and how might you translate that to teaching?

- Your education: how does your degree or A levels contribute to your subject knowledge, interest and passion?

- Your decision to become a teacher: what informed this? Why now? How did your previous experiences and roles contribute to this?

- Your professional development: what has interested and motivated you as you have trained? What makes your subject an invaluable one for pupils to learn? It would

- be good to make a reference to your placement schools, but remember to keep it entirely positive.
- The school and the role you are applying for: why did you apply for this job, in this school? What makes you an excellent fit for the person specification or job description?
- Any issues or problems that your CV might show: do you have an unusual degree? Will a head be able to understand how that equips you to do the job on offer? Did you get into difficulties at school or even with the law as a young person? Be clear about this and what you have learned from these experiences.
- What else can you offer: what about DofE? Sporting clubs? A faith group? Maybe you have an unusual interest that would enthuse pupils – the possibilities are endless.
- A strong sign-off: you need a strong finish. You want to present yourself as a good professional starting out on a career journey. What is it you want the head to remember about your application?

WHAT HAPPENS TO YOUR APPLICATION?

Your application will go into a long-listing process. It will be read by several people, probably the relevant department leader, maybe a governor, and a senior leader. If you get through this phase, there will be a shortlisting process, in which your application will be reviewed with a focus on your statement and, if they've been called, your references. At this point you may be shortlisted for interview.

If you have any live applications, check your emails regularly. Invitations for interview will almost certainly be emailed to you. Sometimes this can be at short notice, so keep your placement school informed.

PREPARING FOR INTERVIEW

The golden rule here is that you need to practise. There are lots of websites where you can find lists of questions for teacher interviews, some of which are subject focused. Use these, and practise answers for them. Take care to plan for difficult questions, which can often be the most simple, such as 'What makes you the best candidate for this job?', which can be off-putting if you're not ready. Practise answers as you're driving or walking to college, university or placement. Ask a friend or your mentor to give you a mock interview and take their feedback on board. If you don't get the job after practising, think about which answers you wish you could have another go at, and practise those for your next application.

Table 13.3 Interview questions – things to prepare for

What makes a good lesson? Tell me about a really good lesson you have taught.	With any sort of question like these, have two or three lessons in mind that you can talk about. You could begin your reply with: "Let me tell you about my second placement lesson on rate of photosynthesis ..." You then talk about how what you did and the impact of this good practice.
What is the worst lesson you have taught?	This is a tough question. Show that you have reflected on why the lesson was not good and what you did about the issues you saw.
Behaviour	Sometimes this will involve a scenario. You should prepare an answer based around your placement school policy and about the impact that this had.
Special educational or inclusion needs	Do not make the mistake of assuming that some schools do or don't have SEN issues to work with. Use clear examples from pupils you have taught and emphasise your high expectations and working with the SEN team and other adults.
Questions from your application form or letter	Have you raised issues there that an interviewer might want to talk about? This could be your unusual hobby, your previous career, languages you speak, or the fact you were brought up abroad. Can you show how any unusual experience could enhance your teaching or be an additional resource for the school?
Safeguarding	There will always be a question about safeguarding. Remember your training, especially that: You need to report all concerns to the safeguarding team in school. Safeguarding isn't just related to physical abuse – it includes issues of political radicalisation, criminal and sexual exploitation and other issues. You *cannot promise* that you will keep secret anything a pupil tells you.

■ ■ ■ —— REFLECTION POINT

- Prepare and practise answers to these questions with someone else from your course. How convincing are your answers?
- What could improve about each other's responses?

THE INTERVIEW DAY

Interviews come in all sorts of shapes and sizes. You might:

- have an opportunity to meet the department;
- have an opportunity to meet (and sometimes be interviewed by) some pupils;

- go on a tour of the school;
- be interviewed by a panel, which may include a governor;
- get a chance to walk around by yourself;
- be asked to teach a demonstration lesson.

Above all remember that you are being evaluated the whole time you are in the school. The pupils, governors, department team, interview panel, school reception team and anyone else you meet will be asked about how you came across. Even while just walking around, your comments will be noted.

Before you arrive, it is important that you think through questions that you want answered and anticipate some questions that you may be asked.

THE LESSON

You will usually be asked to prepare a lesson to teach to a group and will be given a topic and a year group, and often some idea of attainment patterns and any SEN in the group. Schools will be looking to see that you can construct a sensible plan and prepare resources and explanations that address these parameters. During the lesson they will want you to show that you can interact professionally with pupils, understand what pupils are understanding and what they are struggling with, and run the lesson competently. During your preparations, get some advice from your mentor, head of department or others in your placement school so that you're confident about what you're doing. Prepare your lesson plan and bring in copies of this, along with the resources you will use. You will be observed, and your observers will want copies of these. You'll need to reflect on the lesson and discuss this reflection in the interview. Don't panic if the lesson goes badly, but be ready to explain what you would do differently.

ASKING QUESTIONS

There will be opportunities to ask questions in your interviews and panels, but you also need to show interest in the school and its pupils while you are on the tour or meeting pupil panels. Ask pupils about their ambitions, what they like about their school and what they'd like to improve. Take their ideas seriously, and be approachable, but not glib. Pupils are usually proud of their school and want teachers who take it seriously.

You will also want to ask questions in your interview. You don't need to ask lots of them, but it is a good way of showing that you are interested and have noticed important things about the school.

WITHDRAWING

During the interview process you may decide that this really is not the school for you. Do not waste any more time if that's the case. Tell the person running the day that you have decided that you no longer wish to proceed with your application. While it is courteous to offer an explanation, you do not have to go into detail. You might be asked at the end of the interview if you are still interested in the job, or if you are 'still a serious candidate'. If you aren't, this is also a good time to let them know.

DEALING WITH THE OUTCOMES

RESPONDING TO A REJECTION

There can be many reasons why you did not get a job. There could have been an internal candidate who they want to keep, there could be someone with more relevant experience, or you didn't do as well as you wanted on the day.

If you do not get the job, ask for feedback. Listen to and reflect carefully on that feedback. Do you need to develop your knowledge? Improve your explanations? Present yourself differently? Whatever the feedback suggests, do not argue or seek to justify yourself. Arguing changes nothing; what you are being told is how you came across to that panel on that day. If you do argue, you are going to irritate the person providing feedback. No matter how indignant you may feel, you must be professional – especially because you might one day have another interview with this person.

THE JOB OFFER

You might be made a job offer at the end of the day, or even at the end of the interview. Often, you'll get a call in the late afternoon or early evening. If you are offered the position, you will be asked if you will accept the job at a particular salary point and when the job starts. There might be some things that you can negotiate. It's wise not to ask for too much, and some of the ideas below might be more important to you than others. When you make these requests, you need to know what you will accept or say if the answer is no.

- Negotiating your starting salary point upward? You will need to justify this in terms of your experience, expertise or what else you can offer the school.

- A start date at the end of June? The advantage of this is that you will be paid through the summer break.

- Funding for a Master's degree? If you have done PGCE at level 7, you will have 60 Master's credits, so the school only needs to fund 120 credits.

- Second subject teaching or extra-curricular clubs?

13 Your professional future: getting a job and developing your expertise

RESPONDING TO AN OFFER

If your discussions have gone well, and this is the job you want, then you might say "Yes, please" and accept the job at once. A common situation is that you have other interviews lined up and your least favoured school interviewed first and has made you a job offer. At this point you have three options:

1. Accept the job and forget about the other options.
2. Be upfront and say that you have other interviews coming up. Ask the head to give you a few days before accepting.
3. Say no.

You will see there is no perfect solution. If you go for (2), a head may withdraw the job offer. This is a situation that you will have to think through. This really is your decision and there is no perfect answer. What you really should not do is accept a job, go to another interview, get offered the job and then pull out of the least favoured job. When you say "Yes", you are committed. It is unwise to walk away once you have verbally accepted the job.

DEVELOPING YOUR KNOWLEDGE, PRACTICE AND TEACHER-LEARNER IDENTITY AFTER YOU HAVE QTS

The transition to being 'a teacher' rather than a trainee is a rather odd one. It is what you have been working towards and is therefore no great surprise when it happens, but there is something about walking into the school as a teacher with your own classroom that is quite special. At the same time, there is still the two years of the ECF to work through and we must bear this in mind. You are (almost!) there.

All of the principles you have read around being successful as a trainee in terms of working with your mentor, host teachers and other colleagues have real value for you as an ECT. It is easy to think that post-training you are 'done' and full package. The truth of this is that you are just at the start of your career and still at a very formative stage. This is not meant to be discouraging but actually the opposite. You have the chance to become *even* better, develop *further* and grow into your new profession.

Many of the challenges of the training year are stripped away as you become an ECT. There are no more assignments, the lesson planning demands may be less, the need to record your thoughts and actions in as much detail will diminish. In contrast, your teaching load will be higher. You may have a form full-time. Lunchtime duties and expectations of extra-curricular contributions are now part of your normal week. The demands on you are different, rather than less, which means that you need to consider how you will balance these as you develop through the ECT years. Outside of your school there are a number of ways in which you can seek and access support, some of which are outlined below.

ECT DEVELOPMENT

As an ECT you will continue your development through the Early Careers Framework – this will be organised through your school with a local provider. The ECF is designed to offer an ongoing structure and opportunities for continued mentoring over the two years of your ECT year, as evidence suggests that CPD needs to be sustained if it is to be effective (Collin and Smith, 2021). Most ECT programmes and in-school CPD for ECTs also provide chances to meet with others at the same stage of development. It is important that you make the most of the opportunity to talk with other ECTs, particularly if you are one of a small number in your school or department. As with your ITT year, simply knowing that someone else is having some of the challenges you are is often a comfort in itself.

The ECT curriculum framework is very similar to the CCF. This means that many of the ideas will be familiar to you. What the ECT gives you is a chance to develop your use of the ideas and practices you have learned about with a full complement of classes and groups. You will also benefit from a weekly discussion with your ECT mentor, who can help deepen your understanding of the implications for those ideas in the context of your ECT school. Finally, your ECT provider will arrange for sessions and perhaps even conferences where you can meet other ECTs in different schools and understand how their school uses the approaches and ideas in the ECF.

SOCIAL MEDIA

There are a number of subject-specific and generic education groups and communities that can be found through social media channels such as Twitter (Lantz-Andersson et al., 2018). Through these you will be able to access a range of views, positions and approaches to teaching that give you insights into the questions other teachers are asking, the experiences of teachers who have many years of teaching under their belts, and also to pick up on the current debates and thinking around education.

There is a word of caution to be shared in relation to this. The information that is shared through such media is not quality assured and while the significant majority of participants maintain very high professional standards, there are times when heated debates spark more emotional or personal responses (Carpenter et al., 2022). Where there is a limited character count with posting on media, it is important to remember that this diminishes the detail that can be added to the subject and so views may appear to be more extreme than they are in reality or position certain approaches in very polar positions. The situation with teaching is that there is no one right way – there are too many factors that vary by school, class, county ... there is no silver bullet, and it is key that as you engage with education in this way that you bear in mind that many situations are far more nuanced than reading on social media first portrays.

SUBJECT ASSOCIATIONS

Joining your subject association is a way to become involved with a community of people who are able to share experiences, thinking and often resources that relate to the subject you are teaching. There are often wider benefits to this – publications that bring current thinking and practice to you, conferences that highlight best practice in your subject, the ability to explore ways in which your subject can best be accessed by your pupils (Lawson et al., 2020; Perry et al., 2022). Throughout the school, teachers are often bereft of time for discussions – the demands on managing the unexpected, the marking, the classroom organisation, etc., reduce the opportunities to talk about the subject you are teaching more widely. Subject associations may offer a distillation of this dialogue for you and can influence some of the decisions you are making in terms of your classroom practice. They may host events such as TeachMeets where practice is shared as well as social media 'chats' and other focused sessions that enable you to think about the subject-specific ways of the classroom.

Depending on your subject area, you may be offered the opportunity to apply for chartered status for your subject (there is also generic chartered teacher status) after a number of years of teaching. This recognises your continued professional development, expertise and commitment to classroom teaching.

READING AND TALKING – CRITICAL DIALOGUE

It may well be at the end of your training that you do not want to pick up another academic journal or book again. The assignments you had to do through your training should have been closely linked with your practice in schools and beneficial, although when you have relatively little experience, it can be challenging to see the links so explicitly. As you work through your ECT years and beyond, you will gain experiences that you can 'hang' the theory from your reading on. Maintaining reading – even if this is subject association publications and updates – will help. If you can take this a step further and consider this critically with others, then your community and network will support you in being a more discerning teacher than working in isolation.

FURTHER STUDY

If you have undertaken a PGCE through a university, you will have most likely accrued Master's-level credits that you can carry forward through to a full Master's degree – there is usually a time limit on this, so it is worth exploring with your university to ensure that if you choose to do this, it happens within the time regulations.

Further study through a Master's can support your practice in a number of ways. It will allow a structured approach to your thinking about an aspect of education. It might be a focus driven by a personal observation of behaviour, actions or outcomes within your own classroom. That something that you have noted and want to find out a little more about. This form of study will allow you to contextualise your observations and thinking within a theoretical and literature base. It might be that the findings are applicable to only your classroom; however, it is likely that you will have some golden nuggets that can be shared within your department to help influence teaching and/or learning more widely.

The focus of the work might stem from a department or whole school issue – something that from the start you are working towards exploring to shape things across a range of classes. This will have a different feel to it than if you are undertaking something of extremely personal interest; however, it is no less valuable.

CONCLUSION – THE NEXT STAGE IN YOUR JOURNEY

As you go through your ITT year, your ECT years and the first years post-qualification, you will quickly see how much potential for new experience there is in the education sector. Each part of your journey opens up new opportunities to learn, develop and use your expertise. After getting your first job, your career will take you to many different roles, in schools and possibly beyond them. Your pupils, community of practice, your peers and mentors will be a constant source of support and challenge to enable you to meet these new challenges, but the main driver will be your own values, your curiosity and drive to develop.

ASSIGNMENT LINKS

This chapter will help you with the following kinds of assignment:

1. Draft a brief CV for your placement mentor at the start of your placement.
2. Write a draft letter of application or personal statement.
3. Use data sources to find out more about a prospective school.

LEARNING AND CONSOLIDATION ACTIVITIES
KEY THINGS TO LOOK FOR WHEN OBSERVING LESSONS OR TEACHING

Ask your mentor how they work with others from their subject community to develop lesson plans and resources and evaluate the impact of those plans. Do they work with a subject association or its resources, or perhaps online groups and networks through Twitter or Mastodon?

Ask your host teachers and mentors how they found their first job, and what they might look for in a school if they were setting out now.

13 Your professional future: getting a job and developing your expertise

DISCUSSION POINTS FOR TUTORIALS AND SEMINARS

- What kinds of schools have we as a group taught in?
- What are the differences in our experiences of these different schools?
- What are our criteria for looking for a job?
- What kinds of professional literature and knowledge have we relied on during the ITT year?
- What events might subject associations provide that could help new teachers?

IDEAS FOR GUIDED PRACTICE AND FEEDBACK

Collect a set of up to five job adverts and discuss which seem to address your criteria for application with your peers, mentor or tutors.

Join your subject association and use its journal or resources when planning sequences of learning or responding to feedback and assignment briefs.

Prepare for a mock interview with your tutors, mentors or a head teacher from a school in your provider partnership.

▰▰▰ CHAPTER SUMMARY

Now you have read this chapter, you will:

- know how to build criteria to help you decide where to apply
- know about different sources of information to help you research prospective schools
- be able to prepare for and take part in an interview day
- know how to deal with a successful or unsuccessful application
- know about avenues for further development in your ECT and post-ECT years of practice.

▰▰▰ REFLECTION POINT

- Where can I work that enables me to address my values as a subject teacher and that will give me a good grounding in my new career?
- What are subject communities for?
- How can I keep in touch with developments in my subject community and address day-to-day concerns of preparing lessons, teaching and marking?

FURTHER READING

Allen, R. and Sims, S. (2018) *The Teacher Gap*. Routledge.

Priestley, M., Philippou, S., Alvunger, D. and Soini, T. (2021) Curriculum making: a conceptual framing, in M. Priestley, D. Alvunger, S. Philippou and T. Soini (eds) *Curriculum Making in Europe: Policy and Practice Within and Across Diverse Contexts*, pages 1–28. Bingley: Emerald Publishing Limited. DOI: 10.1108/978-1-83867-735-020211002

REFERENCES

Allen, R. and Sims, S. (2018) *The Teacher Gap* (1st edn). Routledge.

Beckett, L. (2020) *How to Stand Out in Your Application Form | TES*. Available at: www.tes.com/jobs/careers-advice/application-and-interview/how-stand-out-your-application-form

Carpenter, J., Tani, T., Morrison, S. and Keane, J. (2022) Exploring the landscape of educator professional activity on Twitter: an analysis of 16 education-related Twitter hashtags. *Professional Development in Education*, 48(5): 784–805. DOI: 10.1080/19415257.2020.1752287

Collin, J. and Smith, E. (2021) *Effective Professional Development* (page 40). Education Endowment Foundation.

Drury, E. (9 January 2019) Job tips for teachers: how to write a winning application. *The Guardian*. Available at: www.theguardian.com/teacher-network/teacher-blog/2013/jan/09/teacher-job-tips-write-winning-application

Lantz-Andersson, A., Lundin, M. and Selwyn, N. (2018) Twenty years of online teacher communities: a systematic review of formally-organized and informally-developed professional learning groups. *Teaching and Teacher Education*, 75: 302–315. DOI: 10.1016/j.tate.2018.07.008

Lawson, H.A., Kirk, D. and MacPhail, A. (2020) The professional development challenge: achieving desirable outcomes for students, teachers and teacher educators, in *School physical education and teacher education*, pages 141–152. Routledge.

Perry, E., Halliday, J., Higginson, J. and Patel, S. (2022) *Meeting the Challenge of Providing High-Quality Continuing Professional Development for Teachers: The Wellcome CPD Challenge Pilot Delivery Report*.

Spencer, P., Harrop, S., Thomas, J. and Cain, T. (2018) The professional development needs of early career teachers, and the extent to which they are met: a survey of teachers in England. *Professional Development in Education*, 44(1): 33–46. DOI: 10.1080/19415257.2017.1299028

INDEX

Locators in **bold** refer to tables.

abuse 38–39
  see also safeguarding
academies 245
accountability
  Core Content Framework 11, 226
  the curriculum 118–119
  education policy 208
  in an educational context 226–228
  and governance 234–238
  national measures 228–230
action scaffolding 155–156
adaptive teaching 139–142
  assessment 143, 150–151
  Core Content Framework 11
  everyday adaptations 151–157
  high challenge / low threat 145–146
  knowing your pupils well 143–145
  meeting pupils where they are 148
  observations 157–158
  supporting personal development 146–148
  teaching assistants 148, **149**
  where to start 142
agency 5
apologising
  pupil behaviour 84–85
  as a trainee 26
Apple, M. 208
assertive discipline (AD) 73–74
assessment 179
  adaptive teaching 143, 150–151
  challenges 186–187
  in the classroom 192–194
  Core Content Framework 11–12
  feedback as key element 195–197
  importance of 180–181
  inclusion 171–172
  inference, validity and reliability 187–189
  IT as tool 61
  managing assessment and marking 197–199
  observations 199
  perspectives on progress 189–191
  and planning 191, **192**
  strategies and assessment in action 184–186
  uses of 181–183
attainment 189–190, 214–215, 229–230
  see also assessment; learning outcomes
autobiographical perspective 6

backward design 126
behaviour management 69
  behavioural theories 73–77
  Core Content Framework 12, 69–70
  learning and consolidation activities 84–85
  meaning of 70–73
  restorative enquiry, circles and conferences 80–84
  restorative practice 78–80
  teacher-pupil relationships 77–78
Biesta, G. 8, 121, 122
bullying 42–44
  sexual harassment 45–46

career progression
  first job 241–254
  learning about your teaching 16–17
  teacher-learner identity after QTS 254–257
child protection 36, 37
  see also safeguarding
Children and Families Act 166
Children's Commissioner 166
classroom behaviour *see* behaviour management
cognitive conflict 103–104
cognitive load 100–101
colleagues' perspectives 6
'common good' 214
contingency planning (lessons) 105
Core Content Framework (CCF) 1–2
  accountability and governance 226
  assessment 180
  behaviour management 69–70
  curriculum 11, 111–112, 113
  how to meet 10
  inclusion 159–160
  planning 89–90

Index

safeguarding and wellbeing 35–36
supporting trainee development 117
teacher wellbeing 51–52
in this book 10–12
wider professional responsibilities 15–16
Covid-19 pandemic 70–71, 141
critical incidents 63–64, **64–65**
the curriculum 111–112
   accountability 118–119
   adaptive teaching 152
   ambitious curriculum and powerful knowledge 121–122
   developing 125–128
   disciplines, subjects and recontextualisation 123–125
   historical context 3
   inclusion 171–172
   Ofsted Inspection Framework 216, 236
   progress 189–190
   purpose of 112–113, 121
   regulatory framework 116–118
   role of knowledge 119–121
   as standard 116–117
   tensions in 122–123
   what we know about our pupils and how to use it 128–132
curriculum making 124, 128–129
curriculum thinking 11, 115–116
cyberbullying 42–44, 45–48

deficit discourses 211–213
Department for Education (DfE) 116
detention 82
Dewey, J. 122, 208
didactic triangle, professional identity 6, 7
diet
   eating disorders 40–41
   teacher wellbeing 58–61
DIRT (Directed Improvement and Reflection Time) 196–197
disabilities *see* Special Educational Needs and Disabilities (SEND)
discipline-specific curriculum 125
   see also subject knowledge
discipline techniques 73–74, **79**
   see also behaviour management
disciplines in the curriculum 123–125
disclosures 39
distress 54
   see also teacher wellbeing
diversity model of disability 162
diversity, reflecting in the curriculum 130–131
   see also inclusion
dual coding 101

Early Career Framework (ECF) 117, 120
Early Career Teachers (ECTs) 168, 171, 226, 241, 254–255
eating disorders 40–41
ecological model of disability 162
Education, Health and Care Plans (EHCPs) 165, 166, 168
education policy 189–191, 205–206
   brief history in England 209–210
   deficit discourses 211–213
   influence of 207–209
   pedagogy and curriculum 113
   'promise of education' 207
   role of the teacher 214–216
   social justice 210–212
   teachers as the change 217
   see also school governance
education, purpose of 8–9, 112–113, 121, 208
Education Reform Act 228
Eisenhower matrix 59–60, *60*
emotional intelligence 57
emotional regulation 57
ending lessons 104–105
endogenous competition 209
English, reasons for studying 24
Equalities Act 130–131, 163
equity perspective 6
eustress 54
   see also teacher wellbeing
evaluation
   lesson plans 106
   Ofsted Inspection Framework 118, 119
examinations *see* assessment
exercise, for wellbeing 58–61
exogenous competition 209
experienced teachers 5
   learning from feedback 21–22
   learning from modelling 21
   observations 19–20
extra-curricular activities 213
extremism 38
extrinsic motivation 73–74, 82

fading 101
faith schools 245
feedback
   behavioural theories 73
   for diverse pupils 171
   learning from 21–22, 31–32
   lesson plans 90
   meaningful and effective feedback 195, 200
   negative feedback 62–63
   teacher wellbeing 66
formative assessment 182

Index

adaptive teaching 143, 148, 151, 152
  distinction from summative
    181–182, 199
  inclusion 171
  learning objectives 93
  success criteria 192–193
formative mindset 182
free schools 245
functional model of disability 162

General Certificate of Secondary
  Education (GCSE) 227–228,
  229–230
goals (lesson objectives) 92–94
governance *see* school governance
group writing 154–155
guidance fading 101

harassment 45–48
Headteachers' Standards 117
hinge questions 193
Hirsch, E. D. 122, 208
historical context 3, 209–210
holidays 58, 246
human rights 208–209

identity *see* professional identity;
  teacher-learner identity
inclusion 159
  in the curriculum 130–131, 171–172
  in the education system 165–168
  meaning of 160
  observations 175
  pedagogy 169–170
  in schools 164–165
  teachers' concerns about 168–169
  teaching strategies 172–174
  who needs including and
    why 160–164
inequality, and social justice 210–213
  see also inclusion
inspections *see* Ofsted Inspection Framework
interventions 147–148, **149**, 180,
  210–212, 215
intrinsic motivation 73–74

job applications 247–253
  see also career progression
job market 243–244
job offers 253–254

knowledge
  ambitious curriculum and powerful
    knowledge 121–122
  curriculum making 124–125, 128–129
  diversity 131

four domains of 19
purpose of education 8–9
Qualified Teacher Status 254–257
role of 118–119
see also subject knowledge

lateness 75
learning
  about planning 106
  how do we learn 96–97
  working out if pupils are
    learning 102–103
learning disabilities *see* Special
  Educational Needs and
  Disabilities (SEND)
learning environments
  safeguarding 40–41
  sense of safety 146–147
  virtual (VLEs) 61–62
learning objectives 92–94, 189, 192–193
learning opportunities, during
  training 19–20, 22
learning outcomes
  accountability measures 229–230
  adaptive teaching 140–141
  evaluation of 106
  lesson plans 94–95
  progress, perspectives on 189–190
  understanding low attainment 214–216
Lemov, D. 92, 208
lesson objectives 92–94
lesson plans
  assessment 191, **192**
  Core Content Framework 11
  importance of 90–91
  reviewing learning 20–22
  step-by-step 91–107
live writing 154–155
local education authorities
  (LEAs) 230
London allowance 243

maltreatment 38
  see also safeguarding
mark books 198
marking 197–199
Master's degrees 256–257
mastery approach 182
media context 207
meetings, learning from 20–21
mental health *see* pupil wellbeing;
  teacher wellbeing
mental models 18–19
mentors
  learning from feedback 21–22
  learning from modelling 21

263

Index

lesson plans 90
negative feedback 62–63
observing experienced teachers 19–20
working with 25–30
metacognition 172
mindsets 182
misconceptions (of pupils)
curriculum making 124–125, 129
lesson planning 97–98, 103–104
purpose of assessment 183
mistakes
as a trainee 26
in worked examples 101
model answers 154
multi-academy trusts (MATs) 230
multi-modal learning 172

National Curriculum *see* curriculum
National Professional Qualifications
(NPQs) 117–118
neglect 38–39
see also safeguarding
Newly Qualified Teachers
(NQTs) 141–142
no hands rule 193

objectives, lesson planning 92–94
observations
adaptive teaching 157–158
assessment 199
experienced teachers 19–20
inclusion 175
key things to look out for 46
Ofsted Inspection Framework 118, 216, 227, 234–238
online activities 61–62
operant conditioning 73

payscales 243, 246
Pedagogical Content Knowledge
(PCK) 7–9, 124
pedagogy
of compassion 217
education policy 113
inclusion 169–170
relational 79
peer assessment 184
personal development of pupils 146–148
placements *see* school placements
planning 89
and assessment 191, **192**
Core Content Framework 89–90
the curriculum 115–116, 128–129
importance of 90–91
reviewing learning 20–22
step-by-step 91–107

policies *see* education policy; school policies
positive discipline (PD) 74, 76
practical perspective 6
Prevent duty 38, 41
private schools 246
profession, meaning of 1, 2–4
professional development 20–21, 255
see also career progression
professional expectations
of teachers 9–10
professional identity 4–5
didactic triangle 6, 7
learning about your teaching 16–17
see also teacher-learner identity
professional responsibilities 12, 25–27, 37–38
progress, meaning of 189–190
'promise of education' 207
protected characteristics 130–131
psychological needs 27
psychological safety 146–147
public trust 10
pupil behaviour *see* behaviour management
pupil wellbeing 35
bullying, cyberbullying and harassment 42–48
learning environments 40–41
see also safeguarding
pupil's views, on the curriculum 129–130

qualifications, as purpose of education 121
Qualified Teacher Status (QTS)
accountability 226
behaviour management 71
teacher-learner identity 254–257
Teachers' Standards 9, 117
quality of education 118
questioning strategies 193–194

racial literacy 131
racism 41
radicalisation 38
reading (post-training) 256
recruitment 245
see also career progression
reflection
adaptive teaching 142
first job 243
how to reflect 5–6
lesson plans 92
theory and practice 23–25
relationships *see* social context
as a teacher; teamwork
relaxation techniques 58
resilience 55–58
see also teacher wellbeing

Index

resources
  IT as organisational tool 61–63
  lesson planning 99–103
  organisation of teacher resources 61
responsive teaching 141–142
  see also adaptive teaching
restorative circles 81
restorative conferencing 81
restorative enquiry 80
restorative practice 78–84
rewards, behaviour management 73–74

safeguarding 35–37
  defining 37
  disclosures 39
  duty as a teacher 37–38
  learning environments 40–41
  meaning of abuse and neglect 38–39
  observations 47
  school placements 47–48
  school policy of 47
safety for learners 146–147
salary 243
scaffolding 155–156
schemes of work 20–22
school governance 225–226
  and accountability 234–238
  educational context 230–231
  effect of school governance on you as a teacher 233–234
  shape and role of the governing body 231–233
school placements 27
  key things to look out for 31
  safeguarding 46–48
school policies 25
  bullying 44–45
  failure to follow 75
  safeguarding 46
  see also behaviour management; education policy
schools
  purpose of 113–115
  recruitment 245
  types of 245–246
Schools Inspection Framework (SIF) 113
self-determination theory (SDT) 27
self-marking assessments 61, 184
seminars 31, 66
sentence starters 152–153
sexual harassment 45–46
sleep, for wellbeing 58–61
social capital 29–30

social context as a teacher 27–30
  in behaviour management 72, 77–78
  emotional intelligence 57
  first job 241–254
  pedagogy for inclusion 169–170
  teacher-pupil relationships 77–78
  teacher wellbeing 56–57
social justice 210–212
social media 207, 255
social model of disability 161–162
socialisation 8–9
Special Educational Needs and Disabilities (SEND)
  behaviour management 71–72
  disability models 161–162
  inclusion 160–164
  in schools 164–165
  teaching strategies 172–174
special schools 245–246
Standard Attainment Tests (SATs) 227
stress 54
  see also teacher wellbeing
structure strips 152–153
student wellbeing *see* pupil wellbeing
students' perspective 6
Style, E. 122–123, 129, 130
subject associations 123, 256
subject knowledge
  accessing teachers' knowledge 18–19
  Core Content Framework 11
  discipline-specific curriculum 125
subjectification 8
subjects in the curriculum 123–125
success criteria
  lesson plans 94–95
  progress 189–190
  using assessment 192–193
summative assessment 182
  in the curriculum 152
  distinction from formative 181–182, 199
support for trainees 55
  see also teacher wellbeing

teacher-learner identity
  accessing teachers' knowledge 18–19
  Core Content Framework 11
  development of 15–16, 17–18, 30
  learning about your teaching 16–18
  learning opportunities during your training 19–20
  after Qualified Teacher Status 254–257
  reviewing lesson plans and schemes of work 20–22
  using theory 23–25

265

Index

working with mentors, teachers and other key staff 25–30
teacher modelling 21
teacher-pupil relationships 77–78
teacher responsibilities *see* professional responsibilities
teacher wellbeing 51–53
  defining wellbeing 53
  discussion points for tutorials and seminars 66
  exercise, sleep and diet 58–61
  getting support 55
  ideas for guided practice and feedback 66
  IT as organisational tool 61–63
  learning from critical incidents 63–65
  recognising threats 53–54
  resilience 55–58
  working with stress 54
Teachers' Standards
  how to meet 10
  introduction of 3–4
  Qualified Teacher Status (QTS) 9, 117
teaching
  first job 241–254
  history of professional status 2–4
  inclusion 172–174
  making a difference 217
  payscales 243, 246
  professional conduct 1
  role of the teacher 214–216
teaching assistants (TAs) 148, **149**

teamwork
  being a team player 28
  teacher wellbeing 56–57
  working with mentors, teachers and other key staff 25–30
terrorism, Prevent duty 38
tests *see* assessment
theory, meaning and role of 23–25, 191
think-pair-share 193
time management 58–61, 197–199
timings in lessons 102
tutorials 31, 66

Unique Pupil Number (UPN) 229
Universal Declaration of Human Rights 208–209

verbal rehearsal 155
virtual learning environments (VLEs) 61–62
vocabulary banks 154

Warnock Report 161, 165
wellbeing *see* pupil wellbeing; teacher wellbeing
word scaffolding 155–156
working memory 101
workload management 58–61, 197–199
writing frames 152–153

Young, Michael F.D. 121–122, 210